GW00501717

In memory
of
my father
and all who have suffered
in exile

Beatrice King

A LONG WAY FROM HOME

CALDRA HOUSE LIMITED
1998

ISBN 1 872286 38 0

Printed by Caldra House Limited,
23 Coleridge Street, Hove, Sussex BN3 5AB England

CONTENTS

ILLUSTRATIONS

INTRODUCTION

In 1993 my father died. As my mother and I went through his papers we discovered documents which set me wondering about his early life and that of his forebears. It was fortunate that so many papers survived in view of the circumstances of my father's life; I found the birth certificates of my grandparents - my grandfather's being written in beautiful but very faint pre-Revolutionary Russian copperplate - and those of my father and his brother and sister. There were old school reports, Diploma certificates, my father's army record, and a newspaper cutting of a letter written by my grandfather in response to an article in one of the Polish newspapers published in Britain. There were also photographs, hundreds of them, some of which I had seen before but others which I had not. Questions began to surface in my mind: why had my father always said that he was born in Poland when it states quite clearly on his birth certificate that he was born in Usole, Siberia? Why did my grandfather settle in an obscure town in Eastern Siberia rather than find work in his native land? Why did my father never tell me that his own mother was Russian? What exactly happened to my father in the Soviet Union during the War? Why did he say that he was a prisoner for four years after 1939 when all Polish prisoners in the USSR had been released in 1941? What had my father's family been like? Why had my father been so reticent about his early life?

With these questions in my mind, I began to search for answers and in doing so uncovered an extraordinary tale which in many ways encapsulates the story not only of a family but of a nation. While each person's story is unique, there are aspects of this story which will resonate with many other Poles and will be part of their shared experience. In the nineteenth century many Poles were exiled to Siberia; despite being in exile, these Poles have contributed greatly to Western knowledge about the Far Eastern past of Russia. In this century, experiences of Poles during the Second World War were terrible and painful, whether they were prisoners of the Germans or the Russians or struggling to survive in occupied Poland. The Polish nation is one I have come to admire more and more, not only as part of my own heritage, but also because of its capacity to rise from the ashes each time it is apparently destroyed. Poland has not been destroyed either by her invaders or by the disparaging remarks of foreigners who know little of her history, because of the resilience in her people which has enabled her to survive all attempts to destroy her identity.

My search for the story of my father's family has led me along fascinating paths and into strange places. In August 1997 I travelled from Moscow to Irkutsk on the TransSiberian Railway; I spent some days in Irkutsk, the city where my father lived as a child. Limited by the obvious constraints of time, geography and politics, I have nevertheless been fortunate to find as much information as I have. Some avenues, such as the relevant archives in Russia, have been closed to me. People have given generously of their time to help me in my quest. I have explored accounts of gold mining practices in Siberia at the turn of the century and traced the last remnants of the gold mining company which my grandfather worked for. I have solved the mystery of the newspaper article and in doing so discovered a new dimension of my family's past. There has been the discovery of an almost certain family connection with Shostakovich the composer.

On my first visit to Warsaw members of my family in Poland told me much of the family history. Friends of my father have generously contributed their own memoirs of what must have been a most terrible period in their lives, and for that I am particularly grateful, recognising the cost of such remembering even after half a century. I have pieced together as best I can the family story and set it against the backdrop of political and historical events which affected them. Thus there are detailed descriptions of events which are not always mentioned in the history books. I have explored each avenue as far as I can, but there are some things which we will never know.

I have been helped in my task by numerous people, without whom I would have given up the quest as being too difficult. Thanks are due first to my husband for his encouragement and to my mother for her unstinting support of the whole project and for her willingness to help wherever she could. Richard Davies, of the Leeds Russian Archive, has freely shared with me his knowledge and expertise. In Minsk, Alexander Bely has carefully unearthed the previously unknown Belarusian / Lithuanian side to the story and has been extraordinarily thorough in discovering facts from documents unavailable in the West. The Sikorski Institute and the Polish Library in London have also been very generous with their time in answering my numerous questions. The Polish Section of the British Army Records Centre in Hayes, West London, let me have a copy of my father's army record. Francis Marten and Emil Skulski both wrote about the time they spent with my father in the 1940s. Joasia Kisielewska translated my uncle's memoir of 1939.

Trevor Mottram has created clear maps and family trees from complex and confused material; I am grateful for his skill and patience. My gratitude to Mr. Filipowicz of the Polish Cultural Foundation is considerable; without his support this book would not be published. I hope it contributes to a wider knowledge and a deeper appreciation of the history and the pain of the Polish people.

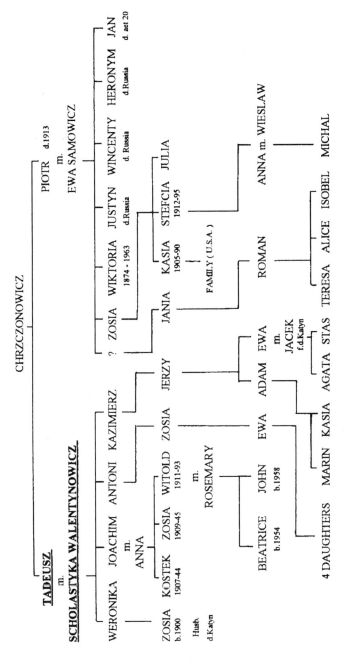

CHRZCZONOWICZ

PIOTR d.1913
m.
EWA SAMOWICZ

TADEUSZ
m.
SCHOLASTYKA WALENTYNOWICZ

WERONIKA JOACHIM ANTONI KAZIMIERZ

? ZOSIA WIKTORIA JUSTYN WINCENTY HERONYM JAN
1874 - 1963   d.Russia   d.Russia   d.Russia   d. aet 20

ZOSIA KOSTEK ZOSIA WITOLD ZOSIA   JERZY
b.1900 1907-44 1909-45 1911-93

Hush.   m.
d.Katyn   ROSEMARY

JANIA KASIA STEFCIA JULIA
       1905-90 1912-95

FAMILY (U.S.A.)

ANNA m. WIESLAW

ROMAN

ADAM EWA
      m.
      JACEK
      f.d.Katyn

BEATRICE JOHN EWA
b.1954   b.1958

TERESA ALICE ISOBEL MICHAL

AGATA STAS

4 DAUGHTERS MARIN KASIA

13

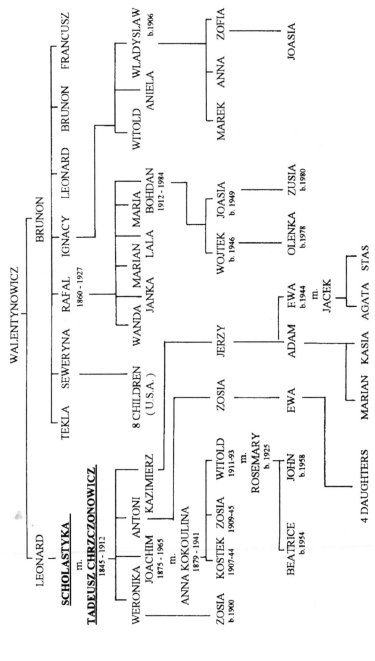

14

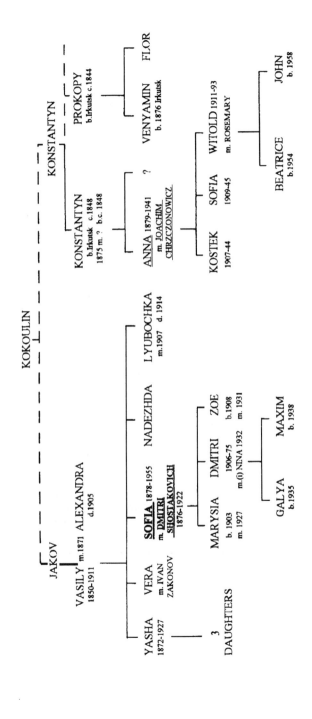

KOKOULIN

JAKOV

VASILY m.1871 ALEXANDRA
1850-1911   d.1905

KONSTANTYN

KONSTANTYN   PROKOPY
b.Irkusk c.1848   b.Irkusk c.1844
1875 m. ? b.c. 1848

YASHA   VERA   SOFIA 1878-1955   NADEZHDA   LYUBOCHKA
1872-1927   m. IVAN   m. DMITRI   m.1907   d. 1914
             ZAKONOV   SHOSTAKOVICH
                            1876-1922

ANNA 1879-1941   ?   VENYAMIN   FLOR
m. JOACHIM   b. 1876 Irkusk
CHRZCZONOWICZ

3   MARYSIA   DMITRI   ZOE
DAUGHTERS   b. 1903   1906-75   b.1908
             m. 1927   m.(i) NINA 1932   m. 1931

KOSTEK   SOFIA   WITOLD 1911-93
1907-44   1909-45   m. ROSEMARY

GALYA   MAXIM
b.1935   b. 1938

BEATRICE   JOHN
b.1954   b. 1958

BALTIC

MOSCOW

•VILNA

GRAND
DUCHY
OF LITHUANIA

WARSAW
•
KINGDOM
OF
POLAND • RADOM

• KRAKOW
(capital)

KINGDOM
OF
HUNGARY

PRINCIPALITY
OF
MULDAVIA

BLACK SEA

Present Day Borders —·—·—

*The Greatest Extent of Polish / Lithuanian Lands (C 15th)
Compared with Present Day Boundaries*

CHAPTER 1

The Background

The history of Poland is a complex story but a summary of it will help to sketch in the background against which the family story unfolds. The following is necessarily a very brief account; for a more detailed picture, see the bibliography. In this chapter it is intended to outline the history of Poland until her independence in 1918 as a way of providing a background to understanding the origins of the family; for the history after 1918, see Chapter 5.

Poland's foundation as a Christian Kingdom – dating from Prince Mieszko's acceptance of Christian baptism in 966AD – was largely as confederation of different Slavic tribes formed to counter the threat from the west, the *Drang nach Osten*, the drive to the east. It was Poland's resistance to the armed struggle, particularly with the Germanic tribes, which prompted her rulers to look to the Holy See in Rome for help, rather than the Holy Roman Empire. It was for this reason rather than as a result of a forced conversion that Poland accepted Christianity. In 990AD, Prince Mieszko drew up a charter making his realm a possession of the Holy See, therefore, and not a possession of the Empire. The evangelisation of Poland was thus from Rome, with the help of missionaries from many different nations. The association of the Kingdom of Poland right from the beginning with the Holy See is important for two reasons in the understanding of Poland's inheritance. Firstly her fierce devotion to the Roman Catholic Church has its roots in the very earliest days of her existence as a nation, and secondly, it marked her out from her eastern neighbour, Russia, who was evangelised from Constantinople, and so followed the Orthodox way of Christianity.

The fledgling Polish State spent the next two hundred years or so gradually forming herself into a distinct entity, although this was no easy task. As she grew stronger, so the surrounding nations felt threatened by her and she was constantly under attack or threat of attack. Moravia and the land bordering the River Elbe was ceded to Poland in 1018 and Boleslaw, Mieszko's son and successor, married his own daughter to Prince Svatopolk, ruler of the Principality of Rus, with its capital then at Kiev. Svatopolk was removed by a rebellion so Boleslaw responded by seizing an area of land between the Rivers Bug and San. Boleslaw had himself crowned the first King of Poland in 1025 with a crown provided by the Holy See.

The area occupied by the Kingdom of Poland was large, but the administration and leadership was weak; on the death of Boleslaw the country was plunged into civil war. Stability was only achieved when Kazimierz I came to power in 1034. Bohemia, Hungary and the Holy Roman Empire all coveted the Polish lands but she succeeded in staving off attempts at this at the Battle of Psie Pole, near Wroclaw, forcing Bohemia and the Holy Roman Empire to renounce their claims. The frontiers of Poland were still fairly fluid at this point but from the twelfth century the State was strong enough for economic and administrative foundations to be laid. Cities began to flourish, Krakow having already been the capital since 1040, but others received their charters in the thirteenth century, including Wroclaw(1242) and Poznan(1253). At about this time, when Jews were almost universally persecuted throughout Europe, they were welcomed into Poland. Their status was confirmed by a charter of 1265 but the flow reached a peak during the following century in the reign of Kazimierz the Great. By then Poland had the largest Jewish community in mediaeval Europe. Other migrants found their way into Poland's cities – the overpopulated areas of Northern Europe meant that there was a steady flow of German-speaking burghers into the towns, and much of Lower Silesia, Pomerania and Neumark was settled by German peasants. The social structure of Poland at this time was unusual in that there was not a feudal system in the way that one existed elsewhere in Europe. In the 13th century a free peasantry was coming into existence as the acceptance of freedom as a basic human right was a fundamental feature of Poland's attitude to society. (In later centuries this belief would be modified and limited to the gentry, or *szlachta*, and serfdom would creep in, especially in the East).

The Prussian threat in the west was greatly increased when the Crusader Order of Teutonic Knights accepted an invitation to move their headquarters from Acre in Palestine to Polish soil in 1226. They quickly established themselves in Marienburg, in the territory of Conrad of Mazovia, who was conducting his own crusade against the pagan tribes of Prussia. The Polish rulers and the Teutonic Knights differed sharply in their views on how pagans should be treated, the Poles favouring toleration, and the Teutonic Knights, forcible conversion and killing the resistors – a policy which they tried to implement in Lithuania. Over the next two centuries there was almost constant warfare between the Poles and the Teutonic Knights, the aim of the latter being to expand their territory eastwards. Eventually they controlled most of the Baltic coastline, and in 1308 they even captured Gdansk. Torun and Konigsberg were also captured by them. It was the ruthless ambition of the Teutonic Order which was a major factor prompting the Union of Poland and Lithuania. This happened informally in 1386 with the marriage of Jagiello, the ruler of Lithuania, and Jadwiga, Queen of Poland.

The origins of Poland's relations with her eastern neighbours, in particular Rus (or Ruthenia) and Lithuania date back to a series of marriages with the rulers of Rus (present-day Belarus). This country had been converted to Christianity only a short while after Poland (in 988 AD), its capital being first at Polock and then at Navahrodal (in Polish Nowogrodek), finally moving to Vilna in 1323. In 1214 Polock had been lost to the Teutonic Knights of the Sword. From the East came another threat – the Mongol (Tartar) invaders from the East, sweeping across Asia, conquering all in their path. Kiev was captured in 1240, and the western advance continued almost unchecked in two major waves, the first one in 1241/2 and the second in 1259.

Indeed, there is the famous and ancient legend of the Krakow Trumpeter. This Trumpeter was on duty at the top of St. Mary's Church tower in Krakow, his normal duties being to sound the hours; on this occasion he sounded the alarm to signal the approach of an invading force of Mongols, but before he could finish playing, a Mongol arrow pierced his throat. To this day the incident is commemorated at midday, when a trumpeter gives the call but stops abruptly in mid-tune at the exact point when the ancient trumpeter was killed. The Mongols also played a significant role in the history of Russia; Genghis Khan and his hordes easily conquered the Russians and kept them under their rule for many years. Poland was finally able to consider eastward expansion only when the Mongols had destroyed the unity of the regions of Kiev and Rus. Fortunately for Poland, and indeed Europe, the Mongols suddenly turned back whence they came, and the threat to Western civilisation was removed.

During the second half of the thirteenth century the lands of Western Rus were seized by the pagan Lithuanians and included in the Grand Duchy of Lithuania, thus initiating a mixture of ethnicity, language and culture whose confusion persists to this day. Byelorussian nationality is said to have begun to take form from this point as the White Ruthenians of Western Rus began to develop their own separate culture and language. The Lithuanians, on the other hand, were a Baltic people, priding themselves on being the last pagan nation in Europe, and her rulers were turbulent, cunning and ruthless. In 1362 the Grand Duke defeated the Mongols and the following year occupied Kiev. The Grand Duchy was now vast, stretching from the Baltic to the Black Sea. However, she had no allies, which she badly needed to consolidate her position, a fact which Grand Duke Iogaila recognised when he came to power in 1382.

Attempts were made during the reign of Wladyslaw I (1306-33) to unify the country, and his son, Kazimierz the Great (1333-70) laid the solid legal and institutional foundations of the Polish nation. Under his reign Poland rapidly began to prosper and acquired a reputation for both tolerance and learning. Her first university was founded in Krakow in 1362, Polish law was codified from 1347, wooden castles and buildings were beginning to be replaced by stone and a new silver currency was introduced.

Unfortunately Kazimierz died in 1370 leaving no heir. For a few years Poland was ruled by the mother of King Louis of Hungary (Kazimierz's nephew) but the future of the monarchy in Poland was very uncertain. Louis himself died in 1382, also leaving no male heir. The situation was by now desperate and the Polish nobles looked to Louis' daughters for the succession. They rejected Maria, the elder and already married, and brought instead the ten year old Hedwig (Jadwiga) to Krakow where she was crowned King [!] in 1384 The plan of the Polish nobles was to marry Jadwiga to Grand Duke Iogaila of Lithuania, and by so doing, unite Poland and Lithuania. On 14 August 1385 an agreement was signed; in February 1386 Iogaila (Jagiello in Polish) was baptised Wladyslaw. On 18 February he married Jadwiga and on 4 March he was crowned King of Poland. By this Union, Poland was joining herself to a backward and largely pagan State three times her size; the advantages to Poland of this Union were not entirely clear, but it would cause problems for the next few centuries. The Union was, however, of great advantage to the Grand Duchy of Lithuania; the Ruthenian and Lithuanian lands would be set on a path of Westernisation and a marked religious and cultural tolerance would evolve as Orthodox and Catholics lived side by side together with the Jewish population. Since the territory is called the Grand Duchy of Lithuania it is often assumed that the population was predominantly Lithuanian speaking Lithuanians. In fact the majority of the population was Ruthenian and the language used from the 1370s onwards for official legal and diplomatic purposes was Byelorussian. It is thought to be one of the first examples of the official use of the vernacular anywhere in Europe.

The Union of Poland and Lithuania created the largest territory at the time in Europe; at its height the lands under Polish-Lithuanian control stretched from the Baltic to the Crimea and included Minsk, Smolensk, Kiev and Odessa. The eastern population consisted largely of Orthodox Christians.

The problems with the Teutonic Knights and the new Kingdom of Poland-Lithuania continued throughout the last decades of the fourteenth century and matters came to a head at the Battle of Grunwald (Tannenberg) in 1410 when the combined forces of Poland and Lithuania, under the command of King Wladyslaw II, won a famous victory over the Teutonic Knights. This effectively ended the threat from this quarter. The Polish-Lithuanian Union was reinforced in 1413 at the Diet of Horodlo, at which 47 noble Lithuanian families received *herby* (or crests) from the same number of Polish nobles (*szlachta*). At the Diet of Horodlo it was decided that high office would only be accessible to Catholics, thus effectively excluding large numbers of Byelorussians who were Orthodox, and any remaining pagan Lithuanians. Throughout the fifteenth century the United territory consolidated its position; for all its size, the whole of the Grand Duchy could only muster fifteen urban centres, seven of them in Byelorussian land, as the population was predominantly rural. Enserfment of the peasantry was permitted by legislation dating from 1447.

The Renaissance came to Poland as to elsewhere in Europe and the new learning was pursued with great enthusiasm. The universities flourished and there was a huge thirst for knowledge of all kinds. The Jagiellonian University in Krakow had been founded in 1364. Scholars such as Nicholas Copernicus (1473-1543) made significant contributions to the rapid advancement of knowledge. The Reformation made a deep impact on religious life and thought in Poland; she continued to welcome persecuted minorities and was a refuge for many of the new religious sects, eg., the Anabaptists and the Menonites, which were springing up. Many considered this to be Poland's Golden Age. Opportunities for Poles to study abroad and to travel opened new horizons and brought about the spread of the new ideas and arts which were sweeping Europe in the fifteenth and sixteenth centuries. Polish literature flourished, much being written in Latin, but there was a sizeable body of literature in Polish as well. The mid-sixteenth century marks the high water mark of Polish culture; the decision of the Polish Parliament, or Sejm, in 1543 to publish its decisions henceforth in Polish marked the beginning of the decline. From then onwards Poland's participation in European affairs necessarily declined as Polish thought became increasingly inaccessible to Europeans.

Having thrown off threats from the Tartars and the Teutonic Knights, Poland then faced a new threat from the east – Russia. This nation was rapidly growing in strength and was wanting to expand westwards; under Prince Ivan III (father of Ivan IV, the Terrible) two wars were waged between Russia and the Grand Duchy (1487-94 and 1500-03) as a result of which great swathes of land were ceded to Russia. The Grand Duke Alexander (1492-1506) and King of Poland from 1501, married Ivan III's daughter Helena in 1494 in an attempt to forge an alliance. Further territorial losses came with the fall of Smolensk in 1514 and that of the ancient Ruthenian capital Polock in 1563.

The links between Poland and the Grand Duchy of Lithuania were formalised at the Union of Lublin in 1569, whereby Poland and Lithuania were recognised as equal parties in the creation of the Commonwealth of Poland and Lithuania – the *Oboja Narodow*. Large areas of the Ukraine were ceded to Poland, and Polish language and culture became more and more dominant in the life of the country. The Golden Age of Byelorussian culture had been exemplified by two important sets of documents, the Statutes of the Grand Duchy of Lithuania, written in 1529, 1566 and 1588, and the Byelorussian-Lithuanian Chronicles, written between 1446 and the 1570s documenting the history of the Grand Duchy of Lithuania. There were other far-reaching effects of the Union. Considerable tracts of land passed into the hands of feudal lords. Large numbers of the Byelorussian and Lithuanian population became Catholic for political reasons and many Catholic Churches were built in Byelorussia and the Ukraine. An attempt was made to unite the Orthodox and Catholic Churches resulting in the 1596 Agreement of Brest and the formation of the Uniate Church, Slavic in outlook but in communion with Rome. It did not prove popular with the people. By the early 1600s the Commonwealth occupied an area of 990 000 sq km and contained a population of 10 million, twice that of England at that time, of whom only 40% were Poles, the rest being a mixture of Lithuanian, Byelorussian, Ukrainian, Russian or Jewish. The land was rich, producing a wide range of goods from grain to fruit, furs to amber, honey to wood.

In 1572 the decision was taken henceforth to elect kings of Poland-Lithuania, these so-called kings being effectively life presidents elected by the *szlachta* or Polish gentry. It is worth spending a few moments considering the *szlachta* as they formed an important part of Polish society, and their influence would increase steadily over the next two centuries. The gentry constituted approximately 10% of the total population, having emerged as a distinct group in the fourteenth century. They were remarkable for their social cohesion as a group, and subscribed strictly to the "noble concept" of treating each other as equals, and to the equality of the sexes in the eyes of the law (so, for example, a Polish noblewoman could, and did, hold property in her own right). Indeed, it often fell to the women to run the estates and to bring up and educate the children. This gave rise to the concept of the "strong-minded female" so prevalent in subsequent Polish literature. Thus they were in a sense the true guardians of the nation's culture. The *szlachta* as a group were not inherently wealthy, in fact many were actually poor, but as only they had the vote, this arguably created a very widely-based franchise. During the interregnum between the death of one king and the election of the next, the acting head of state was not chosen from the *szlachta* but was in fact the most senior Bishop in Poland, the Archbishop of Gniezo, the Primate of Poland.

As time went on, however, the "nobility" of the *szlachta* became apparently diluted; their concepts of the equality of all their number and the dignity of the individual sat uneasily with the parallel rise in serfdom. The principle of unanimity extended to their voting practices in the Sejm, or Parliament, and led to an increasingly clumsy and unwieldy method of passing legislation. The exercise of the veto caused almost impossible delays in the process of government. In due course the Polish nobility became, with a certain justification, a cause for comment and even ridicule throughout the rest of Europe. The parliamentary system, in principle soundly democratic, was largely dismissed as being of no value. The *szlachta* were eliminated eventually by a progressive annulment of their legal privileges. Thousands of families were removed from official lists as a result of successive legislation after the Partitions of Poland, that of Lithuania, for example, occurring in 1818. By 1864 approximately 80% of the *szlachta* were declasse although it was not until 1921 that the Noble Estate itself was formally abolished. The *szlachta* gradually merged with the rest of the population especially after the Partitions at the end of the eighteenth century, and many of their number formed part of a new stratum of society, the intelligentsia, which would play its own part in the more recent history of Poland.

However, in the early days of the elected monarchy Poland was still a great power. Poland's influence in Europe continued – she even conquered and occupied the Grand Duchy of Moscow 1610-13 and fought and won victories over the Swedes (eg., Kircholm 1605). She played a crucial part in blocking Turkish expansion into Europe – most notably at Vienna in 1683 when the Polish King Jan III Sobieski repelled the Turkish army from the very gates of the city.

As the sixteenth and seventeenth centuries progressed the *szlachta* and the people holding power in Lithuania were becoming more and more Polonised. The Byelorussian language was progressively suppressed by Polish feudal lords and many schools and many schools and printing presses were closed. In 1698 the Polish Sejm prohibited the use of the Byelorussian language in institutions and schools. The first conscious stirrings of Byelorussian nationalism date from around this time.

The election of the kings of Poland proved to be a weakness in the government of the country. It was the *szlachta* who had the real power, which increased steadily over the years 1650-1750. Many kings were foreign – in fact only four out of a total of eleven were native Poles. The classes of Polish society did in time become hardened into strata and within the *szlachta* itself an oligarchy of families emerged who eventually shared out all the most powerful positions between them. The Polish magnates became progressively more independent and those in Lithuania were effectively engaged in their own civil war.. This was coupled with the fact that Poland was obliged to wage almost continuous warfare with her neighbours between 1648 and 1717, including a Swedish invasion of 1655-6 and yet more fighting with the Russians over the lands of the Ukraine and Byelorussia in wars between 1654-67. The problems of threats from surrounding countries was a constant throughout her history and it is estimated that between 1240 and 1770 Poland repelled no less than 93 major and minor invasions.

Poland became progressively enfeebled both economically and politically. The Polish Parliamentary system was fragile because it was vulnerable to abuse. The right of veto, one of the fundamental principles of Polish politics, although laudable in theory, meant that it was immensely difficult to pass any laws at all and became hopelessly impractical. The towns, and therefore the trading interests of the nation, were underrepresented in the Sejm. Foreign policy, never a particularly strong feature of Polish political life, was marked by a slowness of response, a lack of consistency and a totally unagressive style. As she decreased, so the power of Russia increased especially towards the Baltic and the Black Sea. As a result of the Austro-Prussian Wars of 1742-1763 Prussia annexed Silesia, an ancient province of Poland. From 1768 Catherine the Great of Russia attempted to reduce the power of Poland to that of a vassal kingdom of Russia. The Lithuanian gentry were involved in their own civil war and ceased to have much interest in the welfare of Poland as a whole. However, there was still a flourishing intellectual life, and agriculture recovered and advanced. Trade also picked up, and the textile and metal industries developed and spread. Mining was revived and modern factories built. Canals were constructed to link up Poland's rivers and facilitate the transport of goods.

The Poles themselves realised that drastic political action was needed, and on 3 May 1791 The Polish Reform Constitution was enacted – the first written constitution in Europe. The State organisation was thoroughly reformed and refounded on a much sounder basis. Zamoyski (p 258) quotes Karl Marx's comments on it:

"With all its faults, this constitution seems to be the only act of freedom which Eastern Europe has undertaken in the midst of Prussian, Austrian and Russian barbarism. It was, moreover, initiated exclusively by the privileged classes, the nobility. The history of the world knows of no other similar noble conduct by the nobility."

Unfortunately this remarkable piece of legislation was too late to save Poland from the designs of her neighbours. Austria, Prussia and Russia each had strong monarchs (Joseph II, Fredrick and Catherine the Great) each keen to expand their own territories. By a series of complex manoeuvres they seized upon the perceived weakness of Poland and carved her up between themselves in three operation, in 1772, 1793, and 1795. For the next 123 years Poland as an independent state did not officially exist and the Polish nation had to resort to other ways of maintaining her national identity

Poland during the Partitions 1795-1918

Although Prussia and Austria had taken some of the Polish lands, it is the fate of the Russian Partition which most concerns us here.

Poland was, not surprisingly, desperate for help and sought for allies. Initially she looked to the French Revolutionaries, and when Napoleon came to power, to him, not least because he had defeated Austria and Prussia . The three occupying Powers of Poland officially maintained that they were merely exercising their ancient rights to those territories of Poland which they had seized; the Russians claimed Kiev and ancient Rus, the Prussians, the patrimony of the Teutonic Knights, and the Austrians, the Kingdom of Galicia, which Poland had seized in 1390. The Poles who looked to Napoleon for liberation joined the Polish Legions in Italy under General Dabrowski, fighting fiercely and famously in the mistaken belief that by fighting for Napoleon they were furthering the cause of Polish independence. They mostly saw action in Italy and unfortunately never even reached Poland. Napoleon himself created the Duchy of Warsaw in 1807, an area carved out of former lands of the Prussian Partition, but later including Krakow and Lublin. This Duchy was administered by Poles and governed according to the Napoleonic Code of Laws. There was a brief period of eight years when life in the Duchy was almost bearable.

Napoleon's invasion of Russia in 1812 was a famous failure. He retreated in defeat after the Battle of Borodino and the disastrous occupation of Moscow, crossing the River Berezina in Byelorussia on his way back to France – even passing through Warsaw without so much as visiting his mistress, Maria Walewska. The Congress of Vienna in 1815 proposed a new solution to the Polish Question. A Congress Kingdom was set up; it inherited much from the Duchy of Warsaw, but put in place a much more repressive system. Its repercussions were felt in the Europe-wide political upheavals a century later.

However, despite the political repression, progress was made in some areas of society. The education system was, for example, the most advanced of its time in Europe, with a National System of Polish Schools (between 1815 and 1827). Vilna University was an important centre of Polish learning until 1822. In 1821 the Patriotic Society was founded at the University; not surprisingly it was carefully watched by the Russian police. In 1823 they decided to suppress the Society as being subversive, and numerous arrests were made, including that of Adam Mickiewicz, the poet and novelist. From this year students from Byelorussia and Lithuania were forbidden to study at Higher Schools in former Poland. The University of Warsaw was founded in 1816 and the Polish Bank in 1828. On the whole, however, the three Powers aimed to render the Polish nation powerless, impoverished, and culturally depressed. Those under Russian rule were subject to a reign of terror, especially under the Tsars Alexander I (1801-25) and his successor Nicholas I (1825-55), who made life progressively harder for the Poles. The repressive measures often took the form of mass deportations to Siberia (of which more later), transfers of population, active suppression of Polish culture, and closure of schools and Universities. According to one estimate Polak (p.49) asserts that no less than 589 schools were closed down in the Eastern Provinces alone. Nicholas I in particular tried to exert an arbitrary influence in the internal affairs of the Congress Kingdom. In 1830 matters came to a head and an attempt was planned by leading Poles to assassinate the Grand Duke Constantine, brother of the Tsar, who was in charge in Warsaw. This was a year of great unrest in general in Europe and many Poles living abroad were taking an active part in revolutionary movements. As a result of the events of November 1830 some 80 000 Poles were exiled to Siberia. In 1831 the Russian army invaded the Congress Kingdom and effectively ended any remaining token independence.

The Polish Constitution was declared null and void, and the ruthless suppression by the Russians caused outrage among the western Powers. Lord Palmerston voiced his protest to Lord Haytesbury, a British diplomat in Moscow, in a letter of 23 November 1831, (quoted in Edwards, appendix) in which he instructed him "to represent to the Russian government how much severities of any kind, not authorised by the laws and constitution of Poland are to be avoided" In 1840 the use of the words "Byelorussia" or "Byelorussian" were forbidden by edict. This caused severe problems for those attempting to keep alive the language and literature. Mickiewicz himself pointed out in 1846 that "Byelorussian – also called Lithuanian – is spoken by 10 million people. Great princes used it in diplomatic correspondence." And yet the literature lacked a readership in the upper strata of society, ie., those with the potential to further the cause. Soon Polish and Russian journals were forbidden even to publish articles in Byelorussian; in fact most Byelorussian writers wrote in both Polish and Byelorussian.

Other harsh measure were imposed. The Universities of Vilna and Warsaw were closed down as was the Warsaw Polytechnic. 2540 families in the Kingdom and 2890 in Lithuania had their lands confiscated. 40 000 families of the *szlachta* from Lithuania and the province of Volhynia were transported to Siberia, and another 40 000 transported from the Kingdom. 254 political and military leaders were condemned to death. It set a pattern that was to be repeated: having imposed a government and constitution on satellite Poland, Russia could not bear to see its legal functioning.

Nationalist feelings were expressed and kept alive by Poles, many of whom were scattered throughout Europe as emigres and who were influenced by the many nationalist movements springing up in Europe at this time. Polish, Lithuanian and Byelorussian nationalism began to emerge as a force, spread and sustained through literature. The nineteenth century was a time of great flowering for Polish literature, much of it with an underlying nationalistic message. Usually expressed in coded form these sentiments would be easily understood by anyone with a knowledge of Polish history. This helped considerably in sustaining the concept of Polish nationhood. However, issues of ethnicity in Eastern Poland are complex, as even a cursory glance at the history of the area shows. An interesting example of this is the poet Adam Mickiewicz (1798-1855), hailed by Poles as their national poet of the Romantic Era. Yet he was born in Nowogrodek, in the former Grand Duchy of Lithuania, and before that a former capital of Ruthenia (Byelorussia). He wrote in both Polish and Byelorussian, and his most famous work, *Pan Tadeusz*, begins with the invocation "O Lithuania, my country". This epic poem describes country life among the *szlachta* (gentry) in Lithuania at the beginning of the nineteenth century (it is set in 1812) and it is a good story – with family feuds and love affairs – against a background of day to day life in an idealised world.

In 1856 the new Tsar, Alexander II, visited Poland and declared an amnesty on any Poles still left in Siberia after exile there in 1831. However, in 1863 another and more serious Uprising against Russia occurred. Numerous towns and cities were centres of unrest, and there were partisan groups hiding in the woods, who harassed the troops sent to put down the insurgents. Byelorussians and Lithuanians were also in revolutionary mood by this time and participated in the Uprising. Now their hope was for independence rather than the restoration of the Polish-Lithuanian Commonwealth. It was this aspiration which was to cause so much bitterness when Poland was trying to re-establish herself after her independence in 1918. The action was widespread and continued in fragmented fashion, for several months, but there was support from foreigners, Garibaldi, Marx and Herzen being among them. The gulf between Russia and Poland was widening.

On 17 October 1863 the National Government ceased to exist as Russia brutally suppressed the Uprising. The *Encyclopaedia Britannica (1911)* expresses it starkly as: "the national history of Poland closes with the Uprising of 1863." in its article on Poland. The identity of the leaders of the Uprising were known to very few, but eventually they were rounded up and five of them hanged on 5 August 1864. Many thousands more were exiled to Siberia.

From 1864 the Kingdom and the name of Poland were formally abolished, and the Tsar relinquished his duties as King of Poland. Repression worsened in many new ways, and there were constant reprisals. For example, the teaching of the Polish language in schools was forbidden, the Polish Education Commission was closed down in 1867 (for the second time), and the Main School in Warsaw was replaced by a Russian University in 1869.

All towns with less than 2 000 inhabitants were deprived of their municipal rights. Russian officials replaced Poles in all administrative positions of importance. After 1873 all teaching at Warsaw University was in Russian. Literacy levels were comparatively high; in 1897 30.5% of the population were literate, compared with 9.3% in 1862, and 19.8% in Russia as a whole (Wandycz). This was partly due to the establishment of clandestine schools in Polish territory; the custom was not as widespread in former Lithuania/Byelorussia, thus giving lower literacy rates in those regions.

The Russians pursued a policy of reconciling the peasants to Russian rule, and breaking the power of the *szlachta*. In 1865 a Russian decree was issued forbidding people of Polish origin to acquire land in the NW Province (former Byelorussia) except by inheritance. Lands previously held by the *szlachta* were granted to the peasants until by the year 1904 the peasantry owned 43.8% of the total land area, private owners, mainly *szlachta*, 40.6%, the Russian court and Imperial family, 6%, public bodies, 2.6%, and Jews, 3%. The peasant holdings were on the whole fairly small (8-13 acres on average); even so, out of an estimated 7 million peasants, no less then 3 million were landless.

The Uniate Church was destroyed in 1875 in a attempt to break the nationalist spirit of its adherents.

By the 1880s the study of isolated works of literature in Polish was grudgingly permitted – on the condition that it was studied as part of the foreign languages curriculum and all the discussion and textbooks were in Russian.

In the 1860s groups of intelligentsia were forming whose concern for Polish nationalism was on a more practical level than primarily idealistic or romantic. The Stanczyk Group, and a little later on, the Warsaw Positivists, realised that Poles must also be trained in skills which would enable them to participate fully in the industrialised world. Factories, railways, mining, and other

30

such enterprises were mushrooming, and there was a perceived need to encourage young men to obtain the best possible training in science, engineering and related disciplines. Realising that there were no suitable places in Poland for training in engineering, for example, they saw that students must either travel to Western Europe or train at the excellent Technological Institute in St.Petersburg (where in fact the Diploma in Engineering was of a higher standard than degree level as it included a professional qualification). So from the 1860s onwards there was a recognisably Polish contingent of students studying there. This will be studied in more detail later.

By the 1870s and 1880s Poles at home and abroad were encountering the tide of socialist, revolutionary and anti-Tsarist thought which was sweeping through Europe. Of course, many of the Polish groups were founded abroad and/or had to carry on their activities secretly. The Polish League was founded in 1887, and renamed the National League in 1897. The Society for National Education was founded in 1899. The Polish Socialist Party (PPS) was founded in Paris in 1892, but also functioned in Warsaw, Lodz, and Bialystok. Many Poles had, of course, emigrated, forming large communities in America, for example, but they supported from afar the new movements in their homeland. In 1904 the PPS held a demonstration in Warsaw. It was cruelly suppressed and this caused widespread outrage. By 1905 the political situation in Russia itself had become so precarious the Tsar was forced to make large concessions to avoid civil war. One concession was to sanction the formation of an elected Parliament, or Duma. Fifty five seats on it were reserved for Poles, but its powers were in practice very limited. The Parliaments of Prussia and Austria were also experimenting at this time with cautiously allowing the Poles some say in national affairs.

The Union for Active Struggle (ZWC) was founded in 1908, financed by a mail train robbery in Lithuania, an enterprise masterminded by Jozef Pilsudski, who was to play such a crucial part in the life of Poland over the next 30 years. The second son of an impoverished *szlachta* family, he was born near Vilna in 1867, and became politically active at a very early age. He was arrested, together with his brother Bronislaw, in 1887 by the Russian police for their supposed part in an assassination attempt on Tsar Alexander III. On the question of ethnicity it is interesting to note that on the occasion of his arrest he apparently gave his nationality as Byelorussian, according to recently discovered documents, and only later changed his nationality to Polish when it became expedient to do so. Both brothers were exiled to Siberia for a time. Bronislaw remained in Siberia, where he pioneered the scientific discovery of much of Siberia, Central Asia, and the Northern Pacific. The ZWC grew under Jozef's leadership, and the force which was formed became known as Pilsudski's Legions. Three of its leaders included men who would play an important part in the future history of Poland, Kazimierz Sosnkowski, Marian Kukiel, and Wladyslaw Sikorski. By June 1914 the Pilsudski Legions had almost 12 000 men trained and ready for action.

At the same time, of course, Russia was struggling in the death-throes of Tsarist rule. Numerous socialist and revolutionary groups were being formed, their leaders arrested, exiled to Siberia or going into voluntary exile abroad. In 1905 Polish as a language was once more permitted to be taught in schools and there was a general easing of conditions in the Russian Partition. In the midst of this ferment, the First World War broke out in August 1914. By this time the Polish nation had succeeded in making herself recognisable as a distinct entity, albeit without any territory or leadership as yet. The Russians were too preoccupied with their own struggles to be over concerned with what they considered to be a minor Western Province. On 15 August 1914 the Governor of Warsaw, Grand Duke Michael, issued a Proclamation promising autonomy for Poland in due course, even though as yet there was no king or clear leader. Poland became a battleground between the Russians and Germans, the Germans laying claim to large areas of land they considered theirs. In the process they caused a huge amount of destruction of crops, fields, buildings, bridges, factories, etc.

Poland turned to the West for help in her hopes for the possibility of a free Poland; in June 1917 France sanctioned the formation of a Polish Army on French soil, and in September of that year France recognised the National Committee in Paris as the Provisional Polish Government.

In March 1918 the Treaty of Brest-Litovsk defined the Eastern and Western boundaries of Poland (to the satisfaction of none of the affected parties) and her right to exist as a free nation, but as yet no clear leader had emerged. On 7 November the Socialist Ignacy Daszynski declared a people's Government, but three days later Pilsudski was released from prison in Germany and returned to Poland where he immediately took up the leadership role. For all his faults, he was considered the only person at that time capable of leading the newly-emerged Republic.

Poland was at last free, although many of the real problems were only just beginning. During 123 years of official non-existence she had maintained her culture, her language, her sense of nationhood, a remarkable achievement in itself, but she now faced the huge task of making herself into a unified nation who could take her place in post-war Europe. Since she had been ruled by four foreign powers, she had inherited four different legal systems, six currencies, three railway networks, and three completely different administrative fiscal and administrative systems. One third of the population were on the verge of starvation and the retreating Germans had destroyed every factory, bridge and railway station in their path.

Truly a formidable task lay ahead; how the problems were tackled is described in Chapter 5.

Such a history, although only briefly described here, sheds light on some of the formative influences in the character of the Polish people, and in particular some of the major factors in the background to the family story.

Poland's fate, given her geographical position, has been to act as a buffer state between East and West – the tribes and groups which became Russia to the east, and the Germanic tribes which became Prussia and Germany to the west. For a thousand years Poland has stood as a barrier to the one expanding westwards and the other eastwards. It is no exaggeration to say that she has in effect maintained the integrity of Europe and with it Western civilisation as we know it, a fact often overlooked in a consideration of European history. She has also championed the cause of Catholicism (even adopting the Virgin Mary as honorary Queen of Poland) as against that of Orthodoxy, which represents the beliefs of the invaders from the East. At times foreign powers have felt it their right to occupy the land – Sweden in the seventeenth century, and Austria, Russia and Prussia in the following century. Nearer our own time, Germany and then the Soviet

Union have had their turn in attempting the annihilation of Poland.

This has given Poland a strong sense of national identity which has been maintained whether Poles are living in Poland itself or emigrated or exiled to some far flung corner of the globe. For all this Poland is historically one of the least military of all the nations in Europe. At the same time she conducted bold and innovative experiments in democratic government, and her written Constitution of 3rd May 1791 was the first one in Europe and only the second in the world (the other being the United States of America). Some of the tragedies which befell other nations in Europe have passed her by; the Black Death did not reach as far east as Poland, nor did Poland become embroiled in bitter religious wars. Her tragedy is her martyrdom at the hands of other nations, but each time she has risen from the ruins to rebuild herself as a nation, despite at best indifference or ignorance of her plight, and at worst, betrayal.

During the nineteenth century there was sympathy from other nations for Poland's plight, but little apparent support. Poles were perceived by many Westerners as backward troublemakers intent on upsetting the status quo. In this century Poland recognised early on the dangers of both Fascism and Communism (note again the threat from her immediate neighbours) and this earned her the reputation of being reactionary and unprogressive. Poland's influence on the making of modern Europe is seen as less than the other great nations of Europe but that may be partly due to the failure to recognise her considerable if less obvious contributions. The situation is made worse by the fact that there was a deliberate smear campaign propagated by the three powers of the Partitions, emphasising Poland's weaknesses, giving rise to attitudes which are still prevalent in some quarters today. Weaknesses there certainly were – the elected monarchy, her unenthusiam for a properly considered foreign policy, her failure to use the opportunists presented for influencing European affairs and lack of an efficient administration and unity in the internal affairs of the country, to name but a few.

The heritage of Poland's history is multicultural. The Poles from the old Kingdom of Poland, with its capital at Krakow, gained ascendancy over their neighbours, the Lithuanians, who in turn had gained power over the Ruthenians (Byelorussians and

Ukrainians). However, there was also a sizeable minority of Jews, Russians, Tartars and Prussians in the population.

The question of ethnicity is complex but has a direct bearing on the family story. Polish history written from a Polish perspective sometimes plays down the role of the minority nationalities in the story. Yet nations such as present-day Belarus and Lithuania have their own distinctive history and culture – that of Belarus stretches back almost as far as Poland herself. The situation becomes confusing when the term "Lithuania" is used to include Byelorussia and even those of Byelorussian origin refer to themselves as Lithuanian, or even Polish. The repression of Byelorussian nationality was almost complete by the eighteenth and nineteenth centuries, the educated and the *szlachta*, originally Byelorussian, preferring to be considered Polish, so eventually only the semi-literate peasants were described as Byelorussian. In fact many of the *szlachta* were almost ashamed of speaking Byelorussain, as being a crude and uncultured language, even though for many it was their mother tongue, and my grandfather certainly spoke it fluently when young.

Ethnicity was no easy matter to resolve. People wishing to make their way in the affairs of the nation might well describe themselves as Polish, especially if they were members of the *szlachta*, although historically and ethnically they could be Lithuanian, Byelorussian or Ukrainian. A good example of this issue is the case of Pilsudski, one of the main architects of the Polish State in the years after 1918, and a passionate Polish nationalist. Yet, as related above, he originally gave his nationality as Byelorussian. Or the poet Mickiewicz, born in Nowogrodek, who could claim to be Polish and Lithuanian and Byelorussian, and has indeed been claimed by each group as "their" national poet. Demographic maps of the Eastern area of the Polish lands show small areas where one or other ethnic group predominates but the areas are so intermixed that it is not always easy to distinguish each group. Perhaps the closest analogy is that of the people of Great Britain, who are all British but who might also describe themselves as English, Scottish, or Welsh. My grandfather's family were *szlachta* living for generations in the Vilna area of Lithuania; his earliest language may have been Byelorussian (the language he heard the villlage children speak) but his nationality was most emphatically Polish.

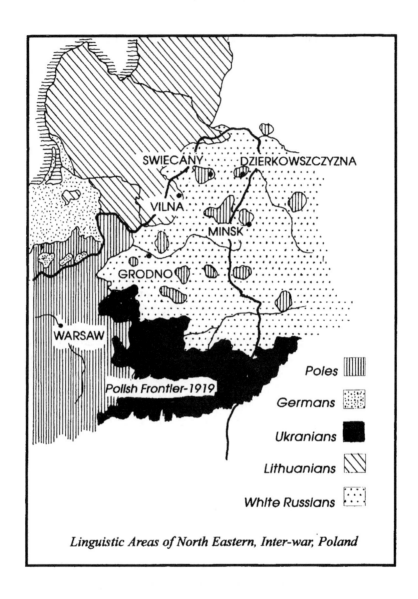

SWIECANY   DZIERKOWSZCZYZNA

VILNA

MINSK

GRODNO

WARSAW

Polish Frontier-1919

Poles

Germans

Ukranians

Lithuanians

White Russians

Linguistic Areas of North Eastern, Inter-war, Poland

Such issues of ethnicity and nationality would assume a new importance in the early years of the newly independent Polish State, particularly between the years 1918-22. The question of the Eastern Territories would cause bitter disagreements and fighting at first and the animosity continued until the outbreak of the Second World War, when once again such issues would be theoretical. Even the Peace Treaties of the Second World War did not properly address the issue. The question will be examined in more detail in Chapter 5.

CHAPTER 2

Origins of the Family

The historical introduction sets the scene for describing the origins of the family. Tracing the family history has proved no easy task, since apart from the obvious geographical and political difficulties, genealogical records were not kept very carefully in this part of Europe. In some instances distinguishing between family legend and facts is not a simple matter. The Chrzczonowicz family lived for centuries in the eastern part of Poland, historically the Grand Duchy of Lithuania (GDL). The population of this area was a mixture of Poles, Lithuanians and Byelorussians, although as time went on the Lithuanian and Byelorussian population was marginalised as anyone who wished to further their career in the Grand Duchy would Polonise their names and adopt Polish customs and dress. The identity of the other two groups was gradually eroded; Polish history has largely been written in such a way as to emphasise the Polish elements and to minimise the contribution of the Lithuanian and Byelorussian strands in her history. Even today many Poles seem reluctant to acknowledge this; one result is that Byelorussian or Lithuanian ancestry may be denied or only grudgingly admitted. Lithuanian nationalism did not emerge as a recognisable movement until the nineteenth century when the idea of national consciousness became widespread throughout Europe. For Byelorussians glimmerings of a national identity had been alive since the seventeenth century. However, the issue was particularly delicate in the lands of eastern Poland where the expression of any kind of nationalism was severely punished. The cause of Byelorussian nationalism was hampered not only by adverse propaganda on the part of the Russians but by the fact that by the nineteenth century the majority of Byelorussian speakers were the country dwellers. These were largely illiterate and therefore least able to take part in a movement whose ideas were spread largely by the written word. The leaders were *szluchta* of Lithuanian or Byelorussian descent who were able to utilise the corpus of Byelorussian literature to further their cause.

The question of ethnicity cannot be ignored when considering the origins of any family living in the eastern borderlands of Poland. Even a quick glance at an ethnographical map will show

how thoroughly mixed geographically these three groups were, and therefore how difficult to separate each one with certainty. The Chrzczonowicz family is no exception. The very origin of the name is uncertain. The root *chrzcz-* is probably derived from the Polish (and Byelorussian) word for baptism. The fact that someone is baptised is noteworthy only in a context where the majority of people are not baptised. This points to a possibility that the first bearer of the name was a converted pagan, as were most of the Lithuanians in the early Middle Ages (and some Byelorussians were calling themselves Lithuanians by this time). The ending of the name, too, is significant. Names ending *-wicz* are typically of Byelorussian origin, while those ending *-ski* are of Polish origin. Family tradition says that until approximately 200 years ago the name took the *-ski* ending (Chrzczonowski) and only changed relatively recently. It was not simply the root *chrzcz-* but rather the name Chrzczon, which obviously derived from this root, which is the origin of the family name. After the Partitions of the Polish-Lithuanian Commonwealth at the end of the eighteenth century those Polish *szlachta* who could prove their pedigree to the Russian authorities were allowed to be treated as gentry, rather than peasants.. It was obviously in the interest of everyone who could do so to register their claim. Some people adapted their name to a similar one bearing a *herb*, others made some very spurious claims to the *szlachta*, and undoubtedly there were cases of bribing the scriveners in Minsk, Vilna and St Petersburg to provide a pedigree. We do know that by the nineteenth century the Chrzczonowicz family were accepted and considered to be part of the Pilawa *herb*, according to the Armorial *Herbarz Polski* (Stupnicki / Niesiecki), even though in official lists of families in the Pilawa *herb* the nearest name to Chrzczonowicz is Chrzczonowski. The surprising fact is that the name appears to have changed from the Polish to the Byelorussian form and not the other way round, which was far more common. Certainly the Chrzczonowicz family considered themselves as Pilawa and the *herb*, the seal and the legends were handed down from one generation to the next. They became widely known and respected as Polish *szlachta* throughout the territory of the Grand Duchy and several held positions of responsibility in the region around Vilna. Any Lithuanian or Byelorussian origins were now quietly ignored. However, the mystery of the true connection with the *herb* remains and any firm links between different aspects of the tale must remain a matter for speculation.

The Pilawa *herb* itself is interesting as it is one of the older Polish *herba*. The crest itself consists of two and a half silver swords on a blue background, the significance of the third, broken sword being that it was a sign of great bravery. Armorials agree that the first person to bear the Pilawa *herb* was one Zyroslaw who was a soldier in the reign of Boleslaw III the Wrymouth (r. 1102-38) and who took part in various battles on Poland's uneasy borders. According to family legend the Pilawa *herb* was conferred upon the Chrzczonowiczs as a reward for bravery at the Battle of Grunwald (Tannenberg) in 1410, in which a combined Polish and Lithuanian force defeated the Teutonic Knights. This was one of the most important battles in Polish history; as a reward 47 Lithuanian nobles were admitted to 47 Polish noble families at Horodlo in 1413. Sadly there is not a single reference in the histories of Pilawa to the Battle of Grunwald or Horodlo, so the truth of this family legend will probably never be known. However, it is almost certain that Chrzczonowicz ancestors took part in the battle as all able-bodied men in Lithuania were called upon to fight. The Chrzczonowskis apparently originally came from the Sandomierz region of Poland, which adds weight to the evidence that the names Chrzczonowicz and Chrzczonowski indicate entirely different families.

If the original form of the name was Chrzczonowicz, which changed to the -*ski* form for convenience and then changed back again, are there any references to them in the historical documents of Lithuania / Byelorussia? The National Archives of the Grand Duchy of Lithuania [*Metryki Litewskie*] are being published volume by volume and they contain numerous references to Chrzczonowiczs. There is no way of knowing, of course, whether they were the family's direct ancestors but they do show that the early Chrzczonowiczs were people of substance and influence even in the sixteenth century onwards in the political and court life of the Grand Duchy. The earliest and most intriguing mention is in Vol. 8 of the Archive in an entry dated 24 June 1508 concerning the sale of a serf, Stan Ozewicz, by Chrzczon Sidorkowicz, to the widow of Martin Jakobowicz. The significance of this text is that the ending -*wicz* is a patronymic meaning "son of", but here we have the name without the patronymic. Could he be the first

The Pilawa 'Herb'

An example of a nineteenth century manor house in the Minsk-Vilna region, of the type built by Polish szlachta. Joachim was brought up in a similar style of house

known ancestor of the family? Chrzczonowiczs feature in the court and diplomatic life of the Grand Duchy from the sixteenth century onwards. One, Jan, was required to pay the special tax for maintaining the hired army needed to fight the war with Muscovy (1561-82); another Jan was one of the witnesses in the election of King Michal Korybut Wisniowiecki (r. 1667-73). This Jan Chrzczonowicz is interesting because he lived in the same *powiat* (roughly equivalent to a county) as the small village of Dzierkowszczyzna, where we know members of our family were living at the turn of the twentieth century. There was also a Francis Chrzczonowicz who was known to be working on the Vilna region as a debt collector in 1785.

When we come to the nineteenth century the situation becomes slightly clearer as any Chrzczonowicz/Chrzczonowski distinction becomes irrelevant. There are several Chrzczonowiczs mentioned in the literature; again, these may or may not be related to our family. The *Polski Slownik Biograficzny* mentions two, one of whom, Jozef (1792-1833) was an engraver. He was a native of Vilna who taught engraving at the University of Vilna. In 1818 he received a prize for his work and in 1819 a grant from the University. His known books of engravings include views of churches in St Petersburg. The other person mentioned, of whom we know even less, was Karol (d. 1850). He was a novelist and poet but earned his living as a schools inspector. Initially he worked in the Bialystok region but at the time of his death he was the Supervisory Inspector for the Swieciany region. His works include a contribution to *New Year Literature 1838* published in St Petersburg and a posthumous collection of poems published in 1861 called *The Messiah. Belarusian Architects* (1993) by U.Dzianisau, lists a Kasimir Chrzczonowicz (1794-1871) who graduated from Vilna University in 1819. Between 1825 and 1863 he was the chief architect for the Minsk region and he designed many of the municipal buildings in Minsk itself. Only a few of his buildings remain standing today, one example being the Central Law Courts; other buildings included the house of Hausman, who was the foremost collector of Byelorussian artefacts in the nineteenth century, and various other buildings in the Minsk area. The artists, architects, etc, of nineteenth century Byelorussia would have been a close-knit circle who met regularly together and who knew each other well. The nineteenth century Chrzczonowiczs would have lived well, in a manor house similar to that owned by Vankovich (see illustration). Other references to Chrzczonowiczs include Konstanty and Leon, who graduated from the Technological Institute in St Petersburg in 1888 and 1897 respectively.

It must be stressed that the story of the Chrzczonowiczs up to this point cannot be definitely traced because of the lack of available records or their inaccessibility (many are in the Archives of St Petersburg, Vilna or Minsk). Given that the family was well-known throughout the former Grand Duchy and were considered at least from the nineteenth century if not earlier to be a respected member of the Polish *szlachta*, one may make tentative suggestions. However, the reader must draw his/her own conclusions as to the likelihood of the different possibilities of ancestry. Many questions remain unanswered, such as the true origins of the family and its connection with the Pilawa *herb*, the links with the Battle of Grunwald and how that came to be part of the family legend and whether Chrzczon Sidorkowicz was indeed the first known ancestor. Do we follow a completely different path and try to trace the Chrzczonowskis back?

However, we can be much more certain about the next generation. Of Ignacy we know nothing except that he was born in the 1810s or 1820s and that he was a direct ancestor. He had at least two sons, Tadeusz-Jozef and Piotr. Piotr was an estate manager near Vilna and was married to Ewa Samowicz, by whom he had seven children. Three of these died in Russia (how we do not know) but one, Wiktoria (1874-1963) qualified and worked as a midwife in St. Petersburg. She gained a great reputation as one of the few trained midwives willing to attend the poor. Her sister, Zofia, fell in love with a man her parents considered most unsuitable – they described him somewhat disparagingly as a "mere postman". They refused to acknowledge the fact that her intended ran the entire postal service in the Vilna region and ran a stable of 17 horses and carriages to do this! However, they did get married and produced three remarkable children. The eldest, Tadeusz Sendzimir, emigrated to America, where he made his name in steel. He produced a large family, most of whom are still in America. The Steelworks at Nowa Huta, originally the Lenin Steelworks, have now been named after him. One of Zofia's daughters, Julia, was a schoolteacher in Zulow near Wilno, the village where Pilsudski was born.

The second daughter, Stefcia, I remember as a gracious white-haired old lady. In her youth she was a noted beauty who, like many women in families of the intelligentsia, had caught the eye of one of the most famous painters of the Formist Movement, Stanislaw Ignacy Witkiewicz (1888-1939), better known as Witkacy. Many of his paintings were executed under the influence of drugs, and he always left a coded clue in his paintings as to which ones he had been using at the time. However, his portrait of Stefcia is sensitive and gentle, a lovely tribute to a friend. When Stefcia and her family returned to their bombed-out flat in the Praga District of Warsaw after the Second World War, in 1945, this portrait was miraculously almost undamaged and has since been restored, to hang in a place of honour in her daughter's home.

Ignacy's other son, Tadeusz, was born in 1845. Here at last is one of my direct ancestors, as he was my great grandfather. We have photographs of him, and a portrait. His marriage to Scholastyka Walentynowicz united two of the ancient *szlachta* families. The Walentynowicz family is very old and includes some remarkable people among its members. One of the female ancestors who lived at the beginning of the nineteenth century was left a widow with eight beautiful daughters. The eldest of these, Tekla, caused a scandal by marrying at the age of fifteen in 1818 a wealthy Russian prince who was well over sixty at the time and who had a reputation for his erotic exploits! However, he died after only a couple of years of marriage, and Tekla married again, more suitably, according to her family. Given the political situation of the time, so soon after the Partitions, for a Polish noblewoman to marry a Russian prince was tantamount to siding with the enemy. Some years later one of the Walentynowiczs was presented with a red velvet and gold monogrammed document cover by the Tsar, Alexander II; we can only guess at the circumstances.

Scholastyka was herself one of a large family – she had seven cousins, of whom three died from typhus fever, and one, Seweryna, emigrated to Chicago. Another cousin, Rafal (1860-1927), fathered six children. One of these, Marian, became a well-known war-time artist and cartoonist and then a nationally-known children's artist, creating the cartoon goat character "Koziolek-Matolek", known and loved by generations of Polish children, and which became classics in his own lifetime. His cousin, Wladyslaw Walentynowicz, has become known throughout Poland as a composer, principally of children's music, and until his retirement he was the Director of the Music Conservatoire in Sopot, northern Poland. I have in my possession a manuscript copy of his "Violin Concerto with String Orchestra" for children, dedicated to my brother, who used to play the violin, and with the orchestra part reduced for piano, so we could both play the piece.

It was Marian's brother, Danek, whom I remember as a child. There was great excitement when he was able to make visits to England in the 1960s. Travel arrangements were a little hit and miss; visas for foreign travel were at that time issued somewhat at the whim of the authorities. An application might lie apparently forgotten in some office somewhere for a couple of years and then be issued for a date two weeks hence, sometimes instead of a pay increase or for some other reason. There was a famous occasion when Witold received a letter from Danek, dated ten days previously, in which he said that he would be arriving at Heathrow in ten days' time – in fact that very morning! I loved Danek's visits to our household. There was always something very special about this cousin of ours who came from my father's country; in fact for some years he was the only Polish member of the family whom I met until his children started to visit as students. Danek spoke very good English, and was a most delightful and entertaining guest, his gentle demeanour and gracious manner hiding great gifts, a brilliant mind and great bravery in service to his country. Danek was a year younger than Witold, and, like him, graduated in Engineering from the Warsaw Technical University – the most prestigious place in Poland for engineers to train. During the Second World War he was a Liaison Officer in the Polish Resistance (Armia Krajowa) working in Warsaw, undermining the German occupation of the city and helping to keep alive the spirit of free Poland. Like many others in the AK he lived largely underground in the sewers of Warsaw for long periods of time, particularly during the Uprising of 1944. There is the story that one day he emerged from the sewers via a manhole in the Praga district of Warsaw, and as it happened, just outside the Transfiguration Hospital where Kostek was working as a surgeon. When Kostek gave him a quinine injection to prevent malaria, Danek had a severe allergic reaction and nearly died. What an irony that would have been! During the Uprising of 1944 Danek's area of operation was the Mokotow district, the scene of much

45

fierce fighting. For the part he played he received distinguished honours including the Cross of Valour and the Distinguished Officers & Commanders Cross for the Revival of Poland. After the War he pursued an academic and publishing career, rising to distinction as Professor at the Institute of Philosophy and Sociology at the Polish Academy of Science, a long-standing Head of the Laboratory of Scientific Research and a lecturer at the Warsaw Technical University. He was also the editor of two publications, *Questions of Science* and *Science of Sciences* as well as the monthly magazine, *Electrotechnical Review*. He was also head of the largest scientific publishing companies in Poland – PWN and WNT. He was truly a remarkable man.

So, although the Walentynowicz side of the family was not very closely related in kinship terms, they were very good friends. Danek, his sister Maria, Witold, Kostek and Zosia spent much time together as they were growing up and as students.

My great grandparents, Scholastyka Walentynowicz and Tadeusz Chrzczonowicz, were married and in due course four children were born to them, three sons and a daughter. Of Weronika, Antoni and Kasimierz we know little, although they would each have their own part to play in the family story.

On 23 October 1875 a son, Joachim, or Chimka for short, was born to Tadeusz and Scholastyka at their farm at Kasperyszki, in the Swieciany district near Wilno. The little baby was apparently baptised a the age of one day – perhaps he was not expected to survive – at the Roman Catholic Church in Swiecianys.

The godparents are listed as the nobleman Ignacy Rakicki and Paulina Zebrowska. The little boy lived on the farm until he was 15 years old, when he was sent away to the Gymnasium at Vilna. However his childhood memories were very vivid, and when he was in his eighties a newspaper article (published in *Wiadomosci* no. 563 13 January 1957) describing countryside similar to that where he had grown up at the end of the nineteenth century stirred such powerful memories in him that he responded with a marvellously evocative piece recalling his own memories of childhood – and this was after a long life of travel, of raising a family, of suffering many tragedies and a final exile in his last years.

The article in question paints a delightful picture of rural life among the *szlachta* of the late nineteenth century in a backwater of Byelorussia and although it describes villages about a hundred miles from his home area, it is worth quoting from it at length for giving a fascinating insight into the background in which Joachim and his brothers and sister grew up.

The broad sweeps of countryside were covered with fields and interspersed with numerous lakes, forests, woods and pastures. Small villages were scattered throughout this isolated part of NE Poland. It was historically the land of the Ruthenians (later Byelorussia and now Belarus) and then by conquest part of the Grand Duchy of Lithuania. The Grand Duchy was joined to the Kingdom of Poland by the marriage of two of its rulers in the 1386. By the mid-nineteenth century it was a sleepy backwater of the Russian Empire, hardly a centre for progress and left largely to the way of life it had followed for centuries. The Polish poet, Adam Mickiewicz, famously captured the atmosphere in his great work *Pan Tadeusz* (1834), with its vivid descriptions of life in this region. Little changed over the next eighty or so years. The population consisted of pockets of Polish *szlachta*, not wealthy or owners of large estates but intensely conscious of their Polish heritage, to the extent of preserving their own customs rather than adapting to those around them. Many of them were effectively free peasants who worked the land but had the courtesy title of *Pan* [gentleman] and who dressed distinctively (in shoes, hats and surtouts). They spoke a strange version of Polish dating from the time of Mickiewicz or earlier and since they learned Polish entirely from literature and by word of mouth one to the other they lost touch with contemporary developments in the language. Children who were sent away to school did acquire a broader vision of the world, but as the language of instruction was Russian they had little chance to learn contemporary Polish. The Polish *szlachta* were very devout Roman Catholics and would travel many miles on a Sunday in order to attend Mass. There were also Jews, Lithuanians and Byelorussians living in the area (in fact they formed the majority of the population), but the Poles kept themselves very much to themselves. The *szlachta* could, and did, obtain a document of proof of their noble origins by applying to the Department of Heraldry in St. Petersburg, but for the well-established families such proof was unnecessary.

Society was organised along strictly defined lines. It was described as a "democratic captivity" – the *szlachta*, no matter how poor they were were always addressed as *pan*, giving an illusion of freedom, but they often only had the tenancy of their small farm. The local manor house was the focus of local life – in return for the "benevolent despotism" of the social structure, the manor house had to allow the peasant to collect firewood from the forest, fodder from the woodlands, and pasture for their cows. Relationships between the Lord of the Manor and the villagers was variable. They were much more lenient regarding the transgressions of their own kind than those of the Lithuanian or Byelorussian peasants and would often overlook the former while punishing the latter. Needless to say this did not foster good relations.

The fields were cultivated by the small peasant farmers, the wealthier ones clubbing together to buy the latest in agricultural equipment, the McCormack Reaper, an import from America. Hay was still cut by hand. The better *szlachta* would lead the haymaking by example, swinging the scythes along with everyone else; the lazy ones would make a token gesture and leave the rest of the work to others.

One such village in this region was that of Backow, in present day Belarus. The road out of the village ran due north-south, so that workers in the fields could tell the time simply by noting when the shadows fell straight along the road . Then it was time for a break in harvesting . The road itself was narrow and raised up on a slight embankment . When carts met each other on the road, the empty one had to give way to the full one. The fine dust from the harvesting clothed everything in a golden light. On the slopes on either side of the embankment there grew chicory and wild garlic, and the area was so densely populated with badgers that it was known as the "Land of the Badgers".

At the end of the road was the Manor House of one of the most ancient of the *szlachta* families, the Huszczas. This was a colourful family with many notable personalities. There was Daniel Huszcza, rumoured to have joined the Polish partisans during the Uprising of 1863, but also renown in the region for his common sense and authority. There was Hipolit Huszcza who surprised everyone by selling his own farm and living in a tiny farm rented from his neighbours, the Irtenskis.

The farm was, by all accounts, a simple building, probably typical of its kind, and was a favourite venue for political meetings. A younger member of the household recollected many years later

48

how students at the meetings would burn with passion as they expounded their beliefs. The farmyard at Ossow was always full of barking dogs; visitors had to wait for a member of the household to come out and control them. The visitor then entered the house, first into a windowless hall where hens scratched around on the floor, and then into the cottage proper. This was simply furnished, with a bed piled high with cushions on one side of the door and a large comfortable sofa on the other side. A polished table and the inevitable religious text on the wall completed the picture. Visitors were welcomed with warm mead and plates of wholemeal bread and honey. Also served were freshly picked cucumbers, which were eaten by scooping the flesh out with a teaspoon which had been dipped in honey, and accompanied by vodka.

The most colourful member of the family was undoubtedly Stefcia Huszcza. She was a whirlwind character, breezing in and out of the *szlachta* houses, bringing news of everyone in the surrounding countryside, and being more entertaining than a newspaper. She had advanced views on education, believing that the education of girls should never stop. When her son married at the age of forty, the story of how she discovered that his bride could never have children was so comical that it passed into local legend.

Life was not always easy for the inhabitants. One of the "bad *szlachta*", Tumilowicz, waged a protracted lawsuit concerning some pigs which had strayed and he refused to pay the set fine for their return. He had wronged another of the *szlachta* by turning her out of her house after the death of her husband, invoking an old law of the Napoleonic Code (parts of which were still in force) to do so. The affair was only settled when someone testified that Tumilowicz had thrown a portrait of the Tsar to the ground and that this act of disrespect would be reported to the authorities unless he paid up and left the poor widow alone. That summer an old Byelorussian custom was enacted. A mysterious charm appeared in Tumilowicz's fields in the form of a stand of rye knotted together. Originally a form of curse against the Tsar, it happened that this year there was much rain and bad weather; the crops did not grow properly being choked with weeds and what little rye that ripened was almost entirely spoiled by the damp conditions. Coincidence or not? asks the teller of the tale.

Sadly, during the turmoil of World War One the front line of the fighting passed along the route of the River Berezino, already with a place in the history books as being on the route of Napoleon's retreat from Moscow in 1812. In May 1920 it was the site of the fierce Battle of Berezino between the Bolsheviks and the Poles. As a result Backow and hundreds of other Polish estates and villages became Bolshevik territory. The Polish partisans formed Intelligence units to relay information about Bolshevik movements to the Polish Army. Many of the inhabitants were rounded up and exiled to the Russian hinterlands, the tundra of Karelia or the steppes of Uzbekistan. Thus passed the end of an era and with it a way of life, never to return.

To this vivid picture of life in countryside so similar to where he spent his early years, Joachim responded by writing an intensely nostalgic article for *Wiadomosci*. The most interesting and significant feature of his reply is that it was written in a mixture of Polish and Byelorussian; it is apparent from this that he spoke both Polish and Byelorussian from an early age. Some of the phrases are pure Byelorussian and he includes quotations from well-known Byelorussian nursery rhymes. Like many of the *szlachta* who spoke Byelorussian he may have been ashamed of this, associating the language with childhood and the village children. Of course he would have spoken Polish as well from an early age, and Russian, too. He learned French at school, so was an accomplished linguist by the time he grew up. His recollections are marvellously sharp and bring to life this bygone era. He writes of shepherds playing tunes on homemade pipes, of amber cherries so full of flavour that they tasted like caramel. Mushroom and berry picking in the forest, baking potatoes in the embers and carrying them in his pockets to keep his hands warm, drinking milk fresh from the cow, milk so creamy it left a white moustache on their faces. Water-lilies on the numerous small lakes, the breeze ruffling the surface of the water, small shrimps nibbling at fingers carelessly trailing in the water. Bird song, the colourful birds flying around, the different sounds of pigs, horses and hens. A lost world except in his memories, and doubtless idealised, it nonetheless conjures up, together with the impressions from the article, an extraordinary picture of how life must have been for a small boy growing up towards the end of the nineteenth century in the rural backwaters of Lithuania/Byelorussia as a member of the *szlachta*.

Joachim could not remain a child forever and at the age of

fifteen he was sent away to the Vilna Gymnasium, which had been founded in 1808. He graduated from there in 1895 at the age of twenty, and was then faced with the question of what to do next. His decision to enter the Technological Institute in St. Petersburg and train as an engineer was very much a product of the philosophy prevailing among enlightened Poles of the time. During this period of Russian rule the situation was very difficult for Poles who were intelligent and who wanted to become professionally trained. Repression and suppression of all things Polish (language, literature, nationalist aspirations) was pursued with vigour by the Russians. Poles were not encouraged to be educated, and certainly it was difficult for Poles to gain a professional qualifications and to practice that profession in their native land. The industrialisation of Europe in the nineteenth century meant that the new learning and skills – engineering, railway building, factory building and manufacturing, for example, were fast becoming essential for a country to play its full part in European life. Poles were discouraged from studying these subjects because an educated intelligentsia would be more likely to breed subversion and trouble, or so the Russians considered.

However, as a result of the increased repressions following the unsuccessful Uprising of 1863 a group of far-sighted intellectuals, the Warsaw Positivists, decided that it was essential that enough Poles were trained in those skills and disciplines which would be needed when Poland was once more a free country. For technology and engineering the only real choices for a proper training were either in the West or at the Technological Institute in St. Petersburg. The best continental Technological Institutes were seen as providing training of a higher standard than the universities as they provided not only a Diploma but also a professional qualification. The coveted Diploma in Engineering from St. Petersburg was no exception to this and was held in the highest regard. In common with continental practice, graduates were entitled to be known as *pan inzynier* [Mr. Engineer], a title which has no equivalent in English, since in English the term can apply to anyone from the person who mends the washing machine to the most qualified researcher in the field. During the 1860s Polish intellectuals began to encourage Poles to study in St. Petersburg and to form a recognised group of Polish students of high calibre within the Institute.

Do we have any idea what the Technological Institute was like in the nineteenth and early twentieth centuries? Fortunately we do, as a book of Memoirs was published in 1933 to commemorate the centenary of the founding of the Institute, and particularly the part played by the Polish students. This is fascinating reading as it gives a history of the Institute and the story of the Polish students there.

The Institute was originally founded on 28 November 1828 (Old Style) by Tsar Nicholas II as a gesture of gratitude for the life of the Minister of the Treasury, a man called Kankin. The teaching followed the pattern of the English education system, the aim being to provide a course of general education and practical technology with scholarships provided by the Government. The children of the nobility were not eligible (and indeed, any nobleman who did apply on behalf of his son was liable to lose his noble status). There were two sections, Junior and Senior. The Junior section gave priority to boys from families of limited means and was non-denominational – significant in an era when Orthodoxy was almost synonymous with Russianness. The course lasted three years, between the ages of 13 and 15, and the boys could then enter the Senior section where specialist subjects, eg., applied mechanics and technology, were taught in addition to the general ones. This course lasted for three years as well and practical tuition was included from the beginning. There were workshops for the teaching of work with lathes, anvils, carpentry skills, and there was even a foundry. Laboratory work included chemistry and dyeing.

The Institute was refounded in 1833 and over the years its reputation steadily increased. By the early 1860s the course had become a five-year technical one designed for those who had already completed their secondary education. Until the late 1860s there had been a mere sprinkling of Polish graduates, but following the conscious decision to produce a group of well-qualified Poles, the numbers increased markedly. There were between 30 and 50 Polish graduates a year until 1908 and then a further boost between 1911 and 1917. In 1865 the Institute closed and was completely reorganised along the lines of the Parisian school, "Ecole Centrale des Artes et Manufactures". There were now two levels of the course, I and II, Level I leading to the title and qualification of Technical Engineer and Level II to that of Technician.

The years 1870-1902 were the heyday of the Institute, many of the reforms being put into practice by Wyszniegradzki, who was the Director between 1875 and 1879. Between 1837 and 1913 the Institute produced approximately 5 700 Engineering graduates, two-thirds being mechanical and one-third chemical graduates. Of these approximately 1 300 (23%) were Poles. The peak years for Polish students were in the 1890s, coinciding with the time that Joachim was there (1895-1900). After satellite Technological Institutes were founded in Karkhov, Tomsk, Kiev and Warsaw, the Polish contingent of students at St Petersburg dropped considerably.

As may be imagined, a closely-knit group of Polish students with a burning sense of national identity and no great love for the Tsar himself or for the Russian Empire was potentially a dangerous situation, so certain restrictions were placed on the students – of movements, of how they spent their free time, on where they could obtain jobs afterwards. One of the Polish students from Grodno, Hryniewiecki, played an important role in the assassination of Tsar Alexander II in 1881. Following this the students were even more closely watched by the Russian administration

Numerous groups and organisations were founded to assist the Polish students, some acting as a front for anti-Tsarist activities. There were organisations such as the "Roman Catholic Charitable Association of the Church of St. Catherine in St. Petersburg" which provided financial help for students. There was an annual "Catholic Ball" held to raise funds – and these funds were secretly used to finance the nationalist cause. There was the "Association for Help for Education in the Faith" which handed out scholarships, the "Polish Kitchen" was an offshoot of this. In 1891 another group was founded, the "Circle for Popular Education". The Polish Socialist Party was founded at about this time and took a distinctly anti-Tsarist stance. It was soon declared illegal. Student unrest was being fuelled on many sides as so many revolutionary groups and ideas were sweeping the capital.

The Polish students performed very well academically and although on the whole not permitted to obtain posts in Polish lands themselves nonetheless secured good jobs in many of the far flung outposts of the Russian Empire. In 1898 graduates of the Institute met in Warsaw in the Victoria Restaurant – on the site of the present Hotel Bristol – to discuss the founding of an offshoot of the St Petersburg Institute in Warsaw. This finally occurred in 1915.

There are close family links with the Technological Institute in St. Petersburg. Danek's father, Rafal, graduated there in 1886 and two others, Konstanty Zorawski (1898) and Mieczyslaw Pozaryski (1897) became professors at the Warsaw Technological Institute and taught Joachim's son, Witold. Leonard Labic (1894) later became Joachim's boss in Poland, and the were at least three cousins of Joachim's, Justyn (1899), Konstanty (1888) and Leon (1897). Other graduates became close family friends, including Konrad Midwid (1900) and Witold Juszkiewicz (1887) and Ignacy Jasiukowicz (1869) who was the relative of another close family friend. Karol Klukowski (1898) obtained a post at the Metallurgy Institute in Ekaterinburg, as we know from a postcard sent him by Joachim in 1904. Klukowski's son became a painter ; in 1968 he bought from Witold the tiny plot of land which was all that remained of the family assets in Poland. As a thank you he presented Witold with his painting of a Polish landscape. Another friend, Stefan Ossowiecki (1898) had clairvoyant gifts. In 1941 he had a vision of Witold, "I see him alive. I see him behind barbed wire in the vicinity of a big river". Witold's note adds, "This agrees perfectly – I was then in a Russian labour camp in the GULAG."

Life as a Polish student in St. Petersburg did have restrictions but for a member of a well-connected family there were plenty of social opportunities. It is almost certain that there were Walentynowicz cousins in St Petersburg and there were other interesting people for Joachim to meet. Although direct proof is impossible to establish at this point in time, it is very likely that through one of his fellow science students at the University Joachim made the acquaintance of a delightful and talented family who were also living in St Petersburg. It is worth spending a little time relating the story of the Kokoulin family, as they would play an important part in the family story, and also present one of the most tantalising puzzles of the whole saga.

Vasily Kokoulin, the father of the family, had returned to St Petersburg with his family in 1898 after a long time in Eastern Siberia where he had been manager of a gold mine in Bodaibo, a small town on the Vittim River and the centre of the large Lena Goldfields. He himself had been born in 1850 in the town of Kirensk in Siberia to a poor family which nevertheless had a long and interesting history. In 1518 a leading Greek Orthodox scholar, Maxim the Greek, had been invited by Prince Vasily III to come to Moscow to correct the sacred writings of the Church. Once in Moscow he exposed and condemned the vice and corruption which he found, which not unnaturally incurred the Prince's displeasure. In 1525 Maxim and his party were exiled, Maxim himself to the Volokolansk Monastery. One of his party acquired the nickname "Kakoboulos", or Bad Adviser. Eventually this became corrupted to Kakosvulin and then to Kokoulin.

The young Vasily Kokoulin started to work in the gold mines of Bodaibo and eventually became the chief manager of the mines in 1889. He introduced many reforms – the lot of the miners at the time was appalling, hardly better than slavery – new machinery and easier techniques for mining the gold, for example. Vasily had married Alexandra Petrovna in 1871 and he was much influenced by Tolstoy's ideas. With the aid of his wife he introduced health insurance and medical care for the workers and their families and started a school for the miners' children, which the Kokoulin children also attended when small. The miners, largely exiles or ex-convicts, and whose lot in life had been very poor, greatly respected Vasily Kokoulin and would refer to him as "Our Father." Vasily summarised his philosophy in an article in the periodical *Gold and Platinum* dated January 15 1909. Six children were born to Vasily and Alexandra. Jasha was the eldest, born in 1872, then there was Vera, Boris (who died young of TB), Nadezhda, Lyubov, and Sofia, who was born on 10th March 1878. Sofia and Nadezhda finished their schooling at the Irkutsk First School for Noblewomen (founded by Tsar Nicholas I). Sofia's great moment came when at the age of 12 she was chosen to dance before the future Tsar, Nicholas II, when he visited the school in 1890.

By 1898 Vasily had had enough of the problems of the goldfields and the way that his superiors in St Petersburg were so slow in making administrative decisions, so he and Alexandra decided to move to St Petersburg. Jasha was already there, studying at the University, and Sofia had passed the difficult entrance exam to study piano at the Conservatoire . Nadezhda and Lyubov remained in Irkutsk to finish their schooling, then they rejoined the family.

It is easy to imagine Joachim making the acquaintance of this lively family and that as his time as a student drew to a close, seeking the advice of Vasily as to where he could work as a Polish civil engineer (his homeland was barred to him, some versions say simply because he was a Pole and others that he had been a student member of one of the numerous anti-Tsarist student organisations). Perhaps Vasily suggested that the Bodaibo goldmines had plenty of opportunities for a keen young man and that he himself had family there who would help set the young man on his feet. We do know that Joachim graduated in 1900 and we next hear of him working in Bodaibo as an engineer, and that soon after he was courting Anna Kokoulina, daughter of the Director of the Gymnasium in Bodaibo.

Meanwhile, in St Petersburg, Sofia had been introduced to an acquaintance of her brother Jasha. The Kokoulin and Shostakovich families had known each other in Siberia – there were members of both families living in Irkutsk – so Dmitri was probably a distant acquaintance. Sofia and Dmitri were immediately attracted to each other and shared a common interest in music. Dmitri himself came from a long line of Polish exiles, illustrating in a personal way the complexities of survival for Polish intellectuals and dissidents. Dmitri had been born in the huge exiles camp at Narim, Siberia, where his father, Boleslav, had been exiled following his implication in the assassination of Tsar Alexander II in 1881. Boleslav's father had been exiled for hiding a revolutionary and taking part in the Uprising of 1863, and his father (Dmitri's great-grandfather) had taken part in the Uprising of 1830. This pattern of exile and return, exile and return was a common experience for Polish intellectuals of the nineteenth century. Dmitri was a histology student, who later worked with Mendeleyev, who devised the Periodic Table of the Elements .

Dmitri and Sofia were married on January 31 1903. Their first child, Maria, was born in the October of that year and their son, Dmitri, in September 1906. Another daughter, Zoya, was born two years later. Dmitri Shostakovich, of course, grew up to become one of the most important composers of the twentieth century, and his life is well documented in numerous biographies (see bibliography). As a child he showed an early interest in music but Sofia did not let him start piano lessons until he was eight years old. She carefully guided his musical education and was herself a woman of strong character; when her husband died suddenly in 1922 from a heart attack she had to keep the family together, and went out to work to earn the money to do this. Even young Dmitri had to make time in his musical studies to play as a cinema pianist (in the days of silent films) to earn what he could. Sofia lived until she was 77, dying in 1955.

The revolutionary activities of both families are recorded. Dmitri himself was present at the so-called Bloody Sunday of January 9 1905, when the Tsarist Army fired on unarmed demonstrators gathered to petition for better wages and conditions. He had been active in the revolutionary movement at least since 1897, when he had come under police surveillance. His flat had been used for printing illegal material. His brother, Boris, had been expelled from the University for his participation in student rebellions. He was ordered to live in Irkutsk, where he continued his revolutionary activities. Dmitri's two sisters, Maria and Vera, were regarded by the police as very dangerous, as was his brother, Alexander, and were subject to various persecutions by the police. Marysia married Maxim Lavrentevich Kostrikin in 1903, another revolutionary activist, who was exiled to the Turukhanskiy region for his activities. From here he escaped to Irkutsk, where he was protected by his father-in-law, Boleslav. Dmitri's older brother, Vladimir, was a meteorologist who became a member of the Irkutsk Meteorological Observatory and who did important research into the climatology of Eastern Siberia. Alexander settled in Germany, where he pursued an academic career. Boleslav, Dmitri's father, was permitted to travel from Irkutsk to St Petersburg in 1898 to visit his son and family. He died a few years later, killed by the White Guards in Irkutsk during the violence of the Civil War (1918-20).

Sofia's sister, Lyubov, was engaged to Vyacheslav Janovitsky, also a revolutionary, who was arrested in 1903 for taking part in an armed attack against a police division. They were married in prison before the trial took place. The sentence for this revolutionary activity was execution, but Sofia defended him in court and he was reprieved.

The newly qualified Civil Engineer, Joachim, set off for Bodaibo, probably as a result of his acquaintance with the Kokoulin family, in the year 1900 or 1901. He certainly settled there and began to court the daughter of the Director of the

Gymnasium, Anna Kokoulina. They eventually married in 1906. Unfortunately the most assiduous enquiry has failed to find a direct link between the two groups of Kokoulins, but it seems on the circumstantial evidence that it would be an extraordinary co-incidence to have two unrelated families of the same name moving in the same circles in the same remote places in Siberia. A possible family tree can be constructed which would relate Anna and Sofia as second cousins, but we will probably never know the exact nature of the relationship between the two parts of the family. It is one of the most tantalising puzzles of the whole story.

CHAPTER 3

Siberia

Siberia – the very word conjures up images of vast expanses of fierce cold and of the GULAG, the Soviet prison system. There are elements of truth, of course, in all stereotypes, but the reality of Siberia is much richer and more varied than this. What was the Siberia in which Joachim went to live and work really like?

Even the briefest of glances at a map will give an idea of the sheer vastness of a land stretching from the Ural Mountains to the Pacific Ocean. Most of the land area is uninhabitable, being tundra which is frozen for most of the year, or taiga, the heavily forested part of the land with permafrost only a few feet below the surface even at the height of the brief, hot summer. There are numerous mountain ranges, some very dramatic and beautiful, others more like series of foothills, for example the Urals. There are numerous rivers, many of enormous width, the principal ones being the Ob, the Yenisei and the Lena, all flowing south to north to empty into the frozen seas of northern Russia. When the rivers freeze over they can be used as roads; before the building of the Trans-Siberian Railway this was the only practical way of travel apart from the Great Post Road, or *trakt*, which was little more than a path through the forest. Siberia is an area teeming with wildlife; reindeer, bears, sable, foxes and wolves all abound and there is a rich supply of fish in the rivers, as well as a profusion of plant life which flourishes in the short summer. The landscape has a severe and unique beauty unrivalled anywhere in the world. The native peoples are survivors of the indigenous tribes of Siberia, for example the Buryats, the Evenki and the Yakuts in the Eastern part, but over the years they have been treated rather like the American Indians or Australian aborigines and are now few in number. They are nomadic peoples, expert survivors in the harsh conditions, peaceable by nature and traditionally following Shamanist forms of religion, although many of the Buryats are, perhaps surprisingly, Bhuddist.

The Russian colonisation of Siberia began in the reign of Ivan IV, the Terrible, who ruled from 1533-84. It was organised by a merchant dynasty, the Stroganovs, who hired a band of Cossacks

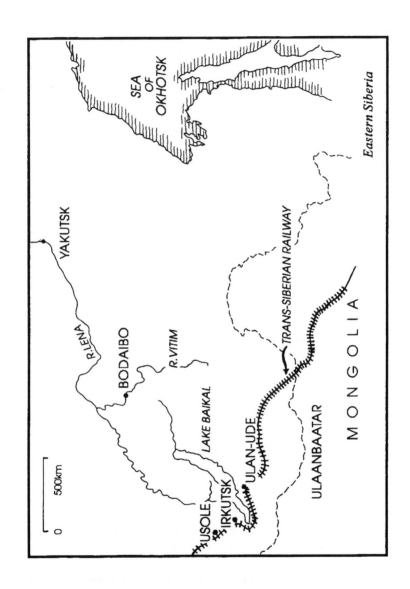

led by a man called Yermak. Their mission was to penetrate deep into the uncharted wilds of Siberia and plunder it for its natural resources – timber, fur and minerals. Yermak succeeded in defeating the Siberian Tartars in 1582 and installed himself in the town which was later to become Tobolsk on the banks of the Irtysh River.

During the seventeenth century bands of adventurers from Moscovy, criminals on the run, and merchants conquered the Lena Valley in the NE of Siberia. The city of Yakutsk, where my grandmother was born, was founded in 1632 by Russian fur traders, furs being much in demand both at home and abroad, the sable being the most prized of all. The colonising Russians demanded tribute, or *yasak*, from the natives, generally in the form of furs. Not unnaturally this was a cause of growing resentment among the native peoples. It was profits from furs which helped to finance the recovery of Russia from numerous wars in the seventeenth century and Peter the Great's ambitious building plans of the eighteenth century.

During the 1760s Catherine the Great published a number of decrees extending the power of the authorities to send serfs convicted of crimes or other delinquents to Siberia either to settle there permanently in exile or for a fixed period of time. There had always been a slow trickle of criminals sent to Siberia as punishment; now the trickle became a flood as a vast eastward tide of exiles made their way on the long and lonely road. Some were criminals, some critical of the Government, others were simply runaway serfs or peasants. The harsh punishments elicited sympathy from the local Siberian inhabitants, but undoubtedly the most renown of the early exiles were the Decembrists. This was a group of aristocrats who decided to assassinate the Tsar, Alexander I, in December 1825, inspired by the liberal ideals which were sweeping Europe in the aftermath of the Napoleonic era. Unfortunately, Alexander rather inconveniently died before the original plan could be carried out, so they hurriedly revised the plot and planned a coup before the new Tsar, Nicholas I, could succeed to the throne. Their plans were discovered and the plot came to nothing. As a result many people were rounded up and questioned. Five were sentenced to death and about a hundred were exiled to Siberia or to army service in the ranks. The Decembrists served as an inspiration for generations to come for all those struggling to bring about reform. They were also remarkable in that the wives of twelve of them, including two princesses, decided to follow their husbands into exile, an action unheard of at the time since spouses would automatically share the same loss of rights as they would. The two princesses, Volkonskaya and Trubetskaya, were the most well-known of the women. The exiles were first of all imprisoned in Chita, beyond Lake Baikal, and then in 1830 moved to the town of Petrovsky Zavod, 400 miles to the southwest. The railway station at Petrovsky Zavod has a memorial and a mural to commemorate the Decembrists. The Volkonskis and the Trubetskis received permission to settle in Irkutsk after the period of exile was over in 1854; the house where they lived is preserved today as a Museum, and they were buried in the grounds of the Znamevsky Convent in Irkutsk.

Each of the Polish Uprisings in the nineteenth century resulted in large numbers of activists or alleged activists being exiled to Siberia. The land was also peopled by an underclass of former prisoners and runaways who wandered from settlement to settlement demanding food from the inhabitants. It was easier to leave out scraps of bread or meat and a jug of milk for them than risk the penalty for non-cooperation, usually in the form of burning houses.

The lot of the exiles was not easy. Before the completion of the Trans-Siberian Railway in the late nineteenth and early twentieth century the exiles had to walk to their place of exile, usually a trek of several thousand miles through inhospitable terrain and bitter cold. Not surprisingly, many did not survive this arduous introduction to life in Siberia. There is an obelisk near the start of the Great Trakt near Perm which marks the point where the convicts had to say farewell to their wives and families who were not accompanying them. The scenes of heartache and tears can only be imagined. The exiles were divided into four categories – the penal colonists, the hard labour convicts, individuals who were simply deported and those who voluntarily followed the exiles, eg., their wives and families. The penal colonists and the hard labour convicts were usually exiled for life; they forfeited all civil and property rights and their spouses were permitted to remarry. They were also tattooed or branded. The third class of exiles were a hotchpotch of religious dissenters, peasants who had been outlawed by their village community and individuals who were simply exiled by a court or by order of the Ministry of the Interior. These were not imprisoned as such but their activities were closely watched. Innocent students were arrested if seen in the company of actual or suspected malcontents. Parents were exiled if their children became revolutionaries (see Tupper, pp142ff). It was an ever-present threat hanging over anyone brought to the attention of the authorities for whatever reason.

Until 1882 administrative exiles were forbidden to teach or lecture, to run a library or printing plant, own a photographic studio, tea house or tavern, participate in theatrical performances or appear in court. They were only permitted to practice medicine, surgery, pharmacy or midwifery with the permission of the Ministry of the Interior. Letters were heavily censored.

It is not difficult to see that groups of like-minded intellectuals would soon band together and form societies and discussion circles to examine the new ideas which were sweeping Europe in the nineteenth century. Many of the activists involved in the formation of the socialist and people's movements of the time were exiled to Siberia and the major towns became, somewhat ironically, centres for dissidents and activists. Lenin himself was exiled to Siberia and Vladimir Ilych Ulyanov in fact took his new name from the River Lena. He was exiled to Shushenskoye in the Krasnoyarsk region. Stalin was sent to Batum from where he escaped and went into hiding. The number of political exiles under police surveillance in 1881 was 2873; in the spring of 1901 alone 16 000 were exiled from St. Petersburg (Harrison Salisbury p.87, quoting Miliukov). The communities of these exiles contributed greatly to the cultural life of Siberia gathering in the largest towns. 80 000 Poles were exiled after the 1830 Uprising; by 1880 75% of the population of Irkutsk was estimated to be Catholic according to Davies (*Heart of Europe* p259), and therefore probably Polish. By and large the exiles were forbidden to return to their original towns after the term of exile had been completed and so learned to settle and make new lives for themselves where fate had put them. Necessity was turned to advantage as people began to study the terrain, the geography, geology, flora and fauna of this vast and largely unknown area. The contribution of Polish intellectuals to the exploration and discovery of Siberia was remarkable. The brother of Jozef Pilsudski, Bronislaw (1866-1918), for example, wrote the first ethnographical survey of the far eastern regions of

Sakhalin and Kamchatka and explorers such as Beniawski (1746-86) had earlier begun the process of making information about Siberia more widely accessible .

This was the region to which Joachim decided to move after graduating in engineering in 1900. We will never know whether he freely chose to work in Siberia or whether he was a member of a forbidden student organisation which meant that he was unable to work in former Polish lands. We do not know for sure whether Joachim went straight to Siberia after graduating or whether he took a year off for travelling. He was certainly living in Bodaibo in 1904 as there is a postcard postmarked Bodaibo sent by him to his friend in Ekaterinburg dated then. Bodaibo, the town where he settled, was not by any stretch of the imagination a great centre of social life.

Not much is known of the details of Bodaibo. Situated approximately 1100km (709 miles) NE of Irkutsk on the River Vittim, a tributary of the Lena River, it was founded as recently as 1863 when a group of Cossacks under the leadership of Ivan Novitskiye was exploring the territory for minerals. There were many such groups searching for gold as NE Siberia was rumoured to have plentiful deposits in the sandy gravels of the river beds. The gold prospectors were looking for river beds with plentiful pyrites, iron, quartz, slate or clay as being likely sites for gold. The gold seam was covered with earth from two to twenty feet thick, but of course the problem was that the permafrost was only six feet below ground. A claim to a piece of land or river could easily be made; the extremities of the proposed territory merely had to be marked and the find registered with the Commissar of Police. A claim was on average three miles long and 500-1 000 feet wide. Once registered the mine had to be worked and tax (5-10%) paid on all gold mined.   Novitskiye was, by all accounts, an impatient and somewhat cruel man, not giving his fellow explorers or his horses much rest on their travels. Their aim was to reach the River Nakatomy as soon as they could. They had heard rumours about the River Bodaibo and that gold had been found there, but no one knew for certain where the river was or where it led to.

The site seemed ideal as a base for further exploration. The confluence of the River Bodaibo with the Vittim formed an ideal natural harbour for setting up trading and the good sandy banks made the discovery of gold there a distinct possibility. The first merchant, Mikhail Sibiryanka, staked his claim to his plot of land in 1863, although his first building was not erected until the following year. The first merchants who bought land were enjoined not to use any gold they might find on their land, although it is difficult to see just how practical and enforceable such a ruling could possibly be. Gold was discovered, in large quantities and easy to pan from the sand and gravel river bed, and the little settlement grew fast. Merchants and gold traders built houses along the banks of the river and the place became a hive of activity as the gold industry brought with it other trade, principally of hay and cattle to help boost the self-sufficiency of the town. Joachim arrived probably in 1901 or 2 but it was not until 10th June 1903 that Tsar Nicholas II officially confirmed the foundation of the city by Decree of the State Council. In 1907 a City Government was established and major administrative centres set up near the principal mining areas of Uspenskoe and Nadezhdinskoye. Originally the town was administered from the Olekim region, but later it was moved to the Vittimsky region. The author of the only book about Bodaibo, Broido, wryly remarks that the most lasting monument left by the city governors to the town was the municipal prison, opened with great pomp and ceremony! However, the authorities were not so keen on building schools and hospitals – in fact the city hospital, although planned, was never built at all. The contribution of Vasily Kokoulin in providing health, welfare and educational facilities for the miners and their families was therefore highly significant in view of the complete lack of alternatives. Pubs and brothels, however, were permitted to operate without restrictions, huge bribes were given to the police and even the army were known to turn a blind eye to some of the suspicious practices. The head of the Gymnasium, or Secondary School, in Bodaibo at this time was Konstantyn Konstantynov Kokoulin. There had certainly been Kokoulins in Bodaibo until 1898 (Vasily and his family). The arguments for conjecturing that the two Kokoulins were related have already been rehearsed (see Ch.2), and it is certainly likely that Joachim settled in Bodaibo because of a family link between the two branches.

The town may have been prospering by this time, but the lot of the miners was scandalous. The story of gold mining in this part of Siberia is very enlightening. The miners and their families lived in atrocious and appalling conditions. The gold was in fact panned from the river bed as well as mined and a photograph of the Bodaibo goldfields taken at this time shows a broad, shallow river with several extremely precarious-looking wooden jetties built out over the water. Presumably this is where the gold was actually extracted.

Gold was first discovered along the Lena River in 1843, the Lena river system covering a huge area of Siberia and draining an area roughly equal to the area of European Russia. The principal goldfields were situated along the Olekma and Vittim rivers. Goldmining did not grow fast in this region as most of the early prospectors and miners were political exiles, ex-criminals or hardy local residents scraping a living out of the harsh environment. The winters were bitter; January temperatures averaged something in the region of -40C, sometimes even lower, with two or three feet of snow. In the short summer the temperature might reach +20C, plummeting to near freezing at night; an added summer problem was the hordes of mosquitoes which thrived on the swampy ground which was frozen for much of the year. The rivers were only fully thawed between June and September of each year, which meant that transport was a problem, and mining itself was impossible between October and May because the ground was frozen.

Conditions were terrible at the mines . Worker unrest broke out at intervals when they became particularly bad, as in the 1870s, 80s and 90s. The first regulations governing conditions were only issued by the Imperial Government in St.Petersburg in the 1870s, but unfortunately proved unenforceable in these remote parts of Siberia. The government legislated for the use of penal labour in the mines, so gradually hard labour prisoners and political exiles began to dominate among the workforce. General causes of unrest listed in 1898 included poor food, low pay and the officials' hard attitude to the workers. The Lena Goldfields, of which the Bodaibo deposits formed a part, were run by one company, the Lenskoe Zoloto-Promyshlennoe Tovarishchestvo, or Lenzoto for short, which had been founded in 1861. In the early 1880s Baron Horace Ginzburg and the House of Meyer Trading Company, a concern with English connections, purchased some shares. In 1896 they assumed control of Lenzoto, which then became the largest goldmining company in Eastern Siberia.

By the 1880s and 1890s there was a ban on using penal labour in the mines. Lenzoto built a small-gauge railway to connect the 25 miles between the Feodosievsk mines and Bodaibo itself and the Company attempted to improve the living conditions of the workers. The Company built churches, chapels and libraries, raised the daily meat ration and enforced the prohibition on women working underground and the restriction of the working day to twelve hours. However, the workers were still heavily fined for minor infringements of the law and could still be easily dismissed (a particularly cruel action as survival in such an inhospitable climate was impossible without proper shelter and provision against the weather).

Not all the mining officials accepted the harsh conditions as inevitable or even desirable. Vasily Kokoulin was at least one manager who protested at the harsh conditions in which the miners worked and he and his wife worked tirelessly to improve their welfare, founding a school for the miners' children and instituting a health care system and a pension scheme among other projects. He was greatly influenced by the ideas of Tolstoy and was later to summarise his philosophy in an article he wrote for the magazine *Gold and Platinum* on January 15th 1909. It was partly because these attempts at improvements met with indifference or even hostility from the management, as well as the frustrations of the extreme slowness of communications between Bodaibo and St Petersburg that persuaded him to leave Bodaibo in 1898. It is a measure of the high regard in which the workers held him that they referred to him as "Our Father".

After the departure of Vasily Kokoulin, conditions steadily deteriorated, particularly after 1907, under the regime imposed by one man, Belozorov. In the extreme remoteness of the Siberian taiga, such a man, and indeed the Lenzoto Company itself, could in practice impose whatever working and living conditions they chose. The workers were effectively prisoners of the mines as they were simply unable to leave them and abandon the area as for most of the year travel was almost impossible due to the harsh conditions. Some conditions were improved; the working day was reduced to eleven hours in winter and eleven and a half in summer, but on the other hand, the workers were beholden to the Company for everything they needed to live. Wages were paid according to the miner's daily output, but they were denied access to the log books where the records were kept. Often the wages were paid (illegally) in coupons which could only be redeemed in the Company's shops which were poorly stocked and where prices were high (on average more than twice the Moscow prices). Some of the wages were paid in food, often in a rotten and inedible state.

The healthcare system was the only area where real progress was made before 1911. Medical care was free and a weekly bath provided. The ratio of doctors to the miners (1:10 000) was higher than that available to the general population of Russia. However, the living conditions were hardly conducive to good health. The barracks where the workers and their families lived were often uninhabitable wooden structures where people were crammed in and lacked even the most basic hygienic and sanitary standards. The rough wooden walls let the moisture in and it was not uncommon for those sleeping next to the outside walls to wake in winter and find their hair frozen to them. An inspection conducted in 1911 found that out of 103 barracks (for 6 700 people) no less than 88 were declared unfit for human habitation. The conditions in the mines themselves were hardly better. The men had to cope with the dangers of inadequate support beams, precarious and unlit ladders, no protection against the gases found underground, and dripping water which froze in their clothes as they walked home. The mortality rate was high, not only from the terrible living and working conditions but also due to the large number of accidents. In the year 1911, for example, there were 869 recorded accidents as a result of which seven were killed and 25 disabled. Employment at Lenzoto was frequently compared with penal hard labour. (See Melancon, M.).

One of the interesting features of Lenzoto, although hardly one to be proud of, was the fact that the Lena Goldfields had a large British interest. By 1906 Lenzoto was producing huge profits and in 1908 the two sons of Horace Ginzburg helped organise Lena Goldfields Ltd, which was an English company owning 70% of Lenzoto shares. This was officially registered as a company on 10 July 1908 with two stated aims:

1. To gain the benefit of a contract between the Ginzburg-Meyer company of St Petersburg and the Russian Mining Corporation for an acquisition of 70% of the capital of Lenzoto.

2. A contract of purchase as a going concern of the Bodaibo Railway connecting with the Trans-Siberian Railway.

The Russian Mining Corporation was another company with interests in the area; originally founded in 1906 it was refounded in 1909 with Baron A. Ginzburg among the Directors.

This large British interest in Russian mining in a remote part of Siberia was part of a drive by the Russian government to encourage foreign investment in Russian, especially in the areas of mining, engineering and manufacturing. Although later derided or ignored by the Bolsheviks after the 1917 Revolution, it was this very investment from capitalist countries which had enabled such phenomenal strides to be taken in bringing Russian industry into the twentieth century. Levels of production were attained which were not equalled for several decades after the Revolution and Civil War which followed. Entries under "Lena Goldfields" in the *Mining Manual* for the years 1908-16 make fascinating reading as the fortunes of the Company, with its British office in Moorgate St, London EC1, can be traced year by year. The Directors obviously had little knowledge of conditions at the mines and one wonders if they would have taken action if they had known what was happening in what was, after all, a remote part of the Russian Empire. It is noted, however, that "very little washing [of the gravels] is carried on at the mines during October to March owing to the gravels and water being frozen." (*Mining Manual 1912*). Lena Goldfields owned an interest in the Russian Mining Corporation and there were also links with the Lenskoe Company.

It is a matter for speculation as to how Joachim felt about the situation at the mines. From what we know of his character it is unlikely that he would have tolerated obviously unfair conditions if he were in a position to change them. To judge by surviving anecdotes there are numerous occasions when he did speak his mind. He was working in Bodaibo certainly from 1900/1 to 1909/10; perhaps he decided to move when Lenzoto became Lena Goldfields and working conditions deteriorated even more, perhaps his particular job came to an end, perhaps the offer of a new job in either Usole Sibirskoe or Irkutsk made them decide to move.

Whatever the reason for the move it is worth sketching in subsequent events in the Bodaibo goldmines as they are interesting in the light of the history of the moves towards the Revolutions of 1917. The most famous occurrence was the Massacre of 1912, an event whose after effects changed the course of history. By early

1912 the plight of the workers, who now numbered 5514 (4383 miners) had become desperate. By February the quality of the meat supplied to the workers was being questioned as being unfit for human consumption. On 28 February a miner's wife showed some of the offending meat to a Tartar livestock expert, who identified it as apparently originating from the sex organs of a stallion. Upon complaining to the management the workers were told to be patient and matters would improve. This incensed the workers as they knew that this was an empty promise so the miners called for a walk out. By mid-March all the mines had struck; the miners elected delegates and attempted negotiation, submitting their demands in writing. The atmosphere was rapidly becoming in danger of running out of control.

There were no socialist party organisations in the area until this time, although Russia itself was seething with different groups of Social Democrats, Socialist Revolutionaries, Mensheviks, Bolsheviks, anarchists, and so on. Approximately two thirds of the strike leaders were political exiles and it was their political awareness coupled with the dreadful conditions in the Bodaibo mines which created the inflammatory situation. The demands of the miners, published by them on 3 March, included better living conditions, better pay and food, proper regulation of women's labour and the use of the polite forms of address rather than the familiar forms (roughly equivalent to the *tu* and *vous* forms in French), thus showing some respect to the workers. They also demanded technical improvements to the mines, an eight-hour working day and other innovations. From 9 March onwards the Company prepared to sack the entire workforce, a process which was initiated by cutting off the food supply. Seventy five soldiers arrived from Kirensk on 18 March to help enforce the evictions; stalemate was reached on 20 March as by then all the workers were on strike, but the government forbade the Company to take harsh action. The situation was steadily becoming more ugly and on 3 April there was a further complaint about bad meat. The next day the police arrested ten strike leaders. The workers decided to deliver individual workers' complaints by marching to the Company offices en masse. Approximately 3 000 miners began the trek over the snow-covered mountain road. As they approached the township of Nadezhdinsk the management and soldiers stood on the opposite side of the railway line. One of the managers, Treshchenkov, begged the miners to stop, but when they did not the soldiers fired a volley of shots into the crowd of unarmed miners. The carnage was terrible. 170 were killed outright and a further 60 as the result of their wounds, and over 300 were wounded. The pastor of the local church, Fr Alexander Chenykh, testified later that "they slaughtered the workers like cattle." Of one group of injured, 117 were shot when lying down, 79 had back wounds and 62 had side wounds. Only ten had front entry wounds, meaning that most had been shot as they fled or after they had fallen. Military procedure had been violated as no warning shots had been fired and individual soldiers had fired after the volley. There is no doubt that the massacre was a vicious and totally unjustified attempt to subdue workers who had legitimate cause for protest and who had been repeatedly attempting to resolve their problems by peaceful negotiation.

The news of the massacre spread throughout Russia and such was the outrage felt in all sections of society that it proved a crucial factor in fuelling the revolutionary movements. Strikes and unrest swept the country and the fortunes of the Lena Goldfields were affected. It would have shocked Vasily Kokoulin (who had died a year or two earlier) and Joachim, by now living in Irkutsk. In fact it was said that such a situation would never had arisen if Vasily Kokoulin had still been there.

As a footnote, the fate of the Lena Goldfields and the related companies had effectively been sealed as a result of the Massacre of 1912. The politicalisation and radicalisation of the miners was a result of the repressive management whose prime intention was to make money regardless of miners' welfare. The Revolutions of 1917 and the subsequent Civil War of 1919 caused the suspension of the operations of the Lena Goldfields. In 1924 attempts were made to re-invest foreign money in the Company. A mining engineer, Alexander Malozemoff, who had worked at the mines for many years, had emigrated to America in 1920 when the goldmines were confiscated. His return in 1924 was not successful and the attempt to restart the Company was abandoned in the late 1920s. Negotiations continued and Annual Reports for the Lena Goldfield Company were produced until the 1930s. In 1938 the Company was finally wound up and the remaining money transferred to the Lena Investment Trust. The Trust and its descendants continued to exist as recently as 1976, when it was finally wound up, almost fifty years after it had passed its heyday. Another interesting fact is that Alexander Malozemoff's son, Plato, who was born in 1909 in St Petersburg, grew up in America. He followed his father into gold mining management and eventually rose to become the Chairman and Chief Executive Officer of the Newmont Mining Corporation, the largest goldmining company in America (see Johnson).

Bodaibo gradually grew in prosperity, becoming a city in 1925. A prison camp was built nearby in 1935, one of many in that region and part of the GULAG system. In 1979 the population of the city was 14 700 and to this day the principal industry is still goldmining.

Konstantyn Kokoulin had at least one daughter, Anna, and possibly another one, about whom we know nothing. It was Anna, however, who caught the attention of the young engineer, Joachim. Anna was born in Yakutsk, where her parents were living at the time. She was baptised at the age of nine days in the Cathedral of the Holy Trinity on 18 September 1879. Her father was Konstantyn, who taught at the secondary school and her mother was Maria Theodorovna Amosova. The godparents were Evtropi Osodorov Karamulin, teacher at the same school as Konstantyn, and Anna Petrovna Amosova, described as the wife of a State Councillor, and probably a relative of her mother. The baptism certificate (which was effectively the birth certificate at this time) was not obtained until 1886, so this may have been the year when the family left Yakutsk and settled in Bodaibo. Unfortunately we know nothing about her childhood or even whether she had any brothers or sisters. A photograph of Anna taken in her late teens during a visit to Irkutsk shows an attractive girl swathed in an enormous *shuba* or full-length fur coat. There is a second girl in the picture; perhaps this is a sister.

Plans for the wedding between Anna and Joachim were long and involved as befitted the union of two families who were conscious of their social position and lineage. The trousseau was prepared, including monogrammed linen sheets, some of which were still in use when I was a child, table linen, clothes and so on. The wedding rings, which survive to this day, were ordered and engraved with their names and the date of the wedding. As Joachim was working at one of the principal gold mines in Siberia it is likely that the gold for the rings was from Bodaibo itself –

perhaps Joachim panned it personally – as there would be no point in importing it from elsewhere. However, not all plans went smoothly. Anna was baptised as an Orthodox, while Joachim was a Catholic, so this issue had to be resolved. She was also marrying into one of the oldest Polish *szlachta* families, so conditions were set on the marriage. Firstly, Anna had to become a Catholic, and secondly, she had to learn the Polish language. Presumably these conditions were imposed so that any children would be brought up as Catholics and so that the Polishness of the Chrzczonowicz family would be beyond doubt. One cannot help thinking that these must have seemed hard conditions for Anna; it must have felt as if she was denying her Russian heritage, the religion as practised by her forebears and even her mother tongue. In common with every other Polish exile, Joachim would have been looking forward to the day when he could return to a free and independent Poland – so perhaps one day Anna would even have to leave the land of her birth, her family, and every one she knew. What did her family make of all this? Were they supportive or did they disapprove? Witold never talked about his mother's family (except that when I was very small he told me they were distantly related to the composer Shostakovich, hardly a piece of evidence which would stand on its own); was this because there were very few contacts, as we know that there were Kokoulins living in Irkutsk at the same time, or simply that he did not remember?

The wedding plans were finally completed. The nearest Catholic church to Bodaibo was at Irkutsk, 700 miles or so to the southwest of Bodaibo. So it was here that the wedding party came in December 1905 or January 1906, possible staying with Anna's relatives. The church where they were married on 10th January 1906 was the Polish Roman Catholic Church of the Assumption of the Blessed Virgin Mary, a small neo-Gothic building (unique in Siberia) built 1881-3 by Polish exiles in Irkutsk, a well-known landmark in the city. As I sat in that same church in the summer of 1997, it was easy for the imagination to let the years slip back to that January day 91 years previously when a young man of 30 waited at the altar and watched as a shy, nervous bride of 26 walked up the aisle, surely wondering what marriage to this strong-minded Polish nobleman would mean for her. At least she had the support of some of her family; two brothers, Flor and Venyamin Prokopyevich Kokoulin, probably cousins by their ages, were the witnesses to the marriage. Were any of Joachim's family able to make the long and arduous journey to Irkutsk?

The newly weds made the long journey back to Bodaibo after the wedding and settled in the region of the Uspenski mines, where Joachim continued his work and Anna adjusted as best she could to her new role. There is a telling photograph taken only a few months after the wedding in which she already had an unhappy and uncertain look in her eyes, perhaps indicating already that things were not as ideal as she would wish. Apparently she was never happy in her marriage, although Joachim was clearly devoted to her.

Their first child, Konstantyn, or Kostek for short, was born on 10 September 1907, the day after Anna's twenty-eighth birthday. As Catholics the proud parents wanted their son to be baptised in the Catholic Church in Irkutsk, where they had been married. A journey of 700 or so miles in the Siberian autumn or winter was not advisable with a young baby, so the baptism was delayed until the following summer. Also, they wanted Joachim's father, Tadeusz, to be the baby's godfather. Kostek was eventually christened on 4 July 1908 at the Polish Church in Irkutsk, with his grandfather Tadeusz as one godparent and Matrena Kokoulina as the other. One can imagine the happy family reunions and Anna's relations fussing over the baby. Had they become reconciled to Anna's marriage with Joachim by this time? The baptism co-incided with an extraordinary natural phenomenon which has never been satisfactorily explained. On 30 June 1908, at Tunguska, a small place 650km north of Krasnoyarsk, there was a huge but strange explosion whose vibrations were felt and recorded round the world. At the time it was thought to be an exploding meteorite or atmospheric disturbance; trees were flattened or torn up within a radius of several hundred kilometres. The mystery has never been explained to this day, but as Joachim and Anna were only 700 miles away they would certainly have known about it.

The young family returned to Bodaibo, where soon afterwards Anna was pregnant again. Their second child, a daughter, was born on 10 June 1909. She was named Zofia, a traditional family name among the Chrzczonowiczs. This time Joachim and Anna decided to have the baby christened near the Chrzczonowicz family home, thousands of miles to the west of Bodaibo. Taking Kostek (by now a toddler) and little Zofia, or Zosia, they travelled

74

to Joachim's home region. They stayed with Joachim's brother, Antoni, at Dzierkowszczyzna, then part of Lithuania/Byelorussia submerged in the Russian Empire. Dzierkowszczyzna is in present-day Belarus, lying just south of the main road between Vilna (Vilnius) and Glebokie (Hlybokae). Historically the village was built and owned by the Domeyko family in the early nineteenth century. (The founder and first Rector of the Santiago University in Chile was Ignacy Domeyko, of the same family). The tiny brick church, whose photograph Joachim kept until he died, was dedicated to the Ascension, and begun in 1817. It was a small, scattered village, typical of hundreds in the region. In 1866 Dzierkowszczyzna consisted of 56 farms and a distillery. The total population was 1387 souls, of whom 196 were Catholics.

There must have been tremendous excitement when Joachim and Anna arrived with their two young children. It would have been the first time that Anna met her husband's family; as she was shy, this was undoubtedly a daunting prospect. Relatives flocked to see them all, and Joachim had a wonderful time catching up on all the family news and gossip. His family was large and widespread throughout the Vilna region so there would have been a constant stream of visitors. The temptation to stay in Byelorussia must have been strong for Joachim. Zosia was christened on 16 September 1910; by this time Anna was already four months pregnant. The social engagements exhausted her, and there was the prospect of the uncomfortable journey of over 3 000 miles ahead. Soon after the christening Joachim and Anna said their farewells and set off on the long journey back to Siberia.

CHAPTER 4

Siberian Childhood

The family returned to Siberia, but apparently not to Bodaibo. We have little clue as to why this was; as stated in the previous chapter, there could have been several reasons for this. Joachim may have decided that he did not like the new management of the mines and the way the workers were treated, his job may have come to a natural end, he could have been offered one elsewhere, or maybe Anna's family needed her nearer to Irkutsk. The family were certainly in neither Bodaibo or Irkutsk when, on 21 February 1911, Anna gave birth to their third child, Witold, my father. His place of birth was the village of Usole Sibirskoe but we do not know whether the family were living there for a year or two, or whether Anna was taken ill on the return journey and they had to stop there.

By all accounts this was a pleasant place to live in the early 1900s. Situated 42 miles NW of Irkutsk on the banks of the Angara river, it was also on the Trans-Siberian Railway. Until the opening of the salt works in 1852 it was only a small village of 3 000 inhabitants. Usole's claim to fame, apart from the salt works and the associated salt water spa, was the school, founded in the same year as the salt works and beginning with 47 of the village boys. The parents were charged for the schooling and for their part the children had to agree to work in the salt works until the age of 20. The school merited a special mention in the Ministry of Education Report of 1870 because of its high standards, and by 1881 it had become mixed, as well as having a kindergarten section. By 1900 there were 378 children at the school and adult literacy in Usole was said to be almost 100% – a remarkable feat for a small village.

There were several tanneries in operation as well as the salt works and the health spa, and the town had a well-organised cultural life. During the summer the spas were open and the spacious halls and salons of the spa buildings were used for performances by visiting artists or local amateurs, as well as concerts and other events. A brass band from the voluntary fire brigade would entertain the workers. The fine park belonging to the spa was not accessible to the general public, so, as dusk fell on summer evenings the youth of Usole would gather at street corners and play their harmonicas and sing songs.

In the winter entertainment and recreation took a different form. "The Society", a group of local worthies, merchants, tannery owners, Institute Directors and intellectuals, would meet. They leased fairly small premises in 1901, but by 1913 had grown considerably and leased a much larger house on the main street. Here there was an auditorium where groups of artistes – salt works employees, merchants' children and so on performed. During holidays visiting artists came from Irkutsk and performed short plays and music hall comedies. At Christmas a skating rink was set up in the main square, complete with Christmas tree. The young men who wished to show off would skate around the rink to the strains of waltz or mazurka.

Underneath the surface of this seemingly happy and cultured society the seeds of revolution were growing. The 1905 Revolution aroused people's interest in the new socialist-democratic movements, and fear and suspicion in Tsarist circles (although warmly welcomed by some aristocrats). Usole took many of its ideas and thinking from Irkutsk, where many of the would-be revolutionaries were exiled. There were plenty of opportunities for the new ideas to spread and the town became a ferment of revolutionary ideas and clandestine activity. It played its part in the Revolutions of 1917 and the subsequent Civil War. Today the salt works are still flourishing, producing 50% of Russia's table salt. My glimpse of the town from the train in the first light of a misty summer dawn was not very enlightening as all I could see were grey blocks of flats; presumably the more interesting parts of the town are away from the railway line.

We do not know how long Joachim and his family remained at Usole. The little baby, Witold, was baptised a month after he was born, on 22 March 1911, at the Catholic Church in Irkutsk as his brother had been. The godparents were Francis Korytkowski and Evdokia Ostroumova, about whom nothing is known. His grandfather, Tadeusz, was not a godparent; probably by this time he was not able to travel or fulfil his duties as godparent as he died the following year, in 1912.

Several early photographs have survived of the three young children. Mostly studio photographs they nevertheless give an idea of carefree, happy days in Irkutsk. This was arguably the happiest period of the family's life. Joachim was prospering, Anna was unhappy but we know that there were some relatives in Irkutsk so she was not entirely alone, and the dark clouds of Revolution and its subsequent chaos and instability were still a long way away. The children were all photogenic; Kostek is instantly recognisable with his mischievous grin (doubtless he got away with a lot because of it) and an intensity of gaze which already gives a sign of the passionately caring and committed doctor he would become – and which would eventually cost him his life. Zosia's face stares out from the pictures uncertainly, perhaps a foreshadowing of her tragedy of the future. Witold is very much the baby of the three, much fussed over and spoiled; he was a wilful child who was nonetheless the most sensitive of the three children. By the irony of fate he was the only one to reach old age, living until the age of 82.

What was the city of Irkutsk like in the days of the children's early childhood? The story of the city and a description of it sheds important light on the context in which the children were growing up. There was a type of European traveller which thrived on journeying to unusual destinations in remote parts of the world and there were several such people who have left us valuable accounts of life in Siberia and Irkutsk in particular (Fraser, Tupper, Kennan, de Windt to name but four; see bibliography for details). The following account of life in Irkutsk up to and including the early 1900s draws heavily on these accounts among others.

Irkutsk

Irkutsk was the capital city of Eastern Siberia as well as being the largest town. Its beautiful buildings, broad tree-lined boulevards and wonderful impression of space and light reminiscent of a European city earned it the title of the "Paris of Siberia". It was founded as long ago as 1662 on a site of winter quarters for the collection of the yasak, or fur tax, from the Buryat natives and took its present name in 1686. The first school was opened in 1725, becoming the capital of the Irkutsk Province of Eastern Siberia in 1764. The library was opened in 1772 and the museum, one of the first municipal museums, in 1782. It became the city of residence of the local Governor in 1803 and of the Governor-General of the Province of Eastern Siberia in 1822. Historically it was an important transit point on the trade routes to and from Mongolia and China. During the nineteenth century it grew fast despite the vast distance from the capital of the Russian Empire, St Petersburg (3792 miles by rail from Irkutsk). The fur trade, the discovery of gold and other minerals and the tea trade with China all contributed to an enormous expansion of the city during the 1800s.

Many of those who were exiled to Siberia, both Poles and Russians, came to settle in Irkutsk after their term of imprisonment was over. Most notable among these were the Decembrists, punished after the failed plot of 1825, and who included the Princes Volkonski and Trubetski and their wives. Their houses were revered as shrines by generations of would-be reformers and revolutionaries and are preserved as museums today. Other exiles settled there, the intellectuals bringing with them a huge body of knowledge and a thirst for learning; many lived out their time doing pioneering work on extending contemporary knowledge of Siberia. They led expeditions to explore and chart the topography, the geology, the flora and fauna and the climate of Siberia and the results of their findings led to much of the opening up of Siberia's huge potential at the turn of the century. A census of the 1880s found that approximately 75% of the population was Catholic, as opposed to Orthodox, a clear indicator of the large proportion of non-Russians in the city. One third of the population were thought to be exiles. Exile to Siberia under the Tsars was, of course, harsh by any standards; many did not survive even the journey most of which was covered on foot. Once there, however, there were huge tracts of land waiting to be cultivated. As long as the climatic conditions were taken into account a house could be built and a tolerable existence had from the land. Many of those exiled to the area at the turn of the century were key players in the move towards the Revolutions of 1917 and were destined to take part in the history of the new state. The most well-known names include Alexander Radishchev, Felix Dzerzhinsky, Mikhail Frunze, Vyacheslav Molotov and even Josef Stalin himself.

The women of Irkutsk were thought to be particularly beautiful, as, with their red hair and green eyes, they were considered to be the descendants of the members of the aristocracy exiled to Irkutsk in previous generations.

In July 1879 a disastrous fire broke out, which destroyed three-quarters of the town including ten churches, chapels and synagogues, the Customs House, the library, and 3 600 other buildings. Out of a population of approximately 34 000 people no less than 20 000 were rendered homeless. As a result immediate steps were taken to prevent a recurrence of such a disaster. Many of the public buildings and most of the houses which had been destroyed were wooden as timber was in such plentiful supply in the region, but after the fire it was forbidden to build wooden houses in the centre of the city, although those still standing were allowed to remain. Fire towers were constructed, complete with alarm bells and round the clock watchmen. The last word in fire engines was bought from a British firm and a set of procedures instituted for fighting future fires. (In fact, despite all these measures the population still resorted to the old methods of forming a human chain and passing buckets of water from the river to put out the fires.)

By the turn of the century the population had grown to over 50 000 people. A much-acclaimed Opera House was built, completed in 1897, and as long ago as the 1860s the city was linked to St Petersburg by a telegraph line. By 1891 some telephones had been installed and soon afterwards electric street lighting along a few of the main streets. The general impression of the city is described by many of the European and American travellers as being that of a frontier town of the mid-West and they complained that despite appearances, Irkutsk was still a dangerous place to live. Living conditions were not always as refined as the inhabitants apparently thought them to be. The American writer, Harry de Windt, writing in the 1890s, complained that not even the main street was properly paved, the pavements consisting of wooden duckboards laid over open sewers, and there was still no piped water. The water was drawn directly from the river by the citizens; the wealthier ones paid men to deliver barrels of water to the doors of their houses. Crime was a big problem, not least because of the large number of released or escaped prisoners and exiles from the prisons of the region who went round terrorising the citizens. To be out alone at night was unwise because of the risk of being attacked or kidnapped. The footpads thrived in the dark streets and used novel methods for capturing their victims. Some were simply garrotted and then robbed, others were lassoed, even in daylight, dragged into a back alley and relieved at leisure of all their valuables. The citizens had several ways of protecting their property. One method was to employ watchmen who would use metal clappers or wooden rattles to warn off burglars and thieves. Others simply fired a single shot from their windows before retiring, to warn would-be burglars that there were firearms in that house, or they unchained savage dogs to roam their yards. One cannot help thinking that it must have been rather noisy in Irkutsk at night! Life as a criminal was financially worthwhile as the chances of being caught were slight and the pickings were rich. The major gold mining area was in the region NE of Irkutsk; once the summer gold working season was finished the miners thronged to Irkutsk to spend their earnings in a reckless orgy of drinking, gambling and high living, making them easy prey for criminals.

The mining managers also gathered in Irkutsk and whiled away the long winter nights in prodigious drinking and card playing. Many of these people had started life as peasants or were ex-convicts or freed exiles who struck gold bonanzas which earned them vast sums of money. Their lifestyles were a peculiar mixture of the simple village ways they were used to and the sophistication of the middle classes to which they aspired as a status symbol. So, although they hired French chefs and French tutors for their children and their residences were as extravagant as could be found anywhere, with furnishings and fittings imported from all over the world, they themselves may have been illiterate and retained the rough and uncouth customs of their origins.

This was not true, of course, for all citizens. Education was highly regarded and anyone who could possibly afford to employed private tutors for their children or sent them to one of the many schools of the city. One of the most famous was the Institute for Daughters of the Nobility, the school where Sofia Kokoulina completed her education (and indeed, danced before the future Tsar, the ill-fated Nicholas II, when he visited the school in 1892). There was a flourishing cultural life in the city. Plays were frequently performed at the theatre, including the works of Shakespeare and other such notable writers. In the summer there was a variety of other entertainments – travelling circuses, jugglers, tumblers, acrobatic bears, band concerts in the park, trotting races, fishing on the river, excursion boats to Lake Baikal and firework displays. Foreign visitors to the city made use of letters of introduction from important officials and were often entertained by the Governor himself. The largest hotel in Irkutsk, the Metropole, seemed very primitive by western standards. Like many other buildings in the city centre it was originally built of logs with moss stuffed into the cracks to insulate the building against the cold. The rooms were none too clean and sometimes had to be shared with other guests. The standards of hotel accommodation were a frequent cause of complaint by foreign visitors and criticism of the state of the rooms often appears in their accounts. An official letter also permitted a visit to Irkutsk Prison or to the nearby model penal colony of Alexandrovski, 46 miles NW of Irkutsk. Joachim would doubtless have taken an active part in the cultural life of the city as we know he was extremely well-read and enjoyed both the theatre and concerts.

An invitation to dinner, another popular pastime, involved eating vast quantities of various imported delicacies and drinking extraordinary amounts of alcohol. Etiquette forbade the guests to depart before 4 or 5am. Public holidays were another chance to show off and the wealthy women of the town would stroll up and down the Bolshaya, the main street, wearing the latest in Paris fashions (which could arrive in Irkutsk only a week after they appeared in the Parisian shops) or drive along in gleaming carriages, well wrapped in expensive furs. Card playing, as already mentioned, was also a popular activity. Joachim used to play bridge, with a foursome including the local Catholic priest. If they played on a Saturday evening, Joachim would apparently put back all clocks and watches in the house as midnight approached so that the priest would not break the strict rule about not playing cards on a Sunday!

The children seemed to be happy in their life in Irkutsk, although Joachim ruled the household with a firm hand, conscious of his heritage and position as a member of one of the oldest Polish *szlachta* families. The children always had to conform to the strict social etiquette of the time. Visitors to the house had to be greeted in strict order of their social standing – and woe betide the unfortunate child who made a mistake. Joachim and Anna often held dinner parties to which the cream of Irkutsk society would be invited. On one occasion Witold was present as a very small child. In order to entertain him, one of the guests took him on his knee and said to him, "Witold, show me your mother," so the little boy looked round the room until he found his mother.

"There she is!" he shouted pointing to her. "And show me your father." the guest continued. Witold looked puzzled for a minute and then shouted triumphantly, "Mr. X is my father!" He could not understand why the assembled company collapsed into fits of laughter.

Witold's memories of his childhood, particularly of the early years, were not very clear and he never talked at length about this part of his life. Perhaps it was painful to remember these happy days in view of the later tragedies of the family; perhaps he suppressed them because for many years he had to conceal the fact that he had been born in Russia and was afraid that he might inadvertently let some fact or other slip out. Much of the information about what life was like for Joachim and Anna and their three children has to be deduced from contemporary descriptions; unfortunately most of the literature is slanted towards giving an account of events leading up to and including the Revolutions of 1917 and the subsequent Civil War. While such accounts are important in themselves, and indeed the events they describe have a direct impact on the life of the family, there is a dearth of material on the social history and day to day life of Irkutsk citizens in the years just prior to 1917.

One of the best sources for gaining a visual impression of Irkutsk in the years 1899-1917 is a book by Sergei Medvedev called *"Irkutsk in Picture Postcards"* [*Irkutsk na Pochtovikh Otkritkakh*], published in 1996. The postcards are grouped according to particular places or buildings and together give a vivid picture of the city which Joachim and Anna knew and which gave Kostek, Zosia and Witold their first memories. They would have known well the main street, the Bolshaya, two miles long, leading from the monument to Tsar Alexander III near the White House north east to the River Ushakovka and on to the Znamenski Convent. Doubtless they often walked along its broad pavements, passing the Central and Grand Hotels, the Russo-Asian Bank, the large shops, the Lutheran church and the Church of the Annunciation. Or they may have turned off to the left and strolled through the huge market where Kirov Square is now. The Catholic Church, their spiritual home, was just the other side of this vast gathering of stalls and traders. On a warm summer evening once the children had been put to bed Joachim and Anna may well have walked along the embankment by the broad sweep of the

Angara river, admiring the view across to the railway station, and in the far distance, Znamenski Convent once more.

There were parks for the children to play in and trips along the river in the summer. Lake Baikal was only 42 miles away up the Angara river. The family went on picnics, fishing trips and boating trips to the Lake and would have known the steep wooded cliffs and the crystal clear but treacherous waters well. It was probably somewhere along the banks of the river or the shores of the Lake that the children were taught to swim, by a method that seems primitive or even harsh – Joachim simply pushed them off the edge of a low cliff into the water and they had to manage as best they could. This was part of Joachim's deliberate policy of toughening up the boys, a strategy which may seem odd to us. Ironically the development of a strong constitution saved Witold's life when he was enduring the rigours of winter in prison in the far north of Russia. The climate in Irkutsk can be harsh; temperatures vary from +17C in July to -20C in the winter and the permafrost is only six feet or so below the surface so there were plenty of opportunities for "toughening up". There were regular visits to the banya or Russian bath house. Witold used to tell how on one occasion the stove used to heat the water was not functioning properly and was giving off carbon monoxide fumes. Joachim only just managed to pull the boys to safety in time and he rolled them naked in the snow to revive them. They suffered no apparent ill effects from this experience.

Despite all the efforts to toughen up the boys they still remained sensitive. Witold was especially so and acutely aware of his mother's unhappiness. Even as quite a small boy he would try to comfort her and cheer her up. In all the surviving photographs she looks sad and uncertain but we have no letters or anything in her writing at all so her story has to remain untold and the photos a silent witness to her private grief. The children were prone to the usual range of illnesses for all the "healthy regime" they were supposed to be following. On one occasion Witold nearly died of diphtheria and his life was only saved by the fact that the doctor spent the whole night scraping his throat free of the deadly membrane. Another time Witold had contracted tetanus and was on the point of death. His brother, Kostek, himself only four years older than Witold, leapt on his horse and galloped through the night to collect some of the precious anti-tetanus serum which was just beginning to be used for treatment. The serum was introduced via a series of small cuts into the skin at the back of Witold's neck, leaving scars which stayed for the rest of his life, but he recovered. The final twist to the tale is that not long after this, hearing that there was some serum left over, a wealthy Jew came to Joachim and begged on his knees in the snow for it for his own child. Of course Joachim gave it to him and his child also recovered.

We do not know where in Irkutsk the family lived or even for certain what type of house they had. There were some stone houses, especially in the city centre, by the time they moved there. Some wooden houses built of a double layer of logs had survived the great fire of 1879 and indeed still stand today being pointed out to tourists as a feature of the city. Witold said that these houses were always very warm and cosy, with the gaps between the logs stuffed with sphagnum moss and the windows triple glazed. They had a good-sized cellar underground and were well able to protect the inhabitants from the harsh Siberian winters. He and his sister were caught one day eating the chemicals put between the layers of glass to reduce condensation. No ill-effects were mentioned.

Milk was bought by weight in frozen blocks, as was fish and other items. Eggs were preserved in isinglass. This gave rise to a curious story which Witold related to my mother and which he assured her was true, difficult though it is to believe. One winter, Anna noticed that the eggs were disappearing from the crock in the pantry. At first she suspected the maid, who protested her innocence. Anna decided to keep watch one night and solve the mystery herself, so she took up a hiding place where she could see what was happening in the pantry. To her utter amazement she watched as a mouse scurried over to the jar, climbed up the side and pulled out an egg. Balancing in the edge of the jar and holding the egg carefully it then fell on its back onto the shelf, thus preserving the egg from damage. It then scurried off to its home and the whole process was repeated. Needless to say, Anna changed the arrangements for storing eggs.

In 1917 the children's cousin, Zosia, the daughter of Joachim's sister, Weronika, arrived from Poland to act as governess to the children. She was herself only seventeen years old and very shy, and presumably had her hands full with three lively children aged six, eight and ten. She has never said why she went to Irkutsk when she did; possibly it was thought to be safer there than at home, or maybe her education was considered unfinished. She must have done a good job teaching the children; when the family returned to Poland and enroled in the local Gymnasium (or Secondary School) they were placed in the class above that according to their age. She noticed how sensitive Witold was to his mother's unhappiness. She remembers that Joachim and Anna used to visit two of Anna's relatives, Flor and his sister Alexandra (Sania) who used to look after him, but she did not know how they were related and she was always too shy to ask. Zosia lives today in a tiny flat in Gdansk in northern Poland and her memories of eighty years ago are still vivid, despite all that happened to her subsequently. She is a remarkable woman, not only for surviving into her mid-nineties, but for preserving a gentleness of character and a warmth that is rarely found. Still alive in 1997, she is the only known living link with the family pre-1917.

The Trans-Siberian Railway

Another important feature of life in Irkutsk was the Trans-Siberian Railway which passed by the city and would play a vital role in the family story. The account of the planning and building of the railway reads like an epic in itself, let alone the essential part it would play in the history of Russia 1917-20. The Railway was a monumental feat of engineering across difficult terrain over thousands of miles. Immensely costly in financial and human terms it made a huge difference to life in Siberia, opening up areas which had previously been inaccessible and giving the country a new potential for growth and trade. Before the arrival of the Railway travel around Siberia had been extremely slow and hazardous; the only "road" was the *trakt*, a highway that was partly roadway and partly dirt track. The numerous rivers were often an easier way of getting around, either by boat in summer or by sledge or tarantas in winter, when the surface would be frozen to a depth of several feet.

We have an account of travel in Siberia just as the Railway was beginning to be built. By a remarkable coincidence my maternal grandfather was given as a child a copy of the 1897 *Children's Friend Annual*. This contains a child's account of a journey through Siberia amazingly similar to those undertaken by my other grandfather. The writer describes arriving at Vittimsk, so

86

must have started very near to Bodaibo, then travelling up the Lena river, through Kirensk and so by tarantas, or sledge, through Irkutsk, joining the new railway at Tyumen and on to the Volga river. The journey continues via Moscow, Berlin, Flushing and so to Queensborough, England. It is a fascinating thought that one of my grandfathers would have read about the lifestyle and way of travel of the other one although they were separated by several thousand miles and a different culture. Obviously travel by sledge or tarantas and boat was slow, uncomfortable and hazardous. The vast distances meant that travel was almost unbearably tedious. The distance between Moscow and Irkutsk via the *trakt* was 3545 miles and the journey took 35 days if the conditions were good.

The idea of a Trans-Siberian Railway linking Moscow and the Pacific Ocean was first mooted by an American, Perry Collins, as far back as the 1860s but the practical problems and the prohibitive cost involved meant that his idea went no further. The idea was raised from time to time until in 1887 the decision was made to build the Railway; the very first section, between Perm and Ekaterinburg, had already been completed in 1878. The Minister charged with overseeing the construction of the Railway was Sergei Witte, who proved to be extremely capable. On 24 February 1891 the decision was made to build from both ends of the route towards the middle, ie., westwards from Vladivostok to Khabarovsk and eastwards from the Ural mountains until the tracks met. The Tsarevich (the future Nicholas II) inaugurated the eastern section at Vladivostok on 31 May 1891. The construction of the Railway was divided into six geographical regions, but was beset with problems right from the beginning. The terrain made the project seem almost impossible; much of the route went through marsh, or steppes, or taiga, frozen for most of the year and an impassible bog for a few weeks in summer. When water freezes it expands, so when the frozen ground melted the track collapsed. This made the work painfully slow and it often had to be repeated. Even a cursory glance at a map of Russia will show the vast number of rivers in the country; bridges had to be built across these. The costs rose and soon became phenomenal, so attempts were made to economise using lighter tracks, more widely spaced ties and less ballast. This would cause huge problems later on.

The eastbound tracks reached Chelyabinsk on 19 July 1892; the first train arrived at Irkutsk station on 28 August 1898. By this time only four sections remained to be completed. The Irkutsk to Baikal section was opened to regular traffic in 1900, and the Transbaikal section was opened in January of that year. However, this section was strictly speaking not railway. In 1893 it was calculated that in winter the ice on Lake Baikal was sufficiently thick to support the weight of tracks laid on its surface so that trains could run across the surface of the Lake. However, this proved a little hazardous as the ice was of variable thickness, and there were several disasters. Experiments were made with icebreaking ferries, one of which, the *Angara*, was actually built in Britain, dismantled for shipping to Russia, and then re-assembled at Lake Baikal. The ferries were not always successful as sometimes even they were defeated by the ice so the passengers had to disembark and complete their journey across the Lake by sledge.

The Russo-Japanese War of 1904 precipitated a crisis in the movement of troops and equipment to the Far East of Siberia. The alternative route was an extraordinarily long one involving travelling eastwards across the Indian Ocean and right round Africa. The problem of the missing section of the Railway was addressed once more and again they tried laying tracks on the ice. While the tracks were under construction the troops were disembarked at Port Baikal and the equipment transported across the Lake on 3 000 sledges. The troops marched across the Lake, beginning at 4am and arriving at the other side at 9pm. There were emergency shelters set up at intervals of four miles across the Lake and a shack at the halfway point. By this means thousands of troops and gun batteries, 65 locomotives and 2 400 fully laden railway cars were transported in five weeks.

In the spring of 1898 the Trans-Siberian Committee investigated the possibility of the circum-Baikal route, which would bring the Railway round the southern tip of the Lake from Irkutsk to Mysovsk, obviating the need for the slow and dangerous crossing of the Lake itself. Construction work began in 1901 and immediately met with immense difficulties. Most of the route was inaccessible by road and could only be reached by water when the Lake was relatively calm and free from fog. By the end of 1903 the constructors had cleared 1 800 acres of forest, 93% of the embankments needed and had dug four miles of tunnels. On 25 September 1904 the whole line was officially opened despite a disastrous test run. The project had taken thirteen years and four months and no less than 5 500 miles of track had been laid eastwards from the Urals. Contemporary pictures give some idea of the scale of the work involved.

Once constructed, the Railway brought undoubted benefits to thousands. Officially convicts were not sent to Siberia after 1900; however, many political exiles found their way there. No longer were there parties of convicts and exiles marching for month after month along a road to oblivion in the unspeakable conditions encountered on the *Trakt* or the river barges. The railway, together with Witte's Tariff Reforms, opened up the country to trade and competition with Western Russia and abroad. It was heavily used for the transport of thousands of Russian emigrants and their possessions (including livestock) as they travelled eastwards to a new life. Here land was being given away to settlers on very favourable terms; since the 1880s St Petersburg encouraged emigration and allotted plots of land of 140 acres to families of three adults and four children and above. In addition the settlers were exempt from conscription for three years and from taxes for the first three years and half taxes for the next three years. It is not surprising that between 1894 and 1914 almost 5 000 000 people had emigrated to Siberia on these terms – 759 000 peasants and artisans in 1908 alone.

The running of the Railway was not without its problems, but by the summer of 1907 there were three fast trains per week in each direction between Moscow and Vladivostok. The times of the trains were unpredictable as the timetable was often ignored. The entire route from Moscow to Vladivostok passed through six time zones, and as is the case today, the timetable ran on Moscow time and the restaurant car on local time. Therefore it was rather disorientating for passengers who were never sure which meals would be served when. Travel by the Trans-Siberian Railway was immediately popular despite these disadvantages and as time went by the trains became more and more elaborate. Some were very luxurious and even included libraries, salons and a complete Orthodox church!

Kostek, Zosia and Witold were, it seemed, growing up in an exciting environment, with plenty of interesting things happening around them. The city of Irkutsk was blossoming, the arts and learning in general was flourishing and some of the best minds of

Russia had settled in the city. The coming of the Railway had opened up Siberia to trade with the rest of Russia and abroad (for example, a high proportion of the butter consumed in Britain before the War was imported from Siberia). However, underneath the rosy surface, the storm clouds of Revolution were already gathering. Many of the political exiles in the Irkutsk region would play key roles in the events leading up to the 1917 Revolutions and beyond. In order to complete the picture of the background against which Joachim and Anna were bringing up their three children, here follows an outline of the contemporary political and social undercurrents as they affected the lives of the children. It is not insignificant that one of Witold's earliest childhood memories is not of some happy picnic by a river bank or an important family occasion, but of seeing the bodies of slain Revolutionaries lying on the streets of Irkutsk – an image which stayed with him for the rest of his life.

The background to the events of 1917-1920

A wealth of literature has been written on the origins of the Russian Revolutions, so for a general account the reader is referred to the bibliography. It is extremely difficult teasing out a comprehensible version of events as they affected the people of Eastern Siberia, but a brief attempt will be made here. It had been obvious for decades that there were serious shortcomings in the Russian Empire – the autocracy of a Tsar out of touch with his people, the persistence of serfdom, (despite its official abolition in 1861), the corruption of the aristocracy and the contrast between their lifestyle and that of the ordinary peasants. It is not surprising that there were anti-Tsarist movements springing up from time to time, the Decembrists of 1825 being the most famous of the early ones. As the new ideas of socialism, democracy and nationalism swept through Europe, they were naturally taken up by free-thinking intellectuals in Russia, in particular students. By the 1880s and 1890s the Russian authorities were fully aware of the dangers to the status quo of such movements and did their best to suppress them and exile the ringleaders. This may be why Joachim had to find a job in Siberia when he graduated from St Petersburg rather than return to his home region.

The first major event which would have affected Joachim was the Russo-Japanese War of 1904-5. It has already been seen how its course was affected by the newly built Trans-Siberian Railway, and the presence of such a large number of troops would have undoubtedly affected the area. Considerable unease was generated among the ordinary people of Russia; some thought that the hour of Revolution may have arrived. Workers at the Puktov Arms and Engineering Works in St Petersburg went on strike there on 8 January 1905, led by an activist priest, Father Gapon. The 200 000 strikers were asking, among other things, for protection by the Tsar, an 8-hour working day, a basic working wage and the release of political prisoners. When a crowd of 100 000 assembled outside the Winter Palace next day, they were met by a cordon of Cossacks and Hussars who fired on the unarmed crowd. Dmitri Shostakovich's father, the husband of Sophia Kokoulina, was present at this shameful event. The slaughter was terrible and provoked outrage throughout Russia. Strikes spread; one in the Polish town of Lodz was particularly savagely suppressed with 300 people killed. The exiled Social Democrats organised the first Associations, or Circles, in Irkutsk at the turn of the century and they organised a series of strikes between 1902-4.

The principal actors in the revolutionary movements were mostly in exile and/or abroad. Both Lenin and Trotsky returned to Russia in late 1905. The pressure for reform continued and the Tsar was forced to concede to the demands for urgent reforms. Accordingly he set up the Duma, an elected Assembly, with representatives from the Poles, Lithuanians, Ukrainians, and Byelorussians as well as Russians. Unfortunately this body had very little real power. In December 1905 there was street fighting in Moscow and Trotsky was imprisoned in the St Peter and St. Paul Fortress in St. Petersburg. In the spring of 1906 Stolypin was appointed Prime Minister and he instituted a reign of terror against dissidents which lasted until his assassination while at the theatre in 1911. Revolutionaries were rounded up and treated with contempt; over 2 000 were shot or hanged in the Baltic Provinces alone. Once again, would-be revolutionaries were scattered, in prison, in exile abroad or in Siberia, or living in hiding. Morale plummeted during this period.

The working people were still very discontented and the waves of strikes continued. In 1910 there were 226 strikes involving 46 623 people, the next year the number more than doubled, and by 1913 there were 2 404 strikes affecting 887 096 workers. It is impossible that Joachim was not affected by such large-scale unrest; some of the intelligentsia did in fact support the workers' case. Despite these problems the summer of 1913 brought a record harvest and a doubling of industrial output since 1906, levels which would not be equalled for many years to come. By 1914 foreign investments had risen to two billion roubles.

2 August 1914 saw the declaration of War against Germany and 1.4 million regular and 3.1 million reserve troops were mobilised. Lenin, by now living in a remote cottage in Nowy Targ near Krakow in Russian-occupied Poland was briefly arrested. On his release he and his wife, Nadezhda, fled to Zurich, where they remained for the next three years.

The War did not begin well for the Russians. Within the first twelve months 1 million soldiers were killed and the army were desperately short of basic supplies such as ammunition, telephone wire and code books for sending messages. They had suffered a disastrous defeat at Tannenberg (Grunwald) where 504 years previously the Polish armies had defeated the Teutonic Knights. The Germans quickly overran Russian-occupied Poland and by 5 August 1914 Warsaw was in German hands. It is hard to imagine what the Poles exiled in far away places, in Siberia or even futher, thought about these events, but at this point no one could have predicted the eventual outcome.

The hated Rasputin, who had held such a grip over the Tsar and his family, was assassinated on 19 December 1916, to the relief of many Russians. The food situation was getting very bad and by February 1917 major cities such as St Petersburg were at breaking point. There was more unrest and the troops remaining in the city (the best ones were fighting at the Front) were unable to control the crowds. Some of the officers mutinied and Kerensky took control of events. On 27 February two Provisional Committees came into being to take over government. One was called the Provisional Government, mostly comprising middle class members, and the other the 1st Petrograd Soviet, whose members were workers and soldiers. The Tsar and his family, realising that all was lost, fled in the early hours of 1 March; the next day Nicholas II formally abdicated.

News of this nature travels fast and on 1 March V. S. Voitinsky, one of the Bolshevik Deputies who had been exiled to Irkutsk, received reports of the revolution. On the following day Irkutsk apparently greeted the news of the formation of the Provisional Duma Committee with jubilation. Crowds marched through the streets waving red flags and singing revolutionary songs.

Other revolutionaries soon heard the news, including several Mensheviks and members of the Social Revolutionaries (the SRs). Word reached I. G. Tsereteli, who was living in Usole (the village where Witold had been born), and he hurried to Irkutsk where the revolutionaries took power, setting up a Citizens' Committee. The mood of the people was, according to the official accounts, one of "happy alarm", although one wonders whether there was more of the "alarm" as people realised how the old order was crumbling away. After ten days in power forty of the revolutionaries departed Irkutsk for Petrograd on a special train decorated with red bunting and slogans. Its progress across the country was slowed down by the numerous celebrations and welcomes at cities along the way. One can only wonder what Joachim made of all this and how anxious he was about the future.

Lenin returned to Russia when he heard of the Revolution, although he did not believe the news at first, and he travelled back in a sealed carriage (courtesy of the Germans).On 3 April 1917 at the Finland Station in Petrograd he made a stirring speech outlining Bolshevik ideals and barely concealing his contempt for the Provisional Government:-

"The people need peace. The people need bread and land. And they give you war, hunger, no food, and the land remains with the landowners." (quoted in Moynahan, B. p.84)

Upheavals continued throughout the summer. The Bolsheviks had played no active part in the February revolution and as they saw the fiasco which followed it they attempted their own revolution in July. However this turned out to be premature and some of the leaders, eg., Trotsky, were arrested. Kerensky was nominally in charge but he lacked the power to hold the government and country together. The country was indeed falling apart – not only was she fighting a major war against Germany but inflation was running at 1000%, food was all but unobtainable and normal life was rapidly becoming impossible. Kerensky became more and more isolated as the Bolsheviks gained more power. Russia as a united country was breaking up as the various nationalist movements gained support, particularly in the Ukraine, Finland and the

Baltic States. The Cossacks, the Bashkirs, the Siberians and the Buryats all declared themselves independent.

The situation worsened and by the end of September Kerensky had formed a new cabinet in the Provisional Government. The Germans were not far from Petrograd and hunger was widespread. By the time Lenin returned to Petrograd on 10 October the Provisional Government were in such a sorry state that they missed their chance to arrest those who were openly planning to overthrow it – Trotsky, Zinoviev, Kollontai, Lenin, Dzerzhinsky, Sverdlov and Stalin. News of the impending coup was so widely known that it was assumed that it would not in fact happen. However, events were moving fast and on 25 October Bolshevik troops seized control of parts of Petrograd. Trotsky held an extraordinary session of the Petrograd Soviet at which he declared that the government had ceased to exist. The Winter Palace was under siege and next day all members of the Provisional Government were arrested. The Bolshevik Revolution had happened contrary to all expectations. However, until as late as the summer of 1918 the only part of Russia under Bolshevik control was European Russia – an area roughly the size of the former Grand Duchy of Moscow.

Siberia after the Revolution

The take over was not straightforward; opposition to the new regime was evident almost from the beginning. The first units of the counter-revolutionaries, the Whites, paraded in Novocherhassk on 26 November 1917 and made some progress in capturing the Provinces, setting up governments in Siberia in January 1918. The Red Army of the Bolsheviks was established by decree on 28 January 1918. The Russian army at this time included a 40 000-strong corps of Czech Legionaries who had been formed from former prisoners and who were seeking the independence of their own country from the Austro-Hungarian Empire. It had been agreed that they could resume fighting the Germans by returning to Europe on the Trans-Siberian Railway, travelling east to Vladivostok and thence by sea to Europe (the western route was closed because of the fighting). The Czechs were fiercely anti-communist who hated the Bolsheviks and supported the Whites. The Bolsheviks were hopelessly disorganised apart from in European Russia and Bolshevik soldiers were easily overcome by crack Czech troops during a brawl in Chelyabinsk in May 1918. This effectively gave the Czechs control of part of the Trans-Siberian Railway and enabled them to link up with the leader of the Whites, Admiral Kolchak. Within two months the Czechs had control of most of the Trans-Siberian Railway.

This was not without its drawbacks, however. The Railway had been built on the cheap over unsuitable terrain and the tracks were far too light and flimsy for the heavy traffic. Originally the rails were supposed to take no more than three trains a week but from the time of the Russo-Japanese War of 1904-5 had been carrying far more than that. Consequently the tracks frequently collapsed, or the engines broke down, especially after 1914, when all available men were fighting at the Front. Without the engineers with the necessary skills to undertake the repairs the tracks soon became littered with broken down trains. Sometimes the trains would be derailed and simply left where they fell down the embankment, in a siding or even blocking the main track. The freight trains, carrying desperately needed food supplies would be unable to reach their destination and their cargo rotted in some siding miles from anywhere. This difficulty of transportation was a major factor contributing to the famine which was gripping the land.

The Czechs realised that they needed assistance in maintaining the Railway so they turned to the Allies for help, since they were on the side of the Whites and against the Bolsheviks. This request for help was discussed at a meeting on 6 June 1918 in the White House, Washington, USA. The Americans were not in favour of direct intervention but did agree to send some troops – engineers – to repair the Trans-Siberian Railway, to protect the troops and to guard the military stores needed. As it turned out, the Americans were never able to advance near enough to the arena of operations to start their work. Large numbers of Allied troops did land in Russia to offer their assistance, including 7 000 American troops, 70 000 Japanese, over 4 000 Canadians and one battalion of British troops.

The Tsar and his family were murdered on 18 July 1918 in Ekaterinburg (where Joachim's friend, Klukowski, worked at the Metallurgy Institute) by order of the Soviet; hardly were they dead when the Czechs seized control of the city, then Kolchak's White forces occupied it. The Reds had fled on 6 August. Other

Czech Units had been steadily fighting their way eastwards, occupying Ufa on 6 July and Irkutsk on 1 September, thereby effectively gaining control of the whole of the Trans-Siberian Railway east of the Urals. The American Expeditionary Force (some of which was to have repaired the Railway) arrived in Vladivostok on 2 September just after the Czechs had broken through to Irkutsk so their presence as a protecting force was now unnecessary. By now the Allied Intervention Forces on Russian soil included 1 100 French, 1 700 Italian, 4186 Canadian troops as well as Romanian, Serbian and Polish troops. In addition the Red Cross had 2 500 workers and even the YMCA had teams. By November 1918 there was a total of 180 000 Allied troops in Russia. The Japanese decided that they had nothing to gain by remaining in Russia so they withdrew most of their troops.

At the beginning of September 1918 a young SR student had shot Lenin in the chest and neck; this led to the decree that all those involved with the Whites were to be shot. The terrible starvation continued; much of what had been harvested was rotting in sidings on the Railway. There was anarchy and confusion throughout the country. There were about twenty bodies claiming to be the legitimate government of Siberia and numerous fiefdoms whose leaders all wanted their share of power.

The story of the execution of the Tsar and his family is one of the most well-known parts of the complex story and accounts can be read in any standard books on the Revolution. What happened to the Imperial treasure is not so well-known, especially the Gold Reserves which existed in the form of bullion. The complete story is recounted in Clarke, W., *The Lost Fortune of the Tsars*. The Bolsheviks took $160 million to Berlin, but $332 million arrived in Kazan and was seized by the Whites when the Reds fled in August 1918. The anti-Red forces – Czechs, Whites and SRs – allied themselves to each other and took charge of moving the gold from Kazan to Samara and then to Ufa and Omsk. Admiral Kolchak, the leader of the Whites, was proclaimed Supreme Ruler of the combined Siberian White Government at Omsk from October 1918. This put him in charge of the $332 million in gold bullion. Some of the money was spent on munitions and military equipment, but $122 million went missing. After the Armistice was signed ending the First World War the Allied Forces lost interest in remaining in Russia so gradually drifted home.

In 1919 four offensives were launched as a result of which the Whites gained considerable ground. There were independent looters, for example the Greens, and regions and cities were constantly changing sides. For example, Kiev changed sides no less than ten times during this period. By 13 October 1919 the Whites were less than two hundred miles from Moscow. However, by this time Kolchak's troops were collapsing from hunger, typhus, and the lack of will to continue. The British ambassador abandoned Kolchak; Lloyd-George said that as anti-Bolshevism in Russia faced a prolonged and sanguinary struggle he had decided that British troops should withdraw.

How did these events affect Siberia, and Irkutsk in particular? For the first two years or so after War was declared, Irkutsk did not seem too badly affected but by 1916 the effects of the food shortages were beginning to be noticed. Inflation soared dramatically and food prices went crazy. Taking prices in December 1916 as 100%, by the end of January 1917 they were as follows:-

Bread	109%
Flour	107%
Butter	83%
Fish	63%
Potatoes	180%

The prices of products which had to be brought in from elsewhere rocketed skywards while those which were a major export from the region, such as butter and fish, plummeted.

Politically, Irkutsk's fortunes were bound up with the Trans-Siberian Railway, so the fortunes of the Czech Legion played a major role in the story of the town. Nevertheless, it cannot have been easy for people such as Joachim, an engineer, and other professionals to know where to put their loyalties for the best. Simply to be a member of the bourgeoisie was becoming dangerous, depending upon who was in power. Events in European Russia were closely and anxiously followed in Irkutsk. At first, the Bolsheviks only had control of European Russia. Early success in seizing Irkutsk on 4 January 1918 was reversed in July 1918, when the Whites retook power, which they held until December 1919. The Czechs supported the Whites (Kolchak's men) against the Bolsheviks. The Whites' first attempt to take the town on 26 May was unsuccessful, though by this time there were two Czech armoured trains at Irkutsk station. The Whites tried to repel the Bolsheviks on 14/15 June 1918, which resulted in them being scattered into the forests surrounding Irkutsk. The municipal authorities decided to evacuate all important administrative establishments to Ulan-Ude for safety, an exercise completed on 11 July. On 12 July a period of bloody struggle began as the Whites gradually gained control of the region and consolidated their power in the town on 1 September. Also fighting in the region was a fiercely cruel and power-thirsty Ataman, Gregori Semenov, who headed a Cossack and Mongol force and who, with the aid of Japanese troops, was hoping to establish his private fiefdom east of Lake Baikal. He killed all who stood in his path and was much feared and hated in the region.

As the year 1918 drew to a close the net which had been thrown round the businesses of the town and the Railway began to tighten and everyone was feeling the effect of living in a state of semi-siege and in the midst of a more or less permanent battleground. The year 1919 saw constant fighting and struggle between the rival groups. Meanwhile throughout Russia the crops were not even sown let alone harvested and the coal and minerals were unmined, so the state of famine increased while the money from exports decreased. Hardship was widespread by now. In the summer of 1919 the Railway line from Krasnoyarsk to Irkutsk came under the protection of the Intervention troops (ie., supporters of Kolchak and the White cause).

By November 1919 Kolchak realised that he had to move his headquarters from Omsk and he decided to travel east to Irkutsk, taking the Imperial gold with him. This was loaded carefully onto a convoy of trains which set off on what was to be a long, slow journey. Disaster struck when a huge fire resulted from a collision with another train; eight railway cars were destroyed, eighty guards killed and boxes containing the gold were scattered all over the tracks, there for the taking. Progress was slow, partly because of the state of the line and partly because of the suspicions of the French commander in charge of the Allied troops, General Janin, and the Czechs. As Kolchak travelled slowly east the Bolsheviks were steadily gaining ground; on 13 December Bratsk was recaptured by the Bolsheviks, followed shortly after by Nizhneidinsk, Tulin and Zima. Unable by now to organise his own protection, Kolchak had to place himself under the protection of the Czechs. Relations had deteriorated between the Whites and the Czechs, who by now merely wanted to get themselves home. The dreadful Siberian winter had set in, so in addition to the starvation faced by Kolchak's men many of those who attempted to escape succumbed to disease or simply froze to death in the trains. On 23 December 1919 Kolchak sent a desperate message to Semenov, the Ataman, appealing for his help.

On the following day, an anti-Kolchak rebellion began in Irkutsk, mostly consisting of an alliance of SRs and Mensheviks calling itself the Political Centre which quickly set about gaining control of the city. The fullest account of the events is that in Kudryavtsev and is written from the Bolshevik perspective, so it is hard to gain a balanced view of the fighting. Semenov arrived in the region on 27 December and sent a message to Kolchak's troops to hold fast and "relentlessly to finish off the insurgents." By this time rebel soldiers were occupying the Znamensky and Glazkov suburbs of the city, putting Kolchak's troops in a very weak position. The rebels swept down in two waves from Znamesky in the north of the city, the first wave occupying Tikhvinskaya Sq (now Kirov Sq) and the Second Khaminovskoy Secondary School (now the Pedagogical Institute). They swept up Amurskaya Street, occupying the Telegraph and Telephone Exchange and the State Bank on the way. On 28 December Sichev, the White commander, moved against the rebel forces and engaged them in hand to hand fighting. Simultaneously the military HQ received the news that Semenov's (pro-Kolchak) troops had taken the Petryushin Hills and the Railway Station and had, with the help of Japanese troops, begun to cross the Angara river, ie., towards the city centre. Apparently this was a ruse to force the rebels to leave the suburbs. The rebels armed themselves with guns and grenades with the help of friendly soldiers and also began to cross the river. They pressed on towards the city centre reaching the Sugar Workers' Building (now the site of the Agricultural Institute) and advanced as far as the Intendantskiy Gardens. The next day the rebel troops reached Laninskaya Street (now Decembrist Street) and as the groups of fighters encountered each other sporadic fighting broke out, even spreading to Bolshaya Street, the main street of the city.

The next day three armoured trains full of Semenov's troops arrived at the station. The locomotive of one of them was badly

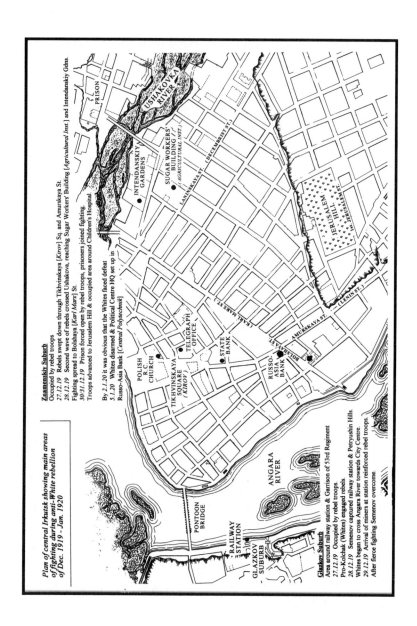

Plan of central Irkutsk showing main areas of fighting during anti-White rebellion of Dec. 1919 - Jan. 1920

100

manoeuvred and collided with the platform, which subsequently collapsed. Semenov merely alighted from the train and strode off to join the thick of the battle in the Glazkov region around the station. The forces of peasant-workers were no match for Semenov's well organised and armed troops so the fighting was fierce and bloody. The citizens on the other side of the River Angara, who could hear the gunfire and the machine guns blazing, anxiously awaited the outcome of this encounter as they realised that this was a crucial stage of the fighting. However, during the afternoon Semenov unexpectedly encountered resistance from troops of miners who arrived at the railway station fresh and ready for battle. Eventually Semenov's troop were overcome and Semenov himself escaped to Baikal, while his men were shown no mercy by the rebels. This defeat of Semenov broke the spirit of the pro-Kolchak men. On the night of 30-31 December 1919 the rebels broke open the prison, thus releasing the pro-Bolshevik supporters, who could then reinforce their own troops. The offensive began in earnest next day as the rebels who were in Znamesky crossed the ice of the Ushakovka river and then advanced to Jerusalem Hill, from where they occupied the area round the Children's Hospital and moved towards Laninskaya Street. Once again the fighting was fierce as the pro-Kolchak troops were forced to hold their position amid a barrage of artillery fire and shrapnel. By evening the outcome was becoming clear and on 2 January it was obvious that the White pro-Kolchak troops were facing certain defeat.

Talks were held in the saloon car of General Zhaneny's train concerning the "handing over of power from the Omsk Government to the Political Centre". A Peace Treaty agreeing to this was signed with effect from 3 January and thus power passed to the Political Centre (the SRs and the Menshevik Alliance) from the pro-Kolchak White Government. They were careful to point out that the "evacuation of the pro-Kolchak army to the east signified the abandonment of all territory to the west of Baikal to the Bolsheviks." They saw the Irkutsk region as a buffer state between the Semenov fiefdom to the east and the Bolsheviks to the west.

The Bolsheviks were anxious for power in Irkutsk and hoped to take advantage of the recent fighting. They threatened to open hostilities with the Political Centre if satisfactory negotiations were not concluded soon. The pro-Kolchak troops took advantage of this confusion to make good their escape. In the evening of 4 January the commander, Sichov, made off in the direction of Transbaikal with the valuables from the State Bank – gold, foreign currency and securities. However, he was ambushed and the valuables recovered. On 5 January the entire pro-Kolchak force was disarmed and the townspeople celebrated. The headquarters of the new Political Centre was set up in the building of the Russo-Asiatic Bank (now the Central Polytechnic).

Thus there were now two groups vying for power in Irkutsk – the Political Centre and the Bolsheviks. Each group sought to discredit the other and a bitter publicity campaign followed. The Political Centre issued their programme of administration, which satisfied the civic bourgeoisie, the village kulaks and the Interventionists, but seemingly few others, and the Bolsheviks published their plans for reform, also with limited support.

During all this time, Kolchak himself was making slow progress by train towards Irkutsk. On 5 January the Czechs detained Kolchak and the trains loaded with the gold in Nizhenidinsky. Realising the failure of the White cause the Czechs decided that they were in a strong position and could either confiscate the gold there and then or have it as a ransom for safe passage to the east. The issue almost provoked riots so the Czechs assumed command of the gold and, under pressure from the Bolsheviks, effectively arrested Kolchak on the train, despite the fact that by now he was flying the flags of all the Interventionist countries. A message concerning his status was relayed to Irkutsk. Some accounts blame the French commander, General Janin, for causing Kolchak's death by not preventing his advance to Irkutsk, where his future was now very uncertain. However, the Interventionists realised by this time that they were powerless to prevent his arrest and would have to hand him and the gold over to the Czechs.

Kolchak's train, now guarded by miners, eventually pulled into Irkutsk station on 14 January. He was met at the station by the Czech commander who handed him over to the Political Centre representatives. He was immediately taken to the prison. The carriages containing the gold were also handed over. They were shunted into a siding, wrapped around in barbed wire, and put under heavy guard. Funerals for those who had perished in the anti-Kolchak struggle were held on 17 January; by this time it was generally agreed that the Political Centre was a spent force and before many more days power in Irkutsk was officially handed over to the Bolsheviks. The first Soviet was convened on 25 January; the Deputies included 346 Bolsheviks, 79 Left SRs, 25 Mensheviks, 18 SRs, and 5 Anarchists.

The struggle was not entirely finished, however. Skirmishes continued along the Railway line and the countryside round Irkutsk still echoed to the distant sound of gunfire. The last remnants of Kolchak's men were roaming round the villages looking for food and shelter.

At first the Soviet Committee advocated peace with the rival groups it had ousted but this idea was soon rejected. The fate of Kolchak had passed into Bolshevik hands after the takeover of power on 25 January. The guard on the train containing the gold was increased and any further movement of the gold eastwards was absolutely forbidden. Surveillance of prominent members of the bourgeoisie of Irkutsk was stepped up to ensure that there was no attempt to rescue either Kolchak or the gold. A list of eighteen people implicated with Kolchak was prepared by the Commissar; Kolchak himself was still imprisoned together with his mistress and his Prime Minister, and subjected to regular interrogation. By all accounts this was a fairly civilised questioning and Kolchak is reported to have conducted himself with great dignity. The Revolutionary Committee selected only two names from the list for death by shooting – Kolchak himself and his Prime Minister, Pepelyaev. Kolchak's appeal to the Interventionists for help after the crushing defeat of Semenov had been in vain, as was Lenin's order not to kill Kolchak. On 6 February 1920 Kolchak was condemned to death and in the early hours of 7 February he was taken from the prison, shot and his body thrown into the Angara river through a hole hacked in the ice. So ended an extraordinary chapter in the story of Irkutsk.

On 10 February the siege of Irkutsk was lifted and the administrative offices returned from Ulan Ude over the next few days. On 1 March the Czechs formally handed the gold over to the Bolsheviks. The 3rd Rifle Division of the V Red Army triumphantly entered Irkutsk on 7 March and thus the town came entirely under Bolshevik control.

The gold rapidly disappeared having gone to pay off wartime enemies, to line the pockets of looters and to finance the armed resistance to the Whites in Siberia. The Whites collapsed at Arkhangelsk on 19 February, the Americans had started to pull out their troops on 11 January, but some Japanese remained in Vladivostok until as late as 1922.

In the space of just two years Irkutsk had therefore come under the control of a number of different groups. On 2 March 1917 the SRs and Mensheviks formed a Citizens Committee. Bolshevik power was established on 4 January 1918. In July the city was seized by the White Guards and on 1 September the Czechs arrived. In December 1919 an alliance of SRs and Mensheviks rose up against the Whites, whom they defeated, and power was handed from the Political Centre to the Bolsheviks on 25 January 1920. The Red Army marched into Irkutsk on 7 March 1920. In addition to this the city was full of Czech troops, Allied troops and groups of other factions and parties. Violence was rife (Shostakovich's father was killed by White Guards at this time) and the extra troops put a further strain on already scarce resources of food. Rumours were abundant; we have the benefit of hindsight to see these events in some kind of perspective and following a pattern, but it must have been thoroughly confusing and frightening to be caught in the middle of this fighting. News from afar must have disturbed the Poles in exile, too. In 1918 Poland at last gained her independence, much to everyone's surprise, after 123 years of official non-existence, as a result of the upheavals in Europe caused by the First World War. Did some of the exiled Poles dare to hope that they might return to their homeland?

What was the effect of witnessing and being caught up in these events upon the three children, aged 12, 10 and 8 in 1919? Surely the memories of such times would have left an indelible mark on their personality, and trying to keep going under such difficult circumstances cannot have been easy for the parents. Food was in constantly short supply, inflation rife and a careless remark overheard by the wrong person could have far-reaching consequences. In the autumn of 1921 Zosia, the children's governess, returned to Poland. The journey westwards across Russia was harrowing as the country was in the grip of a terrible famine and violence was liable to break out at any time. She says of her return, "On that journey, which lasted for two weeks, we had to provide ourselves with sugar and flour, for which I exchanged my clothes and my

104

very best possessions. Flour was the currency at that time throughout Russia. They were very hard and sad times."

Joachim and Anna wanted to move the family to Poland but they judged that it was not yet safe enough. Poland had gained her independence in 1919, more by the collapse of the three Partitioning Powers than any active effort on her part, but the country was by no means stable. The Treaty of Versailles, effective from 28 June 1919, which acknowledged Poland as an independent nation, did not settle the question of her eastern borders, an issue which rumbled on for the next thirty six years. There were several wars with her new neighbours as Poland tried to establish her identity and her borders in the face of a Europe very much changed from the late eighteenth century. The Ukrainian War, from November 1918 – July 1919, established Polish control over East Galicia. The Posnanian War with Germany lasted between 27 December 1918 and the Treaty of Versailles. The Silesian War erupted intermittently until it was settled by the Silesian Convention in 1922. The Lithuanian War, which concerned the possession of Wilno (Vilna), so dear to Polish hearts, began in July 1919 and continued until October 1920. The Czechoslovak War ran from 26 January 1919 - 28 July 1920.

The city of Wilno was captured by Poland in April 1919, and Minsk in August. Pilsudski, the Polish leader, wanted Wilno to remain Polish on the grounds that historically Poland and Lithuania had been united. However, Lithuanians wanted to keep their independence and this dispute was the source of much bitterness. The Bolsheviks captured Wilno in July 1920 only for the Poles to retake it three months later. The Poles refused to give it back to Lithuania. The Poles took Kiev in May 1920, only to be driven out by the Bolsheviks the following month. The Polish-Soviet War was the most important of the disputes as the Poles fought to maintain the independence of the non-Russian areas of the former Tsarist Empire. Lenin wanted to conquer Poland as a stepping stone to bringing the rest of Europe under Communist rule. The fact that Poland won this War meant that his plans were effectively thwarted and Europe saved from Soviet domination. The Red Army was advancing westwards, smashing its way through Polish lines in Galicia in June. By the beginning of August no less than five Soviet Armies were approaching the suburbs of Warsaw; on 10 August they crossed the Vistula river west of the

city. At the very last minute Pilsudski performed a daring man-
oeuvre which outwitted the soviet commander, Tukhachevsky,
slicing through the rear of the Soviet troops and on 18 August
effectively encircled them. The Polish victory was complete – the
so-called "Miracle of the Vistula" – commemorated every year
thereafter by the Polish people. The Poles chased the Russians out
of Poland; by mid-September the Red Army was in disarray.
Lenin suddenly decided to sue for peace just as the Poles were
planning to march on Moscow. The Armistice was signed on 12
October and took effect from 18 October. The final terms were
agreed at the Treaty of Riga on 18 March 1921. The first
Constitution of the new Republic had come into force the previous day.

Given the turbulent events in the newly-independent Poland,
which will be examined in more detail later, it is not surprising
that Joachim and Anna waited until things had settled down a little before moving back to Poland. Life in Russia had become even
harder by 1921 – a severe drought in 1920 had brought about a
dreadful famine in 1921, in which it is estimated that ten million
people died. Many peasant families had lost their breadwinner
during the six years of fighting and war. In some cases people were
reduced to cannibalism or eating acorns and thistles.

The Polish Catholic Church in Irkutsk, the family's spiritual
home, suffered after the Civil War. The building was nationalised
in 1921 and several attempts to close it for worship were made.
The authorities only succeeded in April 1938. The building
became an orphanage, and in the 1960s, a film studio. In 1974-8 the
building was restored and became a concert hall for the Irkutsk
Philharmonia, re-opening on 3 November 1978. In the last few
years it has re-opened for Sunday worship for Irkutsk's Catholics
– the descendants of the original Polish exiles.

The family's preparations for travelling back to Poland were
finally completed in the summer of 1922 and they boarded the
train at Irkutsk for the long journey to Poland. They must have
had mixed emotions – Joachim full of the practical questions such
as where they would live and where would he work. The children,
now aged fifteen, thirteen and eleven, were doubtless bursting
with excitement at the adventure. Anna, quiet and long-suffering,
was leaving the land of her birth and all that was familiar to her,
her family and her friends – what must have been going through

her mind? Surely she must have been filled with apprehension about the future.

The railway journey was not the straightforward five-day run to Moscow that it is today. The country was still licking its wounds after the terrible effects of war and famine. Inflation was running at 1000% and industrial production just a fraction of pre-1914 levels. The driver of the train they were on was no less keen than anyone else to take advantage of a trainload of passengers, some of whom were obviously wealthy, travelling westwards. Therefore he often stopped the train, refusing to drive further without bribes. The passengers had to give him their jewels and other valuable possessions in order to continue. The journey took three long months of slow travelling interspersed with long stops and must have been very tedious for the lively, though well-behaved, children.

Eventually the family did arrive in Poland in the autumn of 1922 and at first they stayed at Dzierkowszczyzna with Joachim's younger brother, Antoni, whom they had last seen twelve years before.

North East Poland / Eastern Byelorussia 1921

CHAPTER 5

Polish Interlude

What was this new country to which Joachim and his family were travelling with such anticipation? Was this really the Promised Land dreamed of by generations of Poles during its 123 years of "non-existence"? As so often happens, the reality did not match up to the ideal. The land to which the family were journeying was emerging from a nightmarish existence and her troubles were far from over. By 1922, when the family returned, some of the initial problems had been tackled, but in order to understand the situation in Poland in 1922, one must go back to 1918.

Poland gained her independence in November 1918 more by an accident of fate as the result of the disintegration of the Partitioning Powers of Poland and the re-drawing of the map of Europe rather than by any positive steps or the struggles of Polish nationalists. The Western Allies were from the outset lukewarm about the concept, despite declarations asserting Poland's right to exist as a free, independent nation state. The Declaration of the Head of the Allied Governments, who were trying to reshape Europe after the First World War asserted at Versailles on 3 June 1919 "the creation of a united and independent Polish State with free access to the sea, constitutes one of the conditions for just and durable peace and of the rule of right in Europe." Woodrow Wilson, President of the USA, pledged the establishment of Poland as a state in point 13 of his Fourteen Point Plan after the end of the First World War (see Polonsky and Halecki).

The task facing Poland was truly formidable and was bravely tackled despite almost overwhelming odds. She inherited a daunting legacy, not only from the recent occupation by the Germans 1914-18, who, during their retreat in 1918, destroyed as many buildings, railway stations, trains, schools, factories, bridges and oil fields as possible. For over 100 years the territory now forged into the one Polish State had been occupied by three different Powers. The task of unification was a mammoth one – there were six currencies in circulation, five regions, (each of which maintained its own completely separate administration), four languages of command in the army, three legal codes, two railway gauges and eighteen registered political parties each wanting their share in the new country. Only 67% of the population were ethnic Poles, the other major groups being Ukrainians (14%), Jews (8.5%), Byelorussians(3.5%) and Germans (2.3%). The total population was 27million (1921 Census). In addition, those entrusted with the leadership of Poland had little or no experience of government or of the parliamentary system, since independence was largely unexpected. During the first six weeks after the Armistice was signed, in November 1918, 650 000 refugees returned from Russia alone; the number soon rose to more than 1.5 million. All the refugees had to be fed and housed somehow; by 1919 it was estimated that a third of the population were on the verge of starvation.

Poland's position was made even more complex by the vexed question of the Eastern Frontier, a question which was to plague her for several decades. Settlements were attempted concerning the borders at the Treaty of Brest-Litovsk on 3 March 1918 and the Treaty of Riga of 18 March 1921. These followed a series of disputes and wars which had severely taxed Poland's meagre resources. Poland's attitude to her eastern neighbours was misunderstood by the Western Powers, provoking comments such as Lloyd George's, "The Poles have quarrelled with all their neighbours and are a menace to the peace of Europe." He, along with other Western statesmen, failed to grasp the historical issues involved in Poland's attempts to include the territory of the former Grand Duchy of Lithuania and the Ukraine in her new borders. Pilsudski's romantic hope was that there could be a revival of the pre-Partition Union of Lithuania and Poland, and her neighbours Byelorussia and the Ukraine, in a kind of Federation of semi-autonomous states which came under a Polish "umbrella". Particularly dear to his heart was the restoration of Wilno to the new Poland. However, the states concerned were unhappy with this idea, which undermined their hard-won independence and suggested Polish domination, so they opposed this idea. The nationalist movements in these countries were particularly vocal in their opposition to this plan.

In October 1920 Polish troops occupied the Wilno region, forcing out the newly-declared Lithuanian Republic and setting up their own state called Central Lithuania with its capital at Wilno. The issue of Wilno became a matter for the Polish-Lithuanian negotiations by the Peace of Riga, although negotiations were conducted in Brussels. In February 1922 Eastern Lithuania was formally annexed to Poland, although as no peace treaty had been signed to end the war Poland and Lithuania were technically still at war in 1939. Poland had also wanted to include the Ukraine in her new State; her troops entered Kiev in May 1920, but even with the support of the Ukrainian nationalist leader, Petlura, she failed to prevent it being recaptured by the Bolsheviks soon afterwards. With the loss of Ukraine to the Soviet State, Pilsudski's dream of a federation was effectively gone. Byelorussia became split into eastern and western halves, the western being ceded to Poland and the eastern to the Soviet Union, not to be reunited until the Second World War when the Soviets took all of it after causing great suffering to the inhabitants. To this day, Lithuanians, Belarusians, and Ukrainians have an uneasy relation with Poles and vice versa. The parts of the territories which were ceded to Poland and had large non-Polish minorities in their populations found their right to the use of their own language and culture progressively curtailed over the next twenty years, despite having these rights enshrined in the Constitution of May 1921. The Polish government reacted to Byelorussian separatist movements by handing over more than 300 Byelorussian schools to Polish teachers, and by breaking up the Byelorussian Commune (Hramada) in 1928. Byelorussians were one of the new State's largest minority; there were an estimated 1.5 - 2 million (sources vary in their estimates) almost all in the most backward region of the country.

The changes in the eastern borders affected the family, which may be remembered was widely scattered throughout the old Grand Duchy of Lithuania (which included much of ethnic Byelorussia). Dzierkowszczyzna where Joachim's brother, Antoni, lived was just inside the new Polish border, which actually ran very close to the village. Sviencionys and Nowogrodek (Navahrudak in Byelorussian) were also in the new Poland. However, Backow and Borsukowa Grzeda, the two small villages near the Berezina river, whose description had brought back childhood memories to Joachim in his old age, were now part of the Byelorussian Republic of the Soviet Union. It is likely that there were members of the Chrzczonowicz family who were likewise caught behind the new borders.

The Soviet leaders' concept of a Europe-wide Communist State led them to plan a great sweep westwards across Byelorussian territory and through Poland conquering Germany and all other countries in their path. However, they reckoned without the fierce resistance they would encounter from the Polish forces, although the Soviet Army did reach as far as the suburbs of Warsaw. Here they were routed and the threat of European invasion disappeared as Lenin subsequently decided to sue for peace. The significance of this defeat is often underrated in Western accounts. However the tactics of this conflict are assessed, it remains true that the defeat of the Soviet army did play an important part in preventing the advance of Communism westwards and thus saved Europe from Soviet domination.

Once Poland's borders (and there were disputes not only on her eastern frontier but also the German and Czechoslovakian borders as well) were more or less fixed by Treaty, it was hoped that she would be able to establish herself as a State without distractions. However, international relations were not easy; few foreigners understood her innate distrust of the Russians and only slightly lesser distrust of the Germans (which a study of Polish history would have clarified). She had little sympathy from her neighbours; even France, once one of her staunchest allies, blew hot and cold. Poland's sympathy for Hungary, with whom she had historical links, inhibited the development of new links with Romania and France. The failure of Western Powers to support Poland during the Polish-Soviet War of 1919-20 obliged her to fend for herself and led to a certain isolation and the feeling that she was not to be taken seriously. Given the huge problems that she faced she did not seem to have any offers of assistance, eg, foreign aid or investment, in their solution. Davies, in *God's Playground* Vol II, p.393, quotes a rich variety of politicians' comments on Poland's situation. They include Lloyd George (already quoted) who dubbed Poland as a "historic failure" and in 1939 said that Poland "had deserved her fate". E.H. Carr, the writer, said that the Polish state was a farce, Stalin, that it was, "pardon the expression, a State." The Soviet Foreign Minister, Molotov, said it was the "monstrous bastard of the Peace of Versailles" (even though it had been established before it). Hitler said, among other things, that it was a "so-called state lacking every national, historical, cultural and moral foundation". This followed more than a hundred years of adverse writing about Poland by the three occupying Powers, whose attitudes influenced European responses to Poland to her disadvantage. With attitudes such as these it is the more remarkable that she achieved what she did. Foreign investment was slow in view of the parlous state of the economy, so she had to struggle on as best she could. In view of the tremendous odds stacked against her she had some remarkable achievements to her credit in her twenty years of independence.

Despite problems on her borders and in her relations with foreign powers, Poland forged ahead with a vigorous programme of social reforms. Within weeks of the new State's existence legislation had been passed to limit the working day to eight hours and the working week to 48 hours. Labour Inspectors were appointed in January 1919 and the complex issues of social insurance tackled in the following few years. Children under fifteen were forbidden to work, and from May 1922 everyone was entitled to eight days' annual holiday, rising to fifteen days after three years' continuing employment. Maternity leave (six weeks before and six weeks after the birth) was introduced and women forbidden to work underground or at night. Unemployment insurance was introduced in July 1924 as well as sickness benefit and old age pensions. There were in addition many private foundations for the provision of aid, some, eg the Holy Spirit Insurance in Sandomierz, dating back to the Middle Ages. Advances were made in the field of health; for example, in 1921 there were 6408 doctors, by 1938 there were 16 088 (including Kostek).

On the education front the situation was worse. The government was faced with the task of educating a population of 25 million, only 68% of whom were ethnically Polish. Almost half the school buildings of Poland had been destroyed by the Germans and there was a desperate shortage of adequately trained teachers. Provision of education varied widely in the different parts of Poland and literacy rates (44% overall in 1918) were especially low in former Russian Poland. Compulsory education was introduced into Poland in 1919 although a uniform system was not fully instituted until the spring of 1923 (Kostek, Zosia and Witold began their Polish school career in September of that year). At first a 7-year programme was introduced after which a further 7 years was spent in a Gymnasium (secondary school) but later this was altered to 6 and 8 years respectively.

Special problems were created by Poland's history and geography when teaching these subjects as also when training Polish children in nationalism and citizenship, since almost one third of children were of non-Polish ethnicity. However, by 1931, literacy had increased to almost 70% of the population.

Economically and politically Poland was in a very vulnerable condition, especially in the early 1920s. There were major splits between the political parties which had opposite views on many issues. As an example of this, Pilsudski saw the greatest threat to Poland as being from Russia, relations with her being traditionally uneasy. To help counter this threat he wanted a federation of states – Poland, Lithuania, Byelorussia and Ukraine – to be able to withstand any planned expansion westwards. This was in addition to his notion of reviving the old Poland-Grand Duchy of Lithuania Commonwealth. Pilsudski's rival Dmowski, however, saw Germany as the greatest threat to Poland and he wanted a Poland which was smaller in area than Pilsudski's but more ethnically Polish, more on the lines of the old Piast concept of the state. The governments of the early 1920s were essentially unstable – there were no less than thirteen governments in the years 1921-26 – partly because it was impossible to elect a government based on a secure parliamentary majority. In the government of December 1922, for example, the Right, Centre and Left parties had almost the same proportion of seats with nearly as many national minority seats.

The first elected Polish President was Narutowicz, elected on 14 December 1922 – and assassinated on 16 December while attending an art exhibition in Warsaw. (We know that Joachim and almost certainly the rest of the family were in Warsaw at this time – what would they have made of this?). Governments were formed and resigned as the task of stabilising the fledgling nation proved too difficult but it hardly gave potential foreign investors confidence in the economy. Inflation was fast running out of control; in November 1918 the mark rate was $1 to 9 Polish marks, in early 1923 it was 1:52 and by the November it had soared to 1:2 300 000. By January 1924 the rate was 1:15 000 000. In April 1924 the Bank Polski was formed to try to stabilise the money, setting up a new currency, the zloty.

In terms of foreign policy there were chronic problems with the Soviet Union, a legacy of centuries of mistrust. The Soviets were

114

not happy with the border settlement ratified by the Riga Treaty of March 1922. In October 1925 the Franco-Polish Guarantee was signed, in March 1926 the Polish-Romanian Alliance was renewed and in the following month the Russo-German Neutrality Pact. In July 1924 attempts were made to meet the demands of the ethnic minorities in Poland by passing legislation that they should be permitted to use their own languages in the courts and in administration. Instruction in schools where 25% or more of the children were non-Polish could be in the minority language if forty or more parents requested it. It should be noted that this seemed to contradict what was actually happening since reports of harassment of the ethnic minorities also seem to date from this time.

Joachim and his family were moving from one unstable situation to another; both Poland and the Soviet Union were promising a new future but Poland seemed to be more likely to be able to fulfil that promise. They arrived at Antoni's house in Dzierkowszczyzna in the autumn of 1922 with a mixture of optimism, apprehension and relief at having safely arrived in Poland at last. How different an arrival this was from the visit fourteen years before when Zosia was baptised!

Joachim's first task was to have his Polish citizenship confirmed and all the family's documents put in order. The birth certificates had to be authenticated and translated and identity cards issued; for this the family would have to travel to Warsaw, which they did in December 1922. Joachim went to the offices of the notary Dunilowski, perhaps a family friend, and the complex process was undertaken 7-29 December as all the certificates bear dates between these two dates. By the end of December all was in order and the whole family were now legally as well as ethnically Polish. Even as this legal process was happening, the first elected President, Narutowicz, was assassinated in Warsaw; perhaps Joachim and Anna wondered whether they had really left the violence and bloodshed behind in Russia. The stay in Warsaw was an ideal opportunity for the family to go sightseeing as well – it must have been a very exciting time for the children as they spent Christmas in the capital, and all business was completed by the New Year. Joachim also had to find a job. Poland was desperate for engineers to help reconstruct the badly-damaged infrastructure of a war-torn and underdeveloped country, so as a fully-qualified civil engineer Joachim doubtless had no problems finding a job. The one he chose took him back, whether consciously or not, to the area of Poland near Sandomierz, where some of his ancestors may have lived many centuries before, to the small town of Skarzysko-Kamienna in the Holy Cross Mountains near Radom in central Poland. His job was to build the State munitions factory in the town. The State armaments factory was in Warsaw and the State firearms factory in Radom (Polonski). Joachim began work there in the spring of 1923. The family settled in a large and comfortable flat in the centre of Skarzysko.

The children's education was a major concern of Joachim and Anna at it had been severely disrupted by the upheavals of the past two years. It must have been with a certain relief that Joachim saw his two sons start at the local Gymnasium on 1st September 1923. Despite all the disruption the boys were very bright and did well at school; so well in fact that they were put into classes ahead of their ages. Zosia had done her work of education well and it stood them in good stead. Nothing is known of their sister's education; not even a matriculation certificate survives. Their final school reports are full of praise for their achievements, with the comment "very good" for most subjects.

The school was known in their time as "A.Witkowski School". It still exists, much altered, but is now called Adam Mickiewicz College. It was situated in the town centre on Stasic Street. One of the former buildings, which the boys used to call the "Kennel," is now a shopping complex. The building where they went for gymnastics was later turned into a cinema called the Comet. Opposite the school was a wonderful bakery where they used to buy little cakes for next to nothing. Photographs of the town show wide spacious avenues; one of the main streets was called Three Poets Street and was where one of the boys' teachers, a Professor Zaleski, lived. Near his house, a picturesque wooden cottage set in its own grounds, there was an old hut. Here there lived an old man who had fallen in love with one of the teachers at the school; when she died he went mad, even though she had moved away from the area some years before and was living with her daughter in Warsaw when she died. Near what is now Independence Square is the church which the family attended Sunday by Sunday and where Witold, if not Kostek as well, was an altar boy.

Their schooldays were obviously happy times. The little town where they lived was picturesque and set amid the beautiful coun-

116

tryside of the Holy Cross (Swientokrzyskie) Mountains, with plenty of forests, hills, lakes and rivers easily accessible for all kinds of activities. The boys loved sports and both owned a horse (Witold's was called Barbara). Kostek's love of horses led him to do his National Service in the Cavalry. They also loved cycling, and one of Witold's proudest moments from this period of his life was winning the local cycle race one year. He also enjoyed a mischievous sense of fun, playing practical jokes on nervous old ladies by pretending to fall off his bike just in front of them or the old trick of tying together two door knockers of doors opposite each other, so when one door is opened, the other door is knocked, opened, and so on. A naughtier trick involved looking up in the phone book for a Mr Bird, then ringing him up. "Mr Bird? Bang! Bang! You are dead!" and putting the phone down.

This was a good and happy time for the family. Joachim was prospering in his job. The first workshop of the Munitions factory was completed in 1924/5, and the event was commemorated by an official photograph of all the people associated with its building – including the local priest.

A number of family snapshots survive from this time, obviously only part of the family collection as there are gaps in dates. Joachim was a keen photographer and it is remarkable that so many pictures are still extant given the events of the War. Witold loved going on long cycle rides as a teenager, often accompanied by his cousin, Danek Walentynowicz, only a year younger than himself. Together they explored the surrounding countryside discovering old ruins and small villages. Kostek matriculated in the summer of 1928 and elected to do his two years' military service in the Cavalry because of this love of horses. Some of his training was done at Modlin, the fortress north of Warsaw built in Napoleonic times, some of it was at Zamosc and Brzesc (Brest). There are many photos of the Cavalry Training School; this was obviously an exciting time for Kostek. Witold was growing up into a quiet, shy, sensitive and serious young man, who was nevertheless capable of coming out of his shell and telling stories which rendered his audience helpless with laughter, a characteristic which he retained until the end of his life. A school essay written when he was sixteen shows a highly developed philosophical way of thinking and a maturity of thought beyond his years.

Christmas 1929 was a fun time for both the Chrzczonowicz and the Walentynowicz families as they spent it together. To judge from the photos the young people had a wonderful few days. They dressed up in Chinese costume, they went for walks in the snow and staged snowball fights; the laughing faces look out of the pictures with no hint of the tragedies yet to come.

The following year, 1930, Kostek enroled in the Medical School in Warsaw, having decided on a last-minute switch from engineering. He studied with enthusiasm and with an earnestness and seriousness which was almost pathological, except that it was tempered with a great sense of humour. The medical students used to play all kinds of practical jokes on each other, mostly of a medical nature. They used to get into dreadful scrapes sometimes. On one occasion Witold was with his brother and a group of friends as they waited in the Common Room playing cards, on call for any patients with interesting conditions who came into the hospital. They were duly summoned but faced with the problem of what to do with Witold. They gave him a white coat and told him to come with them, so they all scurried off to the ward and joined the Professor waiting at the bedside. As luck would have it, the Professor turned to Witold and asked him about the patient's diagnosis! Thinking quickly, Kostek said, "Professor, this is my brother. He's a journalist and is writing an article on the training of medical students." The Professor's reply is not recorded.

In 1931 Witold matriculated and decided to defer his military service until after university. By this time the family also had a flat in Warsaw, at 16 Wozorojska St, and Witold decided to study Electrical Engineering at the Warsaw Technical University, the Institute founded by the Poles who had trained at the Petersburg Technological Institute a generation before and which Joachim had himself attended. The Institute had celebrated its centenary in 1928, an occasion which was celebrated in Warsaw at a dinner attended by Joachim and recorded in the obligatory official photograph. A book was published on the history of the Institute to mark the occasion. Several of Witold's Professors had been his father's contemporaries in St Petersburg. A year later, Danek followed Witold at the Institute.

By this time the political situation in Poland had changed. Five years before, in May 1926, Pilsudski had staged a coup and thus significantly changed the course of Polish politics. The ensuing

118

regime became known as the "Sanacja" or Return to [political] Health and gradually became more and more autocratic until a new Constitution was introduced in April 1935. Although Pilsudski himself died in 1935 the ethos of his regime continued almost unchallenged until 1939. However, cultural and intellectual life flourished in almost every field. Poetry, art, music and literature all developed rapidly and remain one of the lasting legacies of Poland's inter-war years.

It seems that this group of young people – Kostek, Witold, Danek, Marysia, and to a lesser extent, Zosia, were now enjoying life to the full. The anecdotes which survive from this period paint a picture of fun and a busy social life. They were full of practical jokes; a birthday present for a friend, in the centre of Warsaw, was a live goat. The custom at Christmas was for Varsovians to exchange greetings not by Christmas cards but by slipping visiting cards between the door frame and the door of those to be greeted. One year Witold and his friends secretly mixed up the cards, so Mr A, who had not spoken to Mr B for years, found himself greeted by him, and Miss C was startled to find Mr D, a married man, obviously showing an interest in her.

The group went on outings, boating, fishing, cycling, playing tennis, swimming, visiting the sights of Warsaw together. One day Witold was at a restaurant with his friends; it happened that Joachim was also at the same restaurant, but at a different table. When the time came to pay the bill, Witold simply told the waiter to give the bill to "that gentleman over there; he will pay" indicating his father. And he did. Joachim himself attracted a host of anecdotes. As he had a long white flowing beard he was often mistaken for a rabbi, and Jews would stop him in the street asking for a blessing, which he would solemnly give. Once a small boy stopped him and asked him the classic question asked of bearded men – did he sleep with his beard over or under the sheets? Apparently he spent a sleepless night trying to work out the answer. On another occasion Joachim was in the bath and alone in the flat when the postman delivered a letter,. He looked at it straight away, and on discovering that it was wrongly delivered, ran out of the flat naked as he was to catch the postman. Unfortunately a gust of wind at that moment blew the door shut so Joachim was locked naked out of his flat. Fortunately he did not have to wait too long before being "rescued".

119

In March 1932 Joachim was awarded the Gold Cross of Merit (equivalent to the OBE) for "services in the field of the war industry", ie, for his work in building the munitions factory, a showpiece of the Polish arms industry. This was in recognition of his hard work over the best part of a decade. In an ironic twist of fate, his son, Witold, would receive the Silver Cross of Merit fourteen years later, but for very different reasons and in very different circumstances.

How did Anna feel in the midst of all this frantic activity? We can only speculate, and surmise from the photos that she was unhappy as she always appears worried and serious and slightly lost. Her health was beginning to fail and at around this time there are hints that she had spells in sanatoria to rest and recuperate. She must have been anxious, too, about her family in Russia as the stories emerging about life under Stalin can hardly have been encouraging. She must have realised that she was unlikely ever to see them again; she leaves the impression that no matter how many friends she had made in Poland she still felt isolated. Also, underneath all the gaiety and laughter of the young people there was a darker note. Zosia, Witold and Kostek's sister, had been giving cause for concern for some time. Her behaviour was becoming odder and she mixed less and less socially. Danek's twin sister, Maria (Muszka) was quietly asked to encourage her out to social functions and to make friends, but it was obvious that something was not quite right. Doctors were consulted but were evasive; it was only while Kostek was pursuing his medical studies that he realised what was happening – his sister was showing signs of schizophrenia. In an era when mental illness carried a huge stigma and was barely acknowledged even in enlightened circles, this was an enormous blow. Kostek kept an eye on his sister and guided the family's treatment of her, while it appeared that he kept his theory of her true diagnosis from them. When she did finally show an interest in a young man and it was beginning to look serious, Kostek made the couple break up, as he realised the implications of marriage in such a situation. Over the years Zosia became more and more severely ill, despite the family's best attempts to hide her true condition. She, too, had spells in various sanatoria, but the terrible disruptions of the occupation of Warsaw during the Second World War finally meant that she had to be admitted to hospital. The circumstances were obviously so painful that even in old age Joachim could hardly bear to talk about her final years even to Witold without becoming tearful.

However, that was in the future. In the early 1930s the partying continued and the young people studied hard.Poland was experiencing a huge cultural revival in the fields of literature, theatre and the arts. It was an important unifying factor in the relatively new state. Kostek, Witold and Danek enjoyed all the opportunities offered by this flourishing literary scene. (For discussion of the major issues, see Wiles, and Crowley). In 1934 Witold, Kostek and Danek went on a Grand Tour of Europe visiting all the major continental capitals. There are photos of them in Paris, Belgrade, Budapest and little Italian towns. Anna herself was in a sanatorium at this time, as we can tell by the addresses on the cards sent by the family. Her health was becoming poor, as she suffered from heart problems and was a heavy smoker.

There were family holidays in the Tatra Mountains, skiing in Zakopane or Worochta (in the eastern Carpathians and now in Ukraine), and summer holidays in Rabka and Bartodzieje. Joachim was by now approaching sixty years of age and doubtless looking forward to retirement. He had visited the beautiful countryside around Czorsztyn in southern Poland and decided to buy a plot of land there, almost certainly with the hope of building a house there and retiring with Anna. In 1936 he negotiated the purchase of a plot of land 1200sqm from a Stanislaw Drohojowski in the area of Kroscienko, near Krakow. At least the purchase of the land was considered a good investment although the house itself was never built.

Eventually both Kostek and Witold completed their studies, in 1937 and 1936 respectively. Witold was awarded the Dipl.Eng. qualification on 31 August 1936. This Diploma, like his father's, was not only a degree but a professional qualification which entitled him to practise as a fully-fledged chartered engineer (and be addressed as *pan inzynier*). However, before he could start working as an engineer he had to complete his delayed National Service. On 21 September 1936 he was enroled in the Cadets School for Sappers at Modlin, north of Warsaw. He spent exactly a year there and we hear no more of him until he had to do a further six months' training between January and July 1938, this time in the 3 Battalion Willenski Field Engineers.

Kostek qualified as a doctor in May 1937; as he had already

done his military service he began work as a doctor immediately. He worked at the famous Przemienienia Panskiego or Transfiguration Hospital in the Praga district of Warsaw, where he in fact remained until his death. Like all newly-qualified doctors in Poland at that time he started as an unpaid houseman; in due course he received a salary of 30zl./month, as well as his board and lodging and a tram ticket. Eventually he was promoted to doing locum duties, filling in when an assistant went on holiday, for which he earned 8zl. per day. In addition he was trying to gain experience by working in an open air kindergarten for children with TB and, from August 1938, by doing some ambulance work. The head of his department was trying to get Kostek an assistant's post as the next step in his goal to become a paediatric surgeon, but internal politics apparently decreed that this was not easily given. He was faced with the dilemma of continuing the kindergarten work (and the ambulance work) which paid well and which he enjoyed, or giving it all up and working as an assistant for approximately a quarter the salary and with very demanding hours but essential for furthering his career. In the end Kostek decided to keep the ambulance work for one day and one night per month and to take up an assistant's post when one became available.

Christmas of 1938 was the usual family occasion, but sadly would be the last one they would ever spend together, so the photo taken on that occasion has a special poignancy. Only Witold and Anna look directly at the camera, the others are gazing elsewhere, so we can only wonder what was going on under the surface. It seems to have been the only picture to have survived from that Christmas, although it seems a strangely sad one.

What was occupying Kostek, as indeed all thinking people of Poland at this time, was the way events in Germany were going. Hitler's actions were appearing very ominous indeed to the young Polish state, who shared a long border with Germany, and another one with the Soviet Union, and they did not like what they saw. The storm clouds were gathering. Non-aggression Treaties had been signed with Germany in 1934 and the Soviet Union in July 1932. Hitler seemed the greater threat to Poland, especially after his invasion of Austria in March 1938 and the disputed Sudetenland territory in September. The Munich Agreement of September 1938, ceding the territory to Hitler, signed by the leaders of the UK, France, Germany and Italy, led to Neville Chamberlain's triumphant but empty promise of "peace in our time." The rest of Czechoslovakia was invaded by Hitler in March 1939, causing widespread alarm both among the Poles and abroad, the Poles realising that Hitler was turning his eyes eastwards to Poland as his next target. Both Britain and France agreed to come to the help of Poland if she were invaded, but this action was more in the interests of stopping Hitler than helping Poland. (In fact France's commitment had been secretly revoked in the spring of 1939). Chamberlain must have known that Britain did not in fact have the capability to come to Poland's defence. Hitler saw through Britain's declaration and responded by revoking the Polish-German Non-Aggression Pact on 28 April 1939. The next few months saw a war of nerves for Poland, Britain and France, Poland's only other ally. Germany and the Soviet Union were holding talks and a German-Soviet Non-Aggression Pact was signed in July1939; a secret protocol was also signed on 23 August agreeing to the division of Poland between Germany and the Soviet Union. This effectively sounded the death knell for Poland's existence.

How prepared were the Polish Armed Forces to meet any attack by Hitler? Unfortunately, they were singularly unprepared. The legend of the Polish soldiers fighting the German tanks with cavalry has passed into history (but both the German and the Soviet Armies had Cavalry Regiments as well at this time), but it is an indicator of how the Polish commanders failed to take modern advances in military thought into account. Pilsudski's influence was still strong; the prevailing philosophy in military circles was to use First World War tactics. The Air Force was to be a reconnaissance force (as in World War I) rather than a fighting force in its own right so it was never fully developed. There was no proper system for national defence and no effective plans for fighting a future war. The general staff had been downgraded in 1926; the Army Commanders were on the whole opposed to modernisation and the introduction of technological advances (as would be graphically illustrated in considering the fate of the Polish Army in Russia in 1941; see chapter 7).

Kostek intended to write down his memoirs of his experience of the Second World War for Witold; in fact only a tiny but tantalising fragment has survived, which does not even cover the time up to the outbreak of the war. How fascinating it would be if we had a more complete account! He was a keenly observant writer who vividly captured the mood of the people of Warsaw during that last summer of peace and freedom in 1939.

Underlying daily life was the constant anxiety of what Hitler would do next, which made for uncertainty in political circles and for fertile ground for rumour. The Foreign Minister, Jozef Beck, made a speech in Parliament on 4 May, a speech which was full of optimism and included the words, "Poland will not be pushed away from the Baltic." This instilled a false sense of security in people's minds but it was also worrying to see how few soldiers had taken part in the Third of May Parade the day before – most of the army was at the border.

Kostek met Witold on 23 June – the last time the two brothers would ever meet, although they did correspond after Witold was released from the GULAG. It must have been a poignant meeting in view of the ominous situation. Perhaps they had a premonition that they would not meet again. Certainly Kostek told his cousin Danek that he had an intuition that he would not survive the war – despite apparently cheating death on at least eight occasions. Kostek remained in Warsaw until 1 July sorting out his affairs. The newspapers of that day brought news of German tanks passing through Bratislava in the direction of Poland. Next day he visited his mother, who was ill in a sanatorium, and on 4 July he travelled to Lwow for the first time. At that time it was part of Poland. He found it a beautiful city and it called to mind some words of the poet Pawlikowska, words which have not been found in any published collection of her work:-

"I believe in God and Lwow, my heart is beating so fast
and I have this dream again and again, when a frosty morning
wakes me up in Lwow
And those young boys lying dead, so simple and white . . . .
My heart beats thick!
Only this dream can speak about all that we lack in words.
I believe in God and Lwow."

(Maria Pawlikowska-Jasnorzewska (1893-1945) was one of the foremost poets of her generation. During the War she fled to Romania, then France and Britain, where she eventually settled in Manchester, dying of cancer in 1945. She is buried in south

Manchester. The fact that Kostek quotes her poem, probably from memory, indicates his enjoyment and knowledge of contemporary literature.)

Kostek then seems to have travelled around south-eastern Poland, staying in Worochta, the scene of several happy family holidays, and chatting with the Hungarian soldiers along the border. Together with a friend he took part in a horse riding competition and returned to Warsaw via Krakow on 18 July.

On his return to Warsaw Kostek found the atmosphere extremely tense. One of his friends left a note saying that he had to go to Pulawy to drill for six weeks, and Kostek had the feeling that it would be a long time before this friend would take off his uniform. The tense atmosphere even pervaded the hospital and he found that he was doing more and more surgery even though conditions were becoming extremely difficult. Rumours abounded; mobilisation was ordered on 28 August and then hurriedly cancelled in case Hitler should take it to be a sign of Polish aggression and claim that Poland was preparing to attack him. A second, secret, order for mobilisation was given, but the whole issue illustrates the confused command in the Armed Forces of the time.

In the streets and shops people were beginning to panic. There were long queues at banks as people tried to withdraw their money. Profiteers and black marketeers saw their chance and were taking advantage of the situation. Kostek himself felt inwardly restless and yet excited but he realised the importance of keeping calm and carrying on working. On the night of 24 August his friend Stefan left for training at Plock and the next day two doctors from the ward received their call up papers. This left Kostek and two other doctors for the entire ward.

Kostek arranged to go to the Homickis (Danek's sister Marysia and her husband) for dinner on 25 August. Before arriving there he had to visit three patients. On his way to visit the one in Zielonka, just outside Warsaw, he saw signs of the impending war, by now inevitable. Men were leaving with bundles, their womenfolk crying as they said farewell. Horses were being requisitioned for use in the army. The process looked very amicable and seemed suspiciously like mobilisation, although at this point there was nothing official.

He arrived at the Homickis with two bottles of champagne and they had a delicious meal. However, Marysia's husband and his friend were already in uniform, which dampened the occasion. The alcohol had given Kostek a headache but he discovered that his own call-up papers had been delivered to his flat meanwhile, so having seen the other two off at the Station he returned to his flat and packed. He burned all his letters – an action which he later regretted. He also regretted leaving the very first flat of his own. On his way to the station he called in at the Hospital where one of the Nursing Sisters, a nun called Sister Helena Czyzewska, gave him two holy medals. He then boarded the shabby local train for Modlin where he reported for duty. He was assigned to the 8th Division Heavy Artillery. From this time onwards he and his fellow officers were frantically preparing all kinds of military equipment ... and here the narrative breaks off, and we hear no more of Kostek's account. How fascinating it would be if more had survived, if we could continue to have an intimate eye-witness account of life in occupied Poland.

The events of 1 September 1939 onwards are well documented and can be found in any standard history of Poland (Davies, Halecki, Schmitt, Zamoyski, et al). Hitler's invasion of Poland began with an attack on the Polish fort at Westerplatte, near Gdansk, preceded by an attack on a radio station in Upper Silesia. The German forces swept in along the whole length of the Polish-German border overcoming all Polish resistance. The Modlin Army, where Kostek was, held out until 29 September. Of Kostek himself we know nothing for the next six months but it is reasonable to suppose that he escaped capture and went into hiding in the nearby countryside, as did many other soldiers. We next hear of him registering as a doctor in Warsaw in March 1940.

As for Witold, he was called up into the Reserves on 1 September and being stationed to the east of Lwow was captured by the Soviets only one day after they crossed the border into Poland as part of the secret plan to divide Poland up between Hitler and Stalin. On 18 September 1939 Witold was taken prisoner and transported to the Soviet Union.

It seems that Joachim and Anna fled Warsaw and lived in their Radom flat at this point, presumably taking Zosia with them. Doubtless it was considered safer for them, although they had to move around several times, judging by the addresses on the Identity Cards.

Life had changed irrevocably for the family. Gone forever were the days of carefree affluence and busy social life. The future held only uncertainty and sorrow. The anxious parents had no idea whether they would ever see their two sons again, and as events turned out, they would never meet again as a family. It was a fate shared by all Poles as their beloved country, which had so recently gained her independence, was once again plunged into hell, and into a worse torment then there had ever been in the past.

CHAPTER 6

"Free Russian Vacation"

With the unprovoked invasion of Poland by Hitler on 1
September 1939 Poland entered the most tragic phase of her history. The population had begun secret mobilisation at the end of
August, then it had been cancelled, and then ordered again. It had
been kept secret for fear that Hitler should say that Poland was
preparing to attack Germany. Witold was called up on 1
September to join the 3 Wilenski Field Engineers, and was immediately sent to the Eastern frontier region of Poland, somewhere
east of Lwow. Meanwhile, Hitler swept through Poland, over-
powering the Polish Armies who were hopelessly outnumbered by
the Germans. There were legends of Polish soldiers facing
German tanks on horseback, although both the German and the
Soviet armies still used horses themselves to a small extent. By 6
September the Polish command had abandoned its attempt to
defend its frontiers. By 8 September, Warsaw was already under
fire; the threat to the city itself was so great that the President, the
Government, the Commander-in-Chief and the Diplomatic Corps
left for the south of Poland, crossing the border on 17 September
just before it closed, hoping to escape to Romania, which they
eventually reached. The battle for Warsaw commenced on 16
September and lasted for 12 days; the garrison at Modlin held out
another day. Poland was the recipient of the full fury of the
German army; despite the growing conviction in Polish circles that
Hitler was plotting an attack on Poland, its suddenness and ferocity surprised everyone. Britain had already pledged to come to
Poland's aid (more as a threat to Hitler than to assist Poland as
such) in the event of such an attack; on 3 September Britain and
France declared war on Germany. Poland's hope was to be able to
withstand the enemy forces until such time as Britain and France
could assist her; the Polish forces estimated this would take two
weeks at most. In fact Poland was left to fight completely alone
against the aggressor with a hopelessly inadequate army. Neither
France nor Britain came to her aid, as unknown to her, the agreement to do so had been quietly dropped in the summer of 1939.
She had six armies which all told had 1 500 000 troops, including

Scholastyka and Tadeusz Chrzczonowicz, c. 1900

Anna and ? sister, Irkutsk, c. 1900

Joachim in Bodaibo, 1907

Kostek 8, Zosia 7, and Witold 5, Irkutsk, June 1916

The Church in Dzierkowszczyzna (now in Belarus) where Zosia was baptised

Celebrating the opening of the first section of the Munitions Factory in Skarżysko-Kamienna, 1924/5. Witold is standing at far left of front row; Joachim is seated behind the priest's right shoulder on the second row, and Anna is 3 seats the other side of the priest

Danek, Marysia, Witold and Kostek, Warsaw, mid-1930s

Christmas 1938 in Radom, Poland. The last surviving photograph of the whole family. L. to R, Witold, Anna, Joachim, Zoasia and Kostek

Witold and Jerzy Gradosielski in Italy, September 1945

Witold with his wife Rosemary, and two children, Beatrice and John.
Middlesex, early 1960s

those hastily called up from 1 September, which were no match against the German forces of 1 700 000 plus their reserves, plus far superior equipment. The Polish Forces held out for four weeks, the last Polish garrison not surrendering until early October. Polish troops had inflicted over 50 000 casualties on the Germans, whereas the Poles lost 200 000 killed or wounded. In addition to this, on 22 August, Molotov and von Ribbentrop, the Foreign Ministers of the Soviet Union and Germany respectively, had signed a Non-Aggression Pact which included a secret clause dividing Poland between Germany and the Soviet Union.

While the Polish forces were concentrating on the German enemy and attempting to hold out on the Western, Northern and Southern Fronts as the Germans took more and more of Poland, there were relatively few Polish troops in the Eastern borderlands. So when the Soviet Army crossed the Polish border on 17 September 1939 it swept through, capturing all Polish soldiers in its path. The Soviet reasoning given by Molotov, the Foreign Minister, for the invasion of Poland ran as follows:-

"events arising out of the Polish-German war have revealed the internal dissolution and obvious impotence of the Polish State. Polish military circles have suffered bankruptcy ... Warsaw as the capital of the Polish State no longer exists. No one knows the whereabouts of the Polish Government ... the Polish State and its Government have virtually ceased to exist..." In view of this, continued Molotov, the treaties operating between the Soviet Union and Poland had ceased to exist (*The Crime of Katyn* p.4).

On 28 September the German and Soviet Governments would formally sign an agreement partitioning Poland between them. Witold's unit was captured just one day after the Soviets crossed the border, and he was taken prisoner by the Soviets on 18 September. It is estimated that approximately 200 000 Polish soldiers were captured this way (see Garlinski, ch.2). As the war progressed, approximately 1 500 000 Poles in the Eastern territories were deported to the Soviet Union, in three main waves, in February, April and June/July 1940. In addition, tens of thousands of individuals were arrested, members of the intelligentsia – lawyers, doctors, engineers, teachers and other professionals – being at particular risk. Of these, it is estimated that approximately 270 000 of the total of 440 000 perished.

We do not have an account of the arrest of Witold himself; however, several accounts of similar arrests do exist and the scene would have been repeated over and over again. Karski, J., in *The Story of a Secret State* (see pp.14-19) describes it thus. The detachment he was with had been left without clear orders or leadership and were marching towards Tarnopol. They heard via a messenger that news of the Russians crossing the border had been broadcast on the radio, but it was not clear whether this was as friend or enemy. More ominous were the words that the Russians had come to protect the Ukrainian and White Ruthenian peoples, ominous not only because of the innate Polish mistrust of Russians borne out by centuries of deception and betrayal, but also in view of the more recent situations of Spain, Austria, and Czechoslovakia, also under "protection." They decided to march to Tarnopol as soon as possible to get some proper answers. As they approached the town the scene was one of confusion, but it was evident that the Soviets were already in charge. One of the officers was designated to act as spokesman. He met a Soviet officer, they conferred for about 15 minutes and then the Polish captain returned with the grave announcement:-

"The Soviet Army crossed the frontier to join us in our struggle against the Germans ... We cannot wait for orders from the Polish High Command. There is no longer a Polish High Command or a Polish Government. We must unite with the Soviet forces... We must surrender our arms and put ourselves under the command of Colonel Plaskov."

This dreadful speech was greeted in complete, horrified silence – the Poles knew very well what this must mean. Eventually a hysterical sob broke out and the cry, "Brothers, this is the Fourth Partition of Poland!" The soldiers complied with the order to disarm (what else could they do?) and then they lined up, with tanks in front and behind them guns trained on them as they marched towards the Soviet Union – and – what?

The narrative is now taken up by Emil Skulski, one of Witold's fellow soldiers, who was arrested at the same time as Witold. Anyone who was in military uniform was immediately arrested and all experienced a similar story of lies and deception on the part of the Soviets. Skulski describes the whole period of time spent in the Soviet Union as a "free Russian vacation" – the first example of many in his memoirs of the sense of humour which was so vital in preserving sanity and dignity for the prisoners. The

Russian captors forced the new prisoners to march across the Soviet borders, giving them neither food nor drink, nor any transportation. However, they were very heavily guarded. Those at the front of the column were lucky as they could grab potatoes, beets, or other vegetables from the fields when the column stopped; those at the back had to get by as best they could.

After several days' marching, the prisoners reached a huge camp filled with men constantly arriving and departing for other camps. The food here was dreadful, so much so that if a cat or a dog strayed into the camp, "that was its last stroll", and it was quickly killed and eaten. It did not take the men long to find out why the diet was so meagre – the whole Soviet population had been starving for years, and the authorities were hardly going to go out of their way to offer tasty cuisine to prisoners. The situation was so bad that in the wake of the military advances into Poland, civilians were robbing the occupied lands of anything they could lay their hands on – furniture, machinery, clothing, watches, food, and carrying it back to Russia as booty.

The camp where Witold, Skulski and thousands of other Poles found themselves was situated near the small town of Szepetowka – about half-way between Lwow and Kiev and just on the Soviet side of the border. It was here that the prisoners were registered. The Soviet Union had not signed the Geneva Convention on the treatment of Prisoners of War, nor did it recognise the International Red Cross, so the Poles realised that their situation was desperate. Solzhenitsyn notes that the USSR did not recognise as binding Russia's signature to the 1907 Hague Convention on the treatment of war prisoners, so she accepted no obligations at all for them, nor did she take any steps for the protection of her own soldiers who were captured. The USSR did not recognise its own soldiers of the day before, and did not intend to give any help to prisoners of war. The Hague Convention was not in fact signed by USSR until 1955 (Solzhenitsyn A. *Gulag Archipelago* Vol I, Ch5, p. 219). Many of the officers were taken away elsewhere (it emerged later that 5 000 of them were murdered at Katyn, near Smolensk in the spring of 1940 and a further 10 000 were missing and never found); by some miracle, Witold, although declaring his rank as an officer, was not one of these. Many of the Poles realised that their true origins and professions might put not only their own lives but those of their families in danger so they concealed

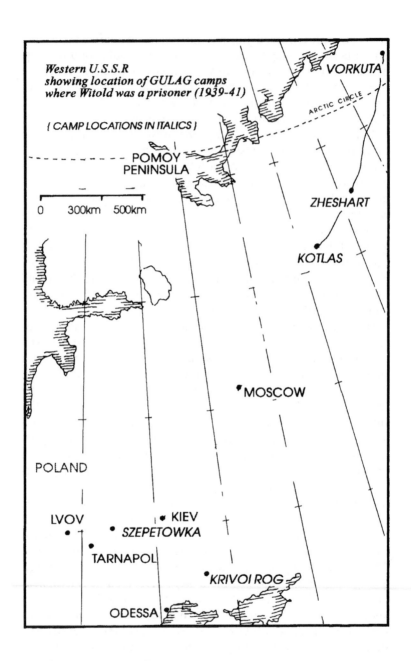

Western U.S.S.R
showing location of GULAG camps
where Witold was a prisoner (1939-41)

{ CAMP LOCATIONS IN ITALICS }

VORKUTA

ARCTIC CIRCLE

POMOY
PENINSULA

0   300km   500km

ZHESHART

KOTLAS

MOSCOW

POLAND

LVOV   KIEV
      SZEPETOWKA

TARNAPOL

KRIVOI ROG

ODESSA

them. At Krivoy Rog (where they were soon to go) there were for example fifty officers hidden among the 6 000 prisoners. So Witold, instead of stating his place of birth as Irkutsk, Siberia, gave Radom, Poland (where he and his family had lived for several years) as his birthplace. Thus he made clear his Polish citizenship. This simple device was to have strange repercussions decades later. The Russian soldier who was registering Witold, Skulski, and the rest was himself a barely literate peasant – when he pointed to Skulski and shouted ,"Name!" to him, Skulski said, "*Ja?... Skulski.*" [ie, "Me? ...Skulski."]. So the soldier carefully wrote his name down as "Jaskulski", a name which he kept throughout his time in Russia and which caused hilarity among the Poles whenever they heard it at roll calls, etc. The camp authorities "promised" that anyone whose family lived in Eastern Poland would be permitted to bring their family to live in the Soviet Union. They would work on a collective farm or in a factory and help build Communism! Indeed, many were deported – but to the Soviet prison camp system. Suspecting the Russian mentality, Skulski also gave a different address, in Warsaw (rather than Lwow) and his occupation as a loader of barges on the River Vistula (rather than an engineering student). Some managed to conceal their ranks, and these devices employed by the quick-witted among the Poles undoubtedly saved lives.

This first camp was a transit camp, and sometime in October 1939 Witold, Skulski, and hundreds of others were herded into trains for transport. The Soviets used cattle trucks for the transportation of prisoners, an unspeakably inhuman way of travelling. Skulski wryly remarks that if horses or cows were being transported, there would probably have been about ten animals in each car, thus giving them plenty of room to move about; as it was only prisoners, eighty people were packed into each car. There was a bucket in the middle of the floor to "refresh the air", as Skulski delicately phrases it; the only ventilation was a tiny slit near the roof. By observing the sun through that tiny window the men calculated that they were travelling south-east.

After a few days, the train stopped at Krivoy Rog, a small town not far from Dniepropetrovsk in the industrial heartland of the mining region of the Ukraine. When they disembarked they were taken to a huge camp with 6 000 inmates, surrounded by a high fence with guard towers and machine guns trained at all times on the prisoners. Accommodation was in long, low huts, each containing about twenty rooms, and each room about twenty people. The beds were bunks but each had a straw mattress as well as a blanket. When Witold and his fellow prisoners arrived they realised that the camp had been hastily vacated by its previous occupants to make room for them. At this time it was common to build what Skulski described as "these Sheraton-Hilton Hotels" for political prisoners near to government factories and projects.

It was here that the Soviet authorities tried particularly hard to indoctrinate the prisoners with Communist ideology. In such situations the characteristic Polish sense of humour came into its own and kept the men sane in a world of lies, suspicion and mistrust. After one particularly grotesque lecture, which was received in silence by the assembled men, one of the prisoners, described by Witold as "a simple peasant", got up from his seat, and silently went up to the front where the Soviet commandant had been lecturing. The "simple peasant" took this man's head in both his hands, shook it, and put his ear close to the man's head to listen to it. Needless to say, this simple gesture brought the house down and negated any effect the propaganda might have had on them. Among other things, the men were urged to be happy and to work hard to build and enrich their Communist country. That way they would prove to the capitalists how wrong they were in their systems and that the great god Joseph Stalin was really the source of their joy and happiness.

The camp was situated in the iron ore mining area of the Ukraine, and the work of the camp was to mine iron and manganese ore, Witold and Skulski being assigned to the manganese mines. This was difficult and dangerous work and the work was done in 10-hour shifts, with a day off every 10 days, although shifts and days off were often changed at short notice. Autumn set in early in 1939 – the first snow fell unusually early at the end of November and the temperature soon dropped to -30C. The warm clothes which they had so eagerly sold or exchanged for a little food a few weeks earlier were now sorely missed. However, at least working in the mine was warm and out of the weather, even if conditions were somewhat grim. The work itself was difficult and dangerous and they had to cope with the ever-present danger of the collapsing walls and roofs of the galleries because of the inadequate props. The rails on which the loaded carts were pulled were often laid crooked, making it hard for the horses to pull the heavy loads. When they were off duty and at night the barracks themselves were inadequately heated due to a chronic shortage of firewood. The food supplied was similar to the "gourmet menu" supplied in camps all over the GULAG – in the morning the men had soup, which mostly consisted of barley water. If they were lucky there might be a few beans floating in it or sometimes cabbage stalks. After this they had a few spoons of solid barley porridge. In the evening the menu was the same, and so on, day after day, week after week, until some different raw material appeared, such as peas or oats.

Witold and Skulski were in the same transport group and began to get to know each other a little. Of similar background they found that they had more in common with each other and the little group which began to gather round Skulski. This helped Witold tremendously and boosted his morale as the group also contained a few more of the "hidden professionals" – there was, for example, a veterinary student, a chemical engineer, and a delightful man who came from the same city as the engineer. The engineer was a heavy smoker and the others in the group worked hard to steal tobacco for him – failing that he smoked a foul-tasting substitute. Witold clearly emerged as the wise man of the group, for despite being quiet and serious, he also had the gift of humour. His fluent knowledge of Russian was much appreciated and made use of. The other groups in the camp respected this group very much.

Life continued in this way until Christmas came. They asked the Commandant (nicknamed the "Hawk") for a day off. He refused and treated them to a tirade about how there is no God and no religion, only Joseph Stalin. Thereupon the prisoners decided to strike, not realising until too late that striking was one of the worst offences it was possible to commit under Communism. By striking, the worker was suggesting that Communism was less than ideal, and thus the striker was the enemy of the people. These "enemies of the people" formed, according to Skulski, a large proportion of the 40 million or so people who were to pass through the GULAG.

The whole camp went on strike – so the Russians led the men outside where they had to stand in the cold snow and freezing temperatures (by Christmas the temperature was -40 C, for the winter that year was particularly severe). When allowed back into the barracks they found that all the mattresses, blankets and firewood were gone. All they had now for bedding was the clothing on their backs. The food ration was cut to one meal a day and only 300g of bread. They were also promised that for their bourgeois approach they would be transported to the land where the "white bears live."

Indeed, this happened soon afterwards. The prisoners were all loaded into the dreadful cattle trucks and packed in like sardines with no room to move and virtually no food or water. It was common at this time to feed prisoners in transit on salted herrings and little or no water. This time the men ascertained their direction of travel to be North. Eventually after several days they arrived at Kotlas, a notorious transit camp many hundreds of miles NE of Moscow, at the point where the rivers Vychegda and Dvina meet. This place was, when Witold and his fellow prisoners arrived, literally the end of the line as the railway ended here. Transport from now on would be by barge. The cold was almost unbearable in the early spring of 1940 in this region which was crossed by the Arctic Circle. During the long Arctic winter the sun barely rose above the horizon at all and during the summer the ground became a swamp where the frozen ground had melted. The temperature was below 0 C for more than two thirds of the year. The region between Kotlas and Vorkuta held the largest concentration of prisoners anywhere in the Soviet Union, with an estimated 1 million people there. (see Conquest, p.480). Many did not survive this far; many were to die of cold, hunger, disease and overwork in what was one of the most desolate places on earth. The conditions here have been described in detail by other authors, notably A. Solzhenitsyn in *The Gulag Archipelago*, Vol II, p.538, and Menachem Begin, also one of the thousands of Polish prisoners of war in the region, in his book, *White Nights*.

Kotlas is situated approximately 470 miles NE of Moscow; 900 miles further NE lies the city of Vorkuta. In the late 1930s rich deposits of good quality coal had been found there, but there was no means of transport to take the coal away. It was the task of these cold, half-starved prisoners to build a railway linking Kotlas and Vorkuta; it became one of the most infamous lines in the whole country because of the human cost of building it. Transport for the prisoners from Kotlas onwards was by barge. When Witold,

Skulski, and the others came off the train they were put onto barges which were waiting for them on the River Vychegda. These barges were crowded, lice-ridden (the prisoners were allowed on deck one by one to brush off the lice into the water) and unspeakably filthy, but below deck, warm. After a few days, Witold's barge stopped and the prisoners were told to disembark. Every 15 or 20 miles a barge stopped, the occupants forced out and they built the railway as far as the next camp, at which point they were again loaded onto a barge and taken further along the river to the next appointed place. The camps were "simple places" – in some cases simply a piece of land divided into cages by fencing with no buildings. The fencing was kept locked, although the chances of escape were minimal as there was absolutely no way of surviving alone in that inhospitable environment. Such buildings as there were had been put together by previous prisoners themselves and consisted of odds and ends of lumber, covered with tarpaulins, totally inadequate protection against the Arctic weather.

The work itself was almost impossibly hard, and as before, many succumbed to the dreadful climate and conditions. The men worked a 12-hour day and had a day off every 10 days. Witold's section was divided into work parties of 20-25 people and there were approximately 10 of these parties. Their task was to dig, using a pick, a shovel and a wheelbarrow, one cubic metre of the permanently frozen ground and to transport it to the place where the railway was being constructed. Other tasks included hauling firewood on sledges, or the iron rails themselves, or the heavy sleepers. The diet for this heavy work varied according to how much of the daily target was completed. If 100% was done, the rations were porridge soup and porridge in more solid form morning and evening, with 800g of bread daily. If the daily norm was only 80% completed the bread allowance was reduced to 600g; less than 80% and 300g of bread were issued. By way of comparison, rations in other parts of the Soviet Union were even worse during periods of famine and siege. In Ukrainian cities during the famine period of the 1930s the bread ration was 800g for industrial workers, 600g for manual workers and 400g for office employees. During the siege of Leningrad 1941-2, the figures were 400g for workers and 200g for dependents in October 1941; one month later it went down to 250g and 125g respectively and then picked up slightly to 350g and 200g. The whole of the country was suffering (see Conquest p. 486). Obviously the diet was hopelessly inadequate – apart from the calories, it was the lack of vitamins which posed the greatest problem, snowblindness and scurvy soon becoming very common among the men. Witold managed to find wild cranberries in the woods, growing under the trees, and as these are rich in vitamin C they ate as many as they could find. It was surprising in later years that he confessed a passion for them; before they were well-known in the UK my mother used to search for them in the shops or order them specially. One might have thought that he would have been totally put off them by his experiences. The men were shaved every two weeks – and to the end of his life one of the things that immediately recalled with painful vividness his time in the camps was the sight of hair cuttings lying on the floor. He also suffered from flashbacks for the rest of his life, for example, a seemingly innocuous Russian folk tune would take him back to this living hell, as he remembered the man who played it constantly on his balalaika. His strict physical training as a child undoubtedly gave him his enormously strong constitution which enabled him to survive – perhaps Joachim was not so eccentric in insisting on training his children so hard.

As spring advanced, midges became a problem and the camp buildings were plagued by rats. To avoid being totally overrun by them the men devised a game which they played on their day off. Most of the rats nested and lived under the barrack floors. Each barrack selected a team of men who would arm themselves with sticks, and making a great deal of noise, chase the rats towards the small pond in the middle of the camp. The team who killed the most rats "won", to the accompaniment of much applause and the promise that their prize would be delivered to them after they left the camp! The men were also plagued by lice, so they decided on the ingenious solution of putting the legs of the bunks in tins filled with water so the lice could not climb up and into the bunks; unfortunately, the lice were cleverer than this and learned to climb up the walls across the ceiling and drop down onto the bunks from above!

Eventually the work on clearing the ground along that particular stretch of railway line was finished and they were loaded onto barges and move further north up the river to Zheshart. The task here was to cut trees to clear the land for the railway. The felled trees were pulled by small Siberian horses to the river bank and were then loaded by the men onto barges. The logs were taken to a sawmill to be cut into planks, which were again loaded onto barges and taken to wherever they were needed.This forestry work was impossibly hard. It was estimated the 50% of workers in these brigades died per annum, as against the overall average of 30%.

The manager of this camp was a pleasant Russian engineer, who was himself a prisoner sentenced to hard labour for expressing dissatisfaction with the Communist regime. This was probably the man with whom Witold had long philosophical conversations, during which he would steal Witold's few remaining possessions, for example, his watch. ("But it was one of the best conversations I ever had with anyone," he later told one of his cousins). When the manager needed help in the camp office he turned to Witold for assistance in devising work plans – an example of how highly Witold was held in regard by the prisoners and the camp authorities. It was no easy option working in the office, although he only rarely needed to visit the work sites. As the months passed he used his wits to cheat the camp authorities and cut down the work norms actually worked. While he was in the office, he devised an ingenious way of letting his family know where he was being held captive. There was a children's book which he and Kostek had enjoyed very much as children. In it the hero disclosed his whereabouts by writing to a friend telling him to sell a piece of land so many metres by so many metres. The dimensions were the longitude and latitude co-ordinates from a map. Witold noticed the map on the office wall and realised that he could send a similarly coded message. The prisoners were occasionally allowed to send letters home, but of course they were heavily censored and could not contain any information such as their location. So Witold sent a letter to Kostek asking him to sell the land 62m x 49m, adding that Captain X [the hero of the children's book] will know all about it. Due to this clever device Kostek knew that in 1940/41 his brother was still alive. (This must have been after Joachim's friend and fellow graduate Stefan Ossowiecki had used his clairvoyant powers to say that he could see Witold "behind barbed wire in the vicinity of a big river"). It must have been a huge relief to the family to know that at least he was still alive.

Witold worked well in the camp office – outside temperatures were still very cold (-40C or even -50C was not uncommon) and the prisoners' clothing was inadequate protection against this. The cotton-lined jacket and trousers (which he was still wearing when he was released from the camps) were reasonably weatherproof and warm, but the boots were crude articles, roughly stitched from old car tyres and offered little protection against the knee-high snow. If the temperature fell below -50C the men were permitted to stay in the barracks and not work outside.

There was another Russian prisoner in the camp, an older man, very quiet, friendly, and well-mannered. Although sentenced to three years' hard labour, he was still in the camps after five years. His health was poor and he was resigned never to see freedom again. His two regrets were that he had had no message from his family and that if he died the world would never know the conditions inside the Soviet prison camps.

His task in the camps was to establish the work norms and he found the task overwhelming. The camp commander asked Witold if he could recommend anyone to help this man, so Witold immediately thought of Skulski. The plan was accepted, another example of the respect in which Witold was held, and so Skulski became the Work-Norm Manager's assistant. A few weeks after this the elderly Russian became very ill and was taken away, nobody knew where, but it did mean that Witold and Skulski could between them plot how to outwit the authorities on work norms.

Skulski knew from experience that it was almost impossible to fulfil even 80% of the work norm, so he began to study the books in order to see how he could reduce the work norm and at the same time appear to have achieved a higher percentage. He found legal tricks to make 80% seem like 100% and gradually introduced the new system. Needless to say the camp commandant was not told, but the men struggling in the cold were very grateful, as they were getting more food for less work. The barges laden with planks arrived daily and were duly stacked by cubic metre, described according to width, length, thickness, and so on. This worked well for several months until one day the camp had visitors from the NKVD (later the KGB). They were known throughout the Soviet Union for their ruthlessness and cruelty. These men began to check the books against the accomplished work. After a couple of days Witold and Skulski were summoned to the office and hauled over the carpet – the stacks of timber were at least 30% short. Skulski showed them all his books and calculations only to be told that the work manual should never be in the camps and that he should never have had access to it and certainly the instructions contained therein were not to be followed. Of course Witold and Skulski knew this but had chosen to disregard this and feigned ignorance. The camp commandant was reprimanded and Witold and Skulski were deprived of their jobs.

So they started to work again with the outside working parties, but in different brigades. The others in the brigades were very appreciative of what they had done, and in return offered to do extra work to help Witold and Skulski make up their work norms. However, they decided that they could not take advantage of this generous offer, so they worked as hard as they could alongside the others.

Thoughts of escape often crossed the minds of the prisoners but was considered impossible by most of the men. For some, however, including Witold, the thought of escape became an obsession. Although we know, from the fact that he occasionally referred to it in later years, that Witold escaped, we have few details on this part of his life. He was understandably unwilling to say much about this experience and there are no known survivors able to fill in the gaps. Piecing together the scraps of information that do exist produces a series of impressions rather than a coherent chronically ordered account. It is likely that the escape took place in the spring/summer of 1941, and that there was Witold and one other in the party. It seems that they were captured before too long and banished to Kamchatka, as Witold mentioned this in later years. They were literally abandoned here and left to survive the harsh conditions without food, water or shelter. Witold's only possessions in the world were the rags he stood up in, a potato sack and half a loaf of bread. The original plan was somehow to make their way to the Chukotskiy Peninsular and once there steal a boat and row across the Bering Strait to Alaska, and hence, freedom. However, they were by this time in far too weak a state to stand any chance of survival. In fact, after ten days or so they became so desperate for food, that coming across an isolated cottage, they asked the woman there for food. She gave them some but also turned Witold and his unknown companion over to the authorities. They spent a couple of weeks in custody before being released again. As the escape plan to Alaska was not feasible, Witold's instinct was to travel westwards across the Soviet Union and escape that way. The obvious way to do this was via the Trans Siberian Railway – so once again it was destined to play a major role in the family story. One can only speculate whether Witold travelled to Irkutsk, or through it on the train – and if so, what his thoughts must have been as he travelled through the town where he spent his childhood – and, indeed, where some of his mother's relatives may still have been living. Witold probably arrived at Omsk, where he hid on a freight train by lying on top of a load of coal, hidden by a tarpaulin, for 1600 miles to Moscow. By this time he was in such poor shape both physically and mentally that he was never able to give any account of himself until the "Amnesty" of August 1941. The only certainty is that he was behind barbed wire by this time as he occasionally referred to his release from the camps.

His experiences while a prisoner were similar to those suffered by thousands of others in the GULAG; he was not singled out for special treatment. A few incidents did stand out in his mind – for example the time when he was interrogated for fourteen hours while standing under a naked light bulb chest-high in freezing water. There was the occasion when he was put into a punishment cell with three known criminals who demanded of him, "Pole! Give us your boots!" Witold's response was to tear a leg off the wooden bench that was in the cell and set about all three of them until, chastened and battered, they grudgingly agreed, "OK, Pole, keep your boots." The authorities tried very hard to break his spirit but did not succeed.

As with everyone who suffered the GULAG system, the prison experience remained with him for the rest of his life. He survived without any physical scars, but the mental scars ran deep. Being of exceptionally strong character, and a person who, unusually, commanded the respect of both the Russians and the Poles among whom he was forced to live, he always maintained that he had no bitterness about his experience. (He was not in fact unique in this respect). Perhaps this was because he realised that nursing such feelings would achieve nothing except to blight whatever else he did in life. He always said that he had no problems with the Russian people (at that time I was unaware that his mother was

142

herself Russian) – it was the Soviet system which was wrong. Most of his prisoner of war experiences he kept to himself and the full story of his personal hell he took with him to the grave. Kostek, always perceptive, and strangely prophetic, was accurate when he said in his letter which was to have described his part in the war to Witold, "When you come back you are not going to talk about yourself as we all know your taciturnity. Like the Polish knight in *The Crusader* – when he came back to Silesia he would not talk about distant countries because nobody would understand him. It is possible that we also will not be able to understand." There is a real sense that only those who have undergone similar experiences can truly understand – and the numbers of survivors who went through that particular experience are diminishing year by year.

"Amnesty"

In the summer of 1941 the whole course of the war was changed when Hitler invaded the Soviet Union on 22 June. It was an event for which Stalin was unprepared, despite warnings from his Intelligence sources, and it ended the German-Soviet Non-Aggression Pact signed in 1939. By Hitler's act, the Soviet Union and the Allied Powers found themselves on the same side. Poland was now expected to consider her erstwhile imprisoners her friends. On 30 July 1941 an agreement was signed between Sikorski (for the Polish Government in Exile in London), Churchill and Eden (for the British Government) and Maisky (for the Soviets) granting the resumption of full diplomatic relations with the Soviet Union. There was to be an "amnesty" – a misnomer as no crime had been committed – for all Polish prisoners, who were to be released from the camps and organised into a Polish Army in the USSR, although they were to be distinctly Polish troops (ie., not absorbed into the Red Army) and were to take their oath of allegiance to the Republic of Poland. They would only be sent to the Front in groups the size of a Division or above. The agreement came into force on 14 August 1941. From the evidence, it seems that right from the beginning Stalin wanted to eliminate the Polish troops by putting them at the Front Line as soon as possible – 1 October was named as the date by which the first of the Divisions would be considered ready. Churchill and Roosevelt had discussed this question of Polish-Soviet relations in detail, issuing a statement which came to be known as the Atlantic Charter, co-incidentally signed on the very day that the "Amnesty" came into effect, 14 August, which stated among other things that all conquests of foreign territory should be renounced, a clause that was to be blatantly disregarded only eighteen months later at the Conference at Teheran. The vexed question of Poland's eastern borders was not raised at this time, although it had been an issue since 1918.

The person chosen to be in charge of this newly-formed Polish Army in the USSR was General Wladyslaw Anders; when the so-called Amnesty was signed on 30 July 1941 he was a prisoner in the notorious Lubyanka Prison in Moscow. He was hastily released on 4 August, and by 8 August he had officially taken up his command as leader of the Polish forces. It was obviously going to be an extremely difficult task as he first had to gather together an unknown number of Poles, but certainly thousands, currently scattered in prison camps throughout Russia. He had his first meeting with the Soviet authorities on 16 August, and on 22 August was informed that the HQ of this new Army would be at Buzuluk, the 5th Division being stationed at Tatishchev, and the 6th Division and the Reserves at Totskoe, these all being places near the city of Saratov on the River Volga. His first task was to ascertain the numbers of men who would form the army. Anders was somewhat aghast on being told that there were approximately 1 000 officers and 20 000 other ranks of Polish military held in the camps. Conservative estimates had calculated the number of officers and men at 200 000; Molotov, the Soviet foreign minister, had even suggested the figure of 300 000. Where were the rest? Anders knew that in 1940 there had been approximately 11 000 officers taken prisoner and held at three camps in the Soviet Union, Starobielsk, Kozielsk and Ostashkov and that almost no men from these camps were joining the new Polish Army. Throughout the following months Anders persisted in asking the Soviet authorities, including Stalin himself, where these men were, only to be given evasive answers – perhaps the Poles had done their calculations wrongly, many Poles had decided to settle in the Soviet Union, or, most bizarre of all, they had perhaps decided to settle in Manchuria! The mystery of the missing officers was not any nearer a solution until April 1943 when the mass graves at Katyn were discovered by invading German forces – and it was an event for which the Russians would not admit responsibility for another fifty years. (At first the Russians insisted that these men had been shot by the Nazis, despite the evidence to the contrary).

General Sikorski summed up the mood of the Poles very well when he declared on 14 August that:-

"It appears that only we, and above all we, who have experienced the purgatory and ill treatment of Soviet prisons, labour camps and exile in often dreadful conditions, could oppose on moral grounds any attempts at agreement with Russia. And yet all of us without exception are coping with the task and our personal misfortunes, since the mere fact that we are able to fight for Poland with a weapon in our hands clearly shows us the path towards a great goal." (quoted in Garlinski, J. p. 116).

The news of the Amnesty spread slowly. Many camp commanders did not believe the news or chose to ignore it. The Poles were told in various ways. Sometimes they themselves did not believe the news – after years of lies and deception it was hard to imagine that the authorities might be telling the truth. For Skulski and his fellow prisoners still in the far North and building the railway line, they could not take in the news at first. For two years the Russians had killed their families, friends and colleagues through overwork, deportation, starvation and exposure, and now they were to believe this fairy tale that the Russians were their friends and now fighting on the same side. It just seemed incredible and was widely thought to be part of a plot to discover yet more Polish professors, policemen, priests, etc., in order to dispose of them. Eventually a large number of guards appeared and the men were told to take their possessions (a rug, a tin bucket and a wooden spoon) and to board the train which was standing on the railway line they had been so painfully building. The attitude of the guards had changed; they were noticeably more friendly. After travelling for a couple of days they were back in Kotlas. Here they changed into "first class" cattle trucks, with only 40 men to a truck instead of 80. The food was marginally better, too, but they still did not believe the guards' story that they were going home.

These men were transported to a huge camp near the small town of Vyazniki. Here officers appeared, this time in British uniforms. The Poles were still suspicious, suspecting these men to be Russians disguised in British uniforms. Eventually they were persuaded, and the process of registration started. Now the real

145

names, ranks and professions of the prisoners were revealed, and it was surprising how many officers of high rank were "discovered" (though not enough to explain the huge shortfall in numbers). One man, a colonel, and later commander of Skulski's regiment, had created an unpleasant scene in the camp – and was now able to reveal that it had been simply to conceal his rank. Witold did not correct his place of birth as stated to the Soviet authorities; for the time being it remained Radom, Poland; Jaskulski became Skulski once more. When Skulski disclosed his true rank (cadet officer) one previously friendly man in his group refused to speak to him; however, later on they became good friends and in fact met up later on during the war.

After the registration process the Poles were put on another train which took them to the main collecting camps for the Army. Witold and Skulski were taken to Tatishchevo, where the 5th Division was being formed.

There are many other example of how the Poles were told of their freedom. Francis Muszytowski, who became one of Witold's closest friends, was imprisoned on the Kola Peninsula by the River Pomoy. (It is Francis' memoirs which have supplied much of the information about Witold's next few years.) Francis also had a hard time in the camps, but they heard unofficially from the guards that Hitler had attacked the Soviet Union. By the end of June the men were evacuated to a vast transit camp at Archangelsk and officially told about Hitler's invasion and that the Poles would be freed. A high-ranking British official told the men that a Polish Army was being formed near the city of Saratov on the Volga. The men were immediately put on board a huge goods train travelling south. On the train there were about 2 500 people, not only Polish military but police officers, priests, civil servants, etc. After two or three weeks this trainload arrived at Tatishchevo. Witold's account was that the prison gates were simply opened and the men told to fend for themselves. "You're free now; let your own Government look after you." Another account states that the men were given a travel document, a pitiful allowance of money based on the estimated days' travelling time to Saratov, and ordered to board the waiting train.

From all over the Soviet Union they came, these freed Poles, by train, by barge, on foot, in enormous train loads or singly, released willingly or reluctantly. Polish liaison officers were stationed on major railway stations to help set Poles in the right direction. The journey took days, weeks, or even months; many never made it to Saratov. Many Poles were directed to the southern Republics rather than the Polish Army HQ. Molotov (whom, incidentally, Witold had met when he visited the camps) claimed that by 28 September all the Poles had been released from captivity. His deputy, Vyshinsky, claimed that by 1 October 345 511 had been released, although 42 241 were still held. By December 1941 37 000 troops had assembled in Tatishchevo and Totskoe. It hardly need be stated that the physical condition of these men was pitiable. Without exception they were emaciated, half-starved and riddled with lice, scurvy, typhus and other diseases. Stalin's desire to send a Polish Division to the Front by 1 October was an obvious fantasy. To illustrate just how weak these men were, Witold used to tell the story of how he and some friends on their release decided to pool their meagre resources and buy something they had not tasted for years – real meat! They persuaded a peasant to sell them a sheep, which was duly killed and roasted. However, as they had had such a poor diet during the previous two years, their stomachs had shrunk, they were unable to eat very much and were all violently ill.

Witold was at Tatishchevo by December 1941 as it was then that Francis recalls meeting him. His army record does not shed much light on the actual date of his arrival as at this point the authorities seem to have been using standardised dates – his date of release from the camps is given as 20 August, which seems too soon, as it was only six days after the Amnesty. He is also listed as a Cadet Officer from this date until 11 September, when he was made 2nd Lieutenant in the 5th KDP (Kresowy, or Borderland, Infantry Division). 11 September was also the date when the 5th KDP was formed as an amalgamation of several groups. It would be possible, but cannot be taken as evidence, that he was in Tatishchevo by then. Whatever the exact details, we can assume that Witold was at Tatishchevo by December 1941 if not before.

The Polish Army in the USSR

What was freedom like for these thousands of Poles? By this time not only military personnel but civilians were being freed and they were offered little or no help by the authorities. ("Let your Polish Government help you Poles"). At this time, too, the

147

Soviets themselves were suffering considerably as a result of Operation Barbarossa, Hitler's invasion of the Soviet Union. The Germans had easily overrun the Ukraine and the Crimea, and they besieged Leningrad from September 1941, causing unspeakable hardship to the inhabitants, as thousands died from starvation and cold. The siege lasted for 900 days. Moscow was also in danger; by November, German troops were in sight of the city. Fortunately they were defeated by the harsh Russian winter, as Napoleon had been almost 130 years before, and were forced to withdraw before reaching the capital. The Government was evacuated to Kuibyshev on the Volga, as was Shostakovich; it was here that he wrote his Symphony No 7, called the Leningrad Symphony, which he wrote to encourage the beleaguered Leningraders. Here, too, the Polish ambassador and some of the Polish Army command were based. There was a chronic shortage of troops for the Front (hence Stalin's idea to send the Poles there); there were few people behind left to grow food, so there was appalling starvation. The Germans destroyed everything they could even when retreating, and the ordinary people suffered appallingly during this war. It is not surprising that the Soviets had very little time or sympathy for the Poles, for whom they had a natural antipathy anyway.

By the beginning of December 1941 37 000 troops had passed through the registration camps, by March 1942 the number was 64 000. The site at Tatishchevo was a hastily evacuated summer camp which had been used for new Red Army recruits. There were a few stone buildings used by the officers, but as for the rest, accommodation was in tents. As the temperature dropped the men dug holes in the ground and erected the tents over them, covering the canvas with leaves, moss, anything they could find for extra insulation. The temperatures plunged to -30C or -40C. At first the food and living conditions were even worse than when they were in captivity, but the big difference was that now they were, at least in theory, free men, even if the NKVD were never far away and sometimes planted informers among them. Disease and lack of adequate clothing were further problems. In the beginning the men were clad in the assortment of rags which they had worn during captivity – tattered Polish military uniforms, or in Witold's case, the cotton padded jacket or *fufaike* and the trousers he had worn in the far North. There were no uniforms or boots available

148

initially; at the first inspection parade General Anders noted that 40% of the soldiers were barefoot. Eventually the men were issued with British uniforms and ammunition. Stalin was still hoping that these troops could be used in front line positions so as to spare his own soldiers. Anders mistrusted Stalin right from the beginning and suspected his real intentions. Anders was held in the greatest respect, even awe, by all the Poles who came under his command because of his wise leadership in the most difficult circumstances and because he always kept the interests of his men and of Poland as his priorities. He refused to be overawed even by Stalin and was not afraid to stand up to him when the need arose.

The cold weather in the camp continued, helped a little by the new uniforms and the use of primitive stoves, fuelled by wood collected from the nearby woods, and with hay and straw stolen from nearby collective farms they improved the insulation of the tents. Conditions were obviously still extremely harsh. Disease was rife among the men; particularly difficult were the head lice and the typhus fever. By December the general situation had eased a little and Christmas was celebrated for the first time for three years – it was a good celebration with food and clothes and the hope that they were going to fight Hitler and create a free Poland once more.

However, this optimism was not shared by all. The senior (older) officers were clearly looking back to the 1914-18 war and the attitudes which prevailed then. If only the Soviets would give them food and arms, ammunition and horses they would be ready to fight with God on their side. The Chaplains, now able to be among the troops and say Mass once more, echoed this sentiment.

The younger men were more realistic and saw that more than the saying of prayers and pious statements was needed for survival. A group of people, including Witold and Francis, formed a cell of "realistic people" whose purpose was to make an assessment of the situation and to try and decide what should be done. The current situation seemed to offer no way out – the choices were either to be killed at the Front by the Germans or to stay behind and die of hunger, cold and lice. The only hope was Great Britain. Witold acted as spokesman of the group and managed to put the group's fears to General Anders himself. Much to their relief, his views were similar to theirs. This whole discussion was conducted almost secretly for fear of betrayal by Soviet informers who were thought to have infiltrated the camp.

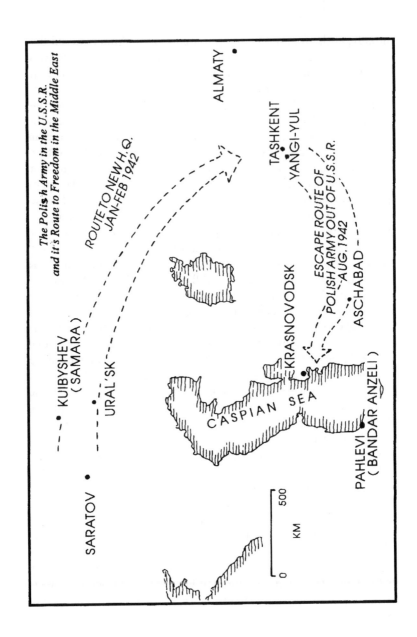

The Polish Army in the U.S.S.R.
and it's Route to Freedom in the Middle East

ROUTE TO NEW H.Q.
JAN-FEB 1942

ALMATY

TASHKENT
YANGI-YUL

ESCAPE ROUTE OF
POLISH ARMY OUT OF U.S.S.R.
AUG. 1942

KUIBYSHEV
(SAMARA)
URAL'SK

KRASNOVODSK

ASCHABAD

CASPIAN SEA

SARATOV

PAHLEVI
(BANDAR ANZELI)

500

KM

0

Once the men had begun to adjust to life in the army camps, there was the problem of how to pass the time usefully. Among themselves, Witold and his little group decided that the best thing would be to start educating the soldiers about cars, lorries, tanks, motorised guns, etc. However, as the winter was very cold, and the men badly fed and sick, they could not do much. So classes of volunteers were set up to teach simple mechanics and Witold taught the electrical aspects of this. There were no teaching aids of any description – not even paper and pencil.

In December 1941 the Commander-in-Chief, General Sikorski, and General Anders met Stalin and Molotov to discuss the dire situation of the men, pointing out that if conditions did not improve all the Poles would die and be of no use to anyone. The number of rations had been reduced from 44 000 to 30 000, and at this point Sikorski suggested moving the Army to Persia for recuperation. In the end Stalin agreed to moving the 5th Division to the East. After much stalling and delaying on Stalin's part this finally happened between 15 and 19 February 1942. The whole of the 5th Division, 18 000 men and some equipment and horses were once more told to board a train going east.

The new HQ was to be at Yangi-Yul, near Tashkent, a journey of 2 500 miles (1 500 as the crow flies) by train from Tatishchevo. Yangi-Yul was in the Republic of Uzbekistan and the different sections of the Polish Army were to be deployed in several locations in the area, but so widely spread apart as to render effective co-ordination very difficult. Witold's section was based at Dzalad-Abad in the Fergana Valley just inside the Kirgyzistan Republic and a mere 100 miles from the Chinese border. The journey was, as most journeys seemed to be, long and indirect, via Saratov, Kuibyshev (Samara), Omsk and Uralsk Tashkent. Even a quick glance at the map will show that Witold was already over halfway to Irkutsk from Warsaw – how frustrating it must have been to be travelling such vast distances east and west! During the journey the transport of Polish soldiers picked up large numbers of Polish refugees – families, women with children, sometimes children on their own. This considerably swelled the numbers of people to feed and care for.

The response of the Soviet authorities was to cut the food rations even further to 26 000, when there were in fact by this time 70 000 to feed. After much persuasion Stalin offered to supply

40 000, then 44 000. Anders persisted and said that in view of this the only solution which would preserve the lives of the Poles was a total evacuation to Persia via Krasnovodsk on the Caspian Sea. At first Stalin was reluctant but he was finally persuaded; all that remained now was to organise the evacuation of thousands of people whose numbers were growing daily, in a hostile country which was ostensibly friendly. It was agreed that there would be 40 000 evacuees; by the end of March 40 000 Poles had been evacuated; by 5 April, 44 000. However, over 40 000 troops remained in the Soviet Union, including the 5th Division.

Conditions in the new surroundings were still poor, but not quite as harsh as in Tatshchevo. The Divisional HQs were spread out over hundreds of miles – in Alma Ata, Frunze, Tashkent, Dzambal as well as Dzalal-Abad. The climate was easier than before as temperatures were in the region of +20C. The food was just as dreadful, and the local Uzbeks were unfriendly. They were not allowed to grow anything but cotton, so their food situation was hardly better than the Army's. Occasionally the men arranged to "buy" a goat , a sheep or a chicken from one of the local farms. There was an abundance of tortoises in the area; the men found that if they boiled them for an hour they tasted delicious.

Again, there was the problem of how to use the time profitably. It was decided to start something that was grandly called the Divisional School of Motoring, Witold being one of the Directors of Study. The first task was to train the officers who would become the future instructors. However, there was a problem in that Witold, being still a Non-Commissioned Officer, could hardly teach lieutenants, captains, etc. So, according to Francis' account, Witold was hastily promoted by special order of the War Ministry in London so that he could do this job, the only promotion in the entire Polish Army in the Middle East at this time. At least, so the story goes, but unfortunately there is no official record of this unless the promotion was backdated to the previous September.

The driving lessons continued with absolutely no equipment; even paper and pencil were still only rarely available. For practical demonstrations, one long stick of wood in the ground was the gear lever, another stick, the handbrake lever, and three flat pieces of wood represented the clutch, accelerator and brake. Francis says that they all recognised that such an arrangement was pathetic, but it was the best they could manage in the circumstances. The shouts of the instructors could be heard from time to time, "Clutch!! Gas!! Stop! Stop! BRAKE! Brake!!" "Oh you idiot!" Witold would shout to his superior officers. By May/June 1942 they had 30 or 40 trained mechanics and 300 trained officers issued with home-made "Driving Licences" – of course these licences were theoretical only as no one had ever actually driven a vehicle.

One day Witold made social contact with a huge collective farm near Dzalal-Abad. This farm had many tractors and lorries. Witold was told to see the farm manager and negotiate a "purchase" of some of the scrap machinery to use on the course. Witold, knowing the Russian soul as he did, facilitated the deal by scrounging a large bottle of vodka from somewhere. However, the manager was unable to help ... but he could let them have the written off equipment as scrap ... for *4 litres* of vodka! Where on earth would Witold find such a quantity? Eventually they came to a deal, and the manager agreed to accept *samogon* or home-made moonshine as a substitute. There was a thriving though unofficial industry in this poisonous liquor throughout the area during the war, especially among the Kazakhs, Ukrainians and Russians.

Agreement was reached and three or four horse-drawn wagons were duly sent to the farm, where the scrap machinery was loaded under Witold's supervision. When the men returned to the camp and unpacked the wagons, they found "by accident" a slaughtered sheep and some butter. Exactly how Witold achieved this no one knows to this day. The sheep was cooked that same day amid great celebrations, with grass as the accompanying vegetable. There was a little moonshine left, too. Incredible though it may seem, within four weeks the mechanics had constructed a complete working lorry from the scraps which Witold bought for 4 litres of what Francis describes as "that terrible drink." It was a tribute to the skill and ingenuity of the mechanics and was a tremendous morale booster.

Meanwhile the situation of the Poles in the Soviet Union was deteriorating. The NKVD was interfering and putting obstacles in the way of running the army. Malaria was rife among the "liberated" Poles in the army, but thousands of Poles remained in labour camps and prisons. General Anders was in frequent contact with Sikorski in London over this issue; it was becoming clear to him that unless an evacuation of troops was urgently undertaken the Poles would have to stay in the Soviet Union for ever.

By the beginning of July 1942 the Soviet authorities had backed down and Molotov agreed to help evacuate the Poles to the Middle East. It is worth noting that this offer was not made to Anders himself but to the British ambassador, Sir Archibald Clark Kerr. The decision was made official on 8 July and plans were quickly put into action to evacuate the remaining 70 000 Poles (in addition to the 43 000 evacuated in April). The number of Poles was swelling daily as civilian Polish refugees found their way to the army camps; of course they could not be refused help. Among this number were 4 000 Jews of Polish origin; the Soviet authorities absolutely forbade the evacuation of Jews of any other ethnic origin. By the end of July Witold was once again travelling a vast distance, this time over a thousand miles by rail from the far west of Uzbekistan and Kirgyzystan to the port of Krasnovodsk on the eastern shore of the Caspian Sea, via Tadzikistan and Aschabad. Witold's section departed from Krasnovodsk on 12 or 13 August 1942. The boats were dreadful. Some were made of planks of wood and logs and propelled by paddles; others were simply empty oil tankers into which people were packed without regard for space, sanitation or air. Many of the army were loaded onto the *Moskovich* and the civilians onto the *Staliets*. Fortunately the sea was calm and after a terrible 20-hour journey the boats landed at Pahlevi (now Bandar e Anzal) in the southwest corner on the Caspian Sea, and in Iran.

The joy and happiness of these Poles, 110 000 in both evacuations, can only be imagined. At last they had left the Soviet "paradise" and were truly free! The Poles had unbounded gratitude for their leader, General Anders, who had looked after them, refusing to be bullied by the Soviet leaders. By holding fast to his purpose, he had saved the lives of so many Poles, bringing them safely out of the Soviet experience, which must have seemed like hell itself.

For the first time for three years the Poles now had their freedom. They could shake off the shackles of the Soviet "paradise" (a phrase used by more than one writer), and once they had their strength back they would be able to fight to win Poland back again. The men were so louse-ridden that they all had to pass through the delousing station at Pahlevi, the clothing they were wearing was burned and they were issued with completely new clothes. Now they could really shake the dust of the Soviet regime from their feet. From now on there was no question: the Poles were directly under British command and the nightmare over. The day that they were given their identity cards, 15 August 1942, by the British army, saying that they were part of the Polish Army in the Middle East was truly a great day. It used to puzzle me that Witold always said that he was a prisoner for three years in the Soviet Union, when the Polish Amnesty occurred in August 1941; the whole Russian experience was so dreadful that he obviously counted the entire time as imprisonment.

CHAPTER 7

The Middle East and Italy

The relief felt by Witold and his fellow Poles at their lucky escape from the "Soviet Paradise" was indescribable. Simply to be alive and under the command of the British Army rather than have the Soviets breathing down their necks was wonderful. Even the fact that they had brought with them as souvenirs of their "Free Russian Vacation" malaria, typhus, jaundice and of course, severe malnutrition, did not dampen their enthusiasm. The arrival of so many refugees in Pahlevi in so short a period of time proved a real headache for the British authorities, as they all had to be fed, housed and given essential medical care. The initial wave of arrivals in March/April 1942 had resulted in nearly 44 000 Poles who somehow had to be cared for. The second wave, of 110 000 Poles, must have stretched the British administration to the limit. Accommodation was in tents on the beach. Everyone had to be thoroughly deloused and hospital care given to the most sick. All their clothing was burned and the military issued with tropical uniforms, cork helmets, and British shoes.

Pahlevi was merely a port and not equipped to deal with this flood of refugees, so arrangements were made to move the Poles on as soon as possible. The civilians, who included a large number of children, many of whom were orphaned, were moved to a transit camp at Ahwaz, 90 miles south of Kharramqhar, from where they were dispersed to any territory in the British Empire which could take them. Many Poles were resettled in East Africa and large numbers of orphaned children were taken to India, where they were given some form of education. Witold's cousin, Zosia, who had been with the family in Irkutsk, was one of the Poles who volunteered to teach the children. It was while she was in India that she learned to speak English so well; so well in fact, that when I met her fifty years later she spoke to me in near-perfect English. Her husband, a military policeman, had been deported to the Soviet Union in the early days of the War and had died there. After the War Zosia settled in Gdansk, living in a tiny flat just a block or two away from where the novelist Gunter Grass had grown up.

The military Poles were almost immediately on the move once more. The HQ of the Polish Army in the Middle East, as it came to be called, was established at Qizil Rabat, but the 5th KDP were on the move westwards towards Iraq, passing through Kermanshah and Hamadan towards Khanaquin where they settled temporarily. Weather conditions were again terrible – the average temperature was over 100°F and the searing heat was accompanied by the *hamsin*, a hot dry wind which whipped up the dust and sand and made the Poles fear for their lives. Within two weeks of their arrival at Khanaquin Witold was put in charge of erecting the tents needed to accommodate the men. He was assisted by men from the Indian Transport Division. The hospital tents were overflowing with patients; none of the soldiers was anywhere even average fitness and certainly in no state to fight. Many, having survived to this point, sadly died in the Iraqi desert. For the rest, as Francis describes in his memoirs, they just "ate, ate, slept and ate", trying to build up their strength so that they could continue to fight for a free Poland.

By the end of September the British authorities were keen to know whether the Polish troops could be formed into motorised units. They requested lists from the Poles as to how many drivers, mechanics and other specialists there were. The numbers were duly listed, but out of the whole of the 5th Division hardly anyone could actually drive. Those who had passed the "Driving Tests" in the Fergana Valley were listed – and with great presence of mind the Polish officers casually asked for some old vehicles so that the drivers could "refresh" their skills. Within a week 25 vehicles – old English, German and Italian cars, lorries and tanks – were supplied. The Polish soldiers, many of whom were of peasant origin and used to driving horses and oxen, very quickly learned to become skilled drivers. Those who had been ordinary tradesmen in civilian life, – butchers, tailors, or joiners for example – became excellent mechanics and repairers. Witold had, of course, been one of the real drivers.

The Polish forces were reorganised into the II Polish Corps, consisting of two motorised Divisions, the 3rd and 5th, a Tank Brigade, and various Cavalry and Artillery Units. Between October 1942 and February 1943 Witold was posted to the 5(15) Workshop Company of the 5th (Kresowy) Division (5th KDP). In October the first proper transport vehicles arrived. These included cars, motorbikes and bulldozers, and were greeted with enthusiasm by the men. Now at last they may be able to start doing something useful. Training on these vehicles was immensely hard work, but the troops approached their task with eagerness, always keeping the cause of Poland before their eyes. Witold was in charge of Electrical Studies at the Central Training School. By this time the 5th Division was 15 000 strong and was stationed in northern Iraq. A group of British officers travelled to Iraq to teach the Polish military the rules and regulations of the British Army, under whose command they were, and the English commands which they would need to know. At the same time the Polish soldiers were offered the chance to serve in the RAF. Some decided to do this, and about 3 500 left Iraq to train in Britain. Training was also given in building Bailey Bridges, reconnaissance, mine detection and other skills. Witold and his colleagues went on numerous training exercises to such exotic-sounding places as Habbaniya on the River Euphrates.

In January 1943 Witold and the other Poles received another blow. Despite all efforts by General Anders and General Sikorski and the Polish Government in Exile in London, the Soviet authorities declared on 16 January that all Poles remaining in the Soviet Union (ie., those who had not been able to escape with General Anders' troops, those deported to the central regions of the Soviet Union and those still remaining in territory currently occupied by the Soviets) would henceforth be considered as Soviet citizens. The news was received with dismay by the Poles abroad, not only in Iraq, but wherever they were scattered, since most had relatives or friends still in the Soviet Union. This declaration meant that those Poles in the Soviet Union would never be able to return home to Poland and their homes and families.

On 15 March 1943 Witold was issued with his official Army Driving Licence. In mid-April there was yet more bad news. The Germans broke the news that they had discovered the mass graves of some 5 000 Polish officers in woods at Katyn, a small Russian town near Smolensk. At last the fate of some of the missing officers whom Anders and Sikorski had been trying to trace was now known. The details of the find made grim reading; although the Germans and the Russians blamed each other, the evidence indicated that the Russians had perpetrated the massacre. The full details of the affair can be read in the various books on the subject, notably Anders and Fitzgibbon (see bibliography). The bare facts were these. Officers from the camps of Kozielsk, Starobielsk, and Ostashkov had been transported in April /May 1940 (judging by the last dates of correspondence, diary entries, newspapers, etc.) to Katyn where almost 5 000 had been lined up and simply shot in the back of the head with a single bullet at point-blank range. Only 448 officers from the three camps had survived – they had been specially selected as suitable for "re-educating" as Soviet soldiers for use as propoganda. All identification papers were found on the bodies, and they were wearing winter uniforms, suggesting that they were killed in the spring of 1940. Names and ranks were clearly identifiable and included three generals, one hundred colonels, and three hundred majors, as well as professors, surgeons, lawyers, engineers, and members of other professions. Of the 2914 bodies which were identified by name, approximately 80% also appeared on the lists drawn up by Anders and Sikorski and handed to Stalin personally on 3 December 1941. Thus perished much of the leadership of Polish society – part of Stalin's systematic plan to eliminate anyone capable of taking responsibility in Poland. In later years, Witold would run his finger down the list of identifiable victims, "I knew him..., I knew him..., that was Irenka's father..., that was Jacek's father..." A sad litany indeed. On hearing the news of the massacre, the Polish Government in London asked the International Red Cross to investigate the affair; this so angered the Soviets that the already fragile diplomatic ties between the two Governments were finally broken by Stalin in May 1943. The Russians would not admit responsibility for the crime until 26 March 1990, almost fifty years later. The worst fears of Anders, Sikorski and other Polish leaders were realised by this discovery, despite Stalin's constant denials of any knowledge as to their whereabouts in December 1941 (and a slip-of-the-tongue admission by one of his underlings that "we had made a terrible mistake there."). The massacre at Katyn accounted for 5 000 missing officers; where were the others? Another, smaller mass grave was discovered in the 1990s, and there may yet be more gruesome discoveries waiting to be made.

Despite these further tragedies in Poland's story, Witold and his colleagues continued their intensive training and exercises. In May 1943 II Polish Corps moved to the Kirkuk and Mosul region of Iraq. Here they practised such tasks as reconnaissance, observing rivers, bridges , oil fields, landing strips, observation posts, water equipment, wells, springs, railways, etc.. One team set off up the Little Zab River and gathered intelligence about river banks, access, bridges and fords. They were still in tents at this point and Witold remembered that he woke one morning to find a scorpion on his pillow – a timely reminder that the desert held other hazards than climate and lack of water.

The supplies for the Polish Army were almost all American and stored at Basra, many miles south of Baghdad, and Witold and Francis often had to travel there on business. During his time in Iraq Witold managed to fit in a certain amount of sightseeing – it seems that he travelled extensively in the region. However, he used to describe his time in the desert as a period of great boredom – either the spells of high activity were interspersed with relatively quiet spells, or he disliked doing the task he was allotted. There were some lighter moments to his time in Iraq, for example the occasion when he and his friends stopped at a restaurant and ordered a steak, which was most delicious. They called the waiter over and asked him what kind of steak it was. The reply, "Why, sir, camel, of course!" caused several of the party to be ill and took away the enjoyment of the meal.

In addition to the training and exercises, the Poles were also given the task of guarding the oil wells and pipelines which were supplying vital oil to the Soviet Union. At around this time rumour was reaching Sikorski in London that the Polish Army in the East was becoming undisciplined and meddling in politics. Anders was able to reassure him that this was not the case, although news of events affecting the Poles was bound to have some effect on the men. The Polish Government had continued to maintain its position on the Polish Eastern Borders (as set down in the Treaty of Riga of 1921) and its position on Polish citizenship (as on 1 September 1939). It redoubled its efforts to evacuate Poles stranded behind Soviet borders.

In July 1943 yet another tragedy struck the Poles. General Sikorski, the Commander-in-Chief of all the Polish Armed Forces was killed in an air crash over Gibraltar in circumstances which were not entirely clear. He was a well-loved and charismatic leader who had served the Polish cause unstintingly from his early years under Pilsudki's command, and since 1939 he had been a particularly strong focus for all Poles everywhere. His loss was a severe blow to Polish morale.

One month later, in August 1943, the 5th Division were moved to a new location, this time in Palestine. The troops were now fully equipped and trained in basic skills and the time had come to practise manoeuvres in a mountainous setting. So Witold moved with the rest through the Arabian desert via Sinai up to Gaza and a station named rather prosaically as "Kilo 89". From here they practised "capturing" Mount Sinai, Nazareth, and other sites in the Holy Land. This was an emotional time for Polish troops, both Roman Catholics and Jews, as Palestine was obviously a special place for everyone. For many of the Jews in the Army, the fact of actually being in the Promised Land was too strong a pull to ignore, and they deserted. Among them was Menachem Begin, who eventually became Prime Minister of Israel. The Poles left their mark on places dear to them in Palestine. For example, they generously subscribed to orphanages for Polish children, perhaps because of those orphans they had met along the way, or maybe because they did not know the fate of their own children. The Ex-Servicemen's Association contributed to one of the mosaic panels in the cloisters of the Basilica of the Annunciation in Nazareth in appreciation of the time they had spent there. In Jerusalem they rebuilt one of the Stations of the Cross (No.3), and the 8th Rifle Division paid for the addition of the Lord's Prayer in Polish to the multi-lingual collection at the Paternoster Church on the Mount of Olives. It was a strange experience for me visiting Israel in the 1990s and finding these small but significant souvenirs of the Polish presence in Palestine in 1943. I could not help wondering what Witold's contribution had been and whether he had been present at the unveiling of these monuments. He would remember this period of time with a certain wistfulness.

Meanwhile the intensive training continued, not always with happy results. In November 1943 a group were exercising in Lebanon when several men fell into a river and were drowned. The British instructors became stricter with the Poles to ensure that they would be able to operate under battle conditions. At this point it was decided that the II Polish Corps was now fit and ready for action. Witold was put in charge of the Field Rescue Unit, whose job it was to recover damaged vehicles from the battlefield. At his disposal he had ten heavy cranes and other specialist equipment. His soldiers always called him "Pan Inzynier" [Mr. Engineer], but contrary to military rules he always called them by their first names. He was held in great respect by all the men.

In November and December 1943 events were once again moving on the political front with regard to Poland's future, although without including any Poles in the discussions. Stalin, Roosevelt and Churchill held a Conference in Teheran whereby among other things Roosevelt and Churchill, seeking to appease Stalin, agreed to the Soviet Union's annexation of the Eastern part of Poland after the War. This would effectively confirm the Ribbentrop-Molotov agreements of August and September 1939. In fact it violated Britain and America's obligations under the Atlantic Charter [whereby all territory conquered after 1 September 1939 would be returned to its original country]. Poland would in exchange receive western territory at Germany's expense. What kind of bargain was that for a country who had not started the conflict, who had been invaded simultaneously by two powers, one of whom was even now deciding her fate, and who had been martyred many times over? There was not a single family who had not suffered some loss; the flower of Polish society had been deported or killed. It was not surprising that the Polish Government in London refused to consent to this annexation by Russia of half of Poland's territory, this illegal agreement in which she had not even been consulted. In retrospect it seems that Churchill was rather embarassed by the Polish Question and rather hoped the whole issue would go away. The Allies failed to understand the strategic importance of Poland's geographical position and to appreciate the heroic sacrifices made by the whole nation. As Witold philosophically remarked, "It is impossible for those who have never suffered occupation of their country to know what it is *really* like to live in that country." It must be remembered that for many years Westerners did not believe the tales emerging from Stalinist Russia about the reality of conditions there, nor did they believe the initial reports of the Holocaust (on the grounds that the accounts were propaganda intended to discredit the accused, as no one could sink so low as to do such terrible things to other human beings). Even today there are some who choose to doubt the reality of such events. The priority at Teheran was in practice to appease Stalin lest he unleashed other more sinister schemes.

162

When the Poles heard of the Teheran Agreement they were near to despair. They understood, as the Western Powers could not, that their old enemy, Russia, had in fact been given the blessing of the Allies to take over Poland and by placing Communists in the positions of power, turn her into a satellite Communist State. As events turned out, this is exactly what happened and Poland was effectively ruled from Moscow for 45 years until she shook off the yoke of Communism in 1990. In a sense there was a certain justification in the argument that there was little point for the Poles to continue fighting as whatever the outcome of the War Poland would be the loser.

However, life did go on. In January 1944 the exercises in Lebanon were completed and on 28 January Witold moved with the troops to Quassain in Egypt. There was great secrecy about future plans, but much rumour. It was probably at this time that Witold visited the Pyramids with some friends. By mid-February the II Polish Corps was definitely on the move in the direction of Cairo. On 9 February 5th Division embarked at Alexandria for an unknown destination; all the II Polish Corps was on the move by 25 February. Witold and Francis were very excited by this voyage as it could mean one of only two destinations – Greece or Italy. The crossing was a very long journey because the ships travelled in convoy due to the danger of mines, and the shallow waters near Alexandria were full of sunken ships. As Witold and Francis' ship approached Crete one night there was a huge explosion and a terrific jerk. All the men were ordered up on deck, as it was thought that they had been torpedoed; when daylight came they noticed that the rest of the convoy had vanished except for one other ship. Their own ship sailed very slowly and finally put in at the port of Taranto in southern Italy on 15 February 1944 after a journey of six days from Alexandria. It was only a couple of days later that the two friends noticed that there was a huge hole at about water level in the side of the ship they had sailed in. The other ship which had completed the journey with them had had its nose flattened like a bulldog. They learned that apparently their ship had been hit by a companion friendly ship during the night (when of course there were no lights above water on any ships for fear of revealing their presence to the ever-watchful Germans).

Italy

What had been happening in Italy during the War? A detailed description of the events of the Second World War can of course be found in any major work on the subject (see bibliography). In brief Mussolini and Hitler had formed an informal alliance in 1936; on 22 May 1939 this had been enshrined in the so-called "Pact of Steel" and Germany and her allies were known as the Axis powers. Italy entered the War on 10 June 1940 as Hitler's ally against France and England, but did not appear to achieve much success in the place where she was active, particularly in North and East Africa. In October 1940 Hitler occupied Romania to safeguard his oil supplies, so Mussolini, not to be outdone, attacked Greece, and which proved to be another disaster. As Hitler could not tolerate the defeat of an ally he sent the Luftwaffe to defend Sicily at the end of 1940, and in early 1941 he sent German forces to Libya. In April 1941 the Germans poured into Greece and yet more territory was overrun. The Germans then took Crete as well, and emboldened by these successes Hitler invaded Russia on 22 June 1941. The Allies launched a new offensive against the Axis forces in North Africa; in the summer of 1942 an Italo-German invasion of Egypt was attempted. The tide had turned against the Axis forces with the significant victory at El-Alamein by the British Eighth Army under General Montgomery. By May 1943 the last of the Axis forces in North Africa were cornered in the northern tip of Tunisia.

By this time it was becoming apparent that now was the time to begin reclaiming the German-occupied territories of Europe, and it was decided to begin by recapturing Italy. An Anglo-American invasion of Sicily was launched in July1943, this being considered the easiest way to enter Italy. Mussolini realised at this point that his cause was lost and he fell from power on 28 July 1943, as the result of a coup led by General Badoglio and backed by King Victor Emmanuel III. On 3 September the Anglo-American forces crossed over into mainland Italy, having taken Sicily from the Germans with much difficulty and bloodshed. The new Italian Government secretly negotiated with the Allies to shake off the hated alliance with Hitler and officially joined the Allied forces in October 1943.

The mainland campaign began in Calabria, in the Toe of Italy, and spread gradually northwards over the next eighteen months.

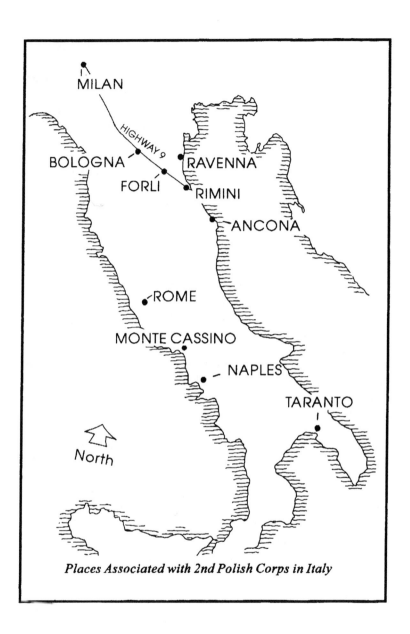

MILAN

HIGHWAY 9

BOLOGNA   RAVENNA

FORLI   RIMINI

ANCONA

ROME

MONTE CASSINO

NAPLES

TARANTO

North

Places Associated with 2nd Polish Corps in Italy

The geography of Italy is such that two invasion forces were needed, one on the west coast and one on the east coast, as the Apennine Mountains (the Backbone of Italy) prevented easy communication east-west. Each force needed its own supply base, so a priority was to capture strategic ports such as Naples (on 1 October) and Taranto and Brindisi on the Adriatic coast. The German strategy was to defend Rome and to hold the Front Line – the Gustav Line – which ran across Italy with the well-fortified monastery of Monte Cassino a pivotal point. Only when the Front had been broken could the Allies hope to capture Rome. This was the situation in Italy when the II Polish Corps disembarked at Taranto.

The Poles, ever romantic and sensitive to their surroundings, were delighted to be in "Bella Italia", the land of wine, beautiful women, olive groves, sunshine and song, although this required a certain degree of imagination in mid-February, when Italy was in the grip of the worst winter weather for decades! They were also thrilled because they were following in a tradition of fighting in Italy for Poland's freedom. One hundred and fifty years before, the Polish Dabrowski Legions had fought alongside Napoleon hoping that as a result of their efforts Poland would at last be free. The Poles would at last see action here in Italy and be able to play an active role in the overthrow of Hitler.

Once all the II Polish Corps had landed at Taranto, by 5 March 1944, they were temporarily encamped in a olive grove in near the village of Sta.Teresa, about three miles from the port, and here they were reorganised ready for action. Witold, with the rest of the 5 KDP, was moved up the Western coast in order to take his place for the next action of the War. By the end of March, General Anders knew that the Polish troops were going to play an integral role in the capture of Monte Cassino. He knew it would be a difficult task and costly in terms of men. Victory, however, would give new heart to Poles both at home and abroad, and give glory to the cause of Poland. It would also put paid to the current Soviet propaganda that the Poles did not really want to fight the Germans. Witold journeyed up the west coast of Italy, stopping in Naples sometime in the first half of April. Naples itself had been severely damaged in the course of its capture by the Allies, but Witold wanted to see Vesuvius. There had been a major eruption of the volcano as recently as 31 March, which had blown off the top of the volcano; by the time Witold arrived in April the lava was still warm, and presumably the ascent was still dangerous because of the possibility of further eruptions. Because of the war, no one had been able to pay very much attention to the volcano. Nothing daunted, the intrepid group of Polish soldiers hired a guide and clambered to the top. Here the guide demonstrated the softness of the lava by dipping a coin into it; it came out coated with the stuff which quickly hardened. As a child I was always fascinated by this coin and its story. Witold used to say that the most beautiful view in the whole world was that from the top of Vesuvius looking over the Bay of Naples. By the time he was there it was spring and it must have been blissful to be able to forget for a few moments the horrors of the war and to enjoy the sunshine, the flowers, the birds and the beautiful sparkling blue sea, with the island of Capri in the distance.

However, this was only an interlude in the real business of fighting the war. The II Polish Corps were soon deployed in assisting the French section of the Allied line in the region of Pozill-Prata. The sappers were active in clearing minefields in the territory bordering the River Sangro as far as the source of the Rapido river. The Poles were also given the tasks of maintaining communications between the British Eighth Army and the American Fifth Army and defending two of the main roads through the mountains, from Monte Curvale to Colle Lettica and the Isemia-Aledina road. In mid-April the II Polish Corps were relieved of these duties and the 5th KDP moved to Venafro. Witold was then moved on to Acquafondata, a tiny place only 12 miles or so from Monte Cassino.

The capture of Monte Cassino, considered essential for the conquest of Rome, was proving an extremely difficult task. The monastery was built at the top of a steep hill and as a fortress was all but impregnable. The Germans knew this and exploited its strategic location by making it an integral part of their defences. The building itself was one of the historic and religious treasure of the Western world, having been founded by St. Benedict himself, the father of Western monasticism, almost 1500 years previously. Most of the priceless art treasures had been removed by the Germans to Naples for safety (and plundered for the Nazi hierarchy in Germany), and the Abbot and the monks advised to leave the building. In fact most of the monks remained as by this time

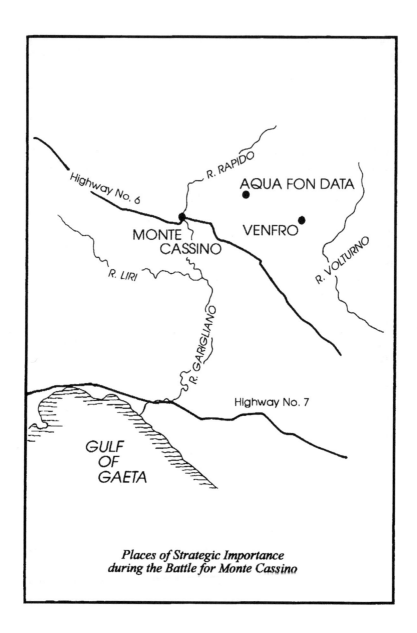

*Places of Strategic Importance
during the Battle for Monte Cassino*

many of the local villagers had sought refuge within the Abbey walls. The American Fifth Army under General Mark Clark had been attempting to capture the monastery without success since the beginning of 1944. They were assisted by the French Expeditionary Force and then New Zealand troops and Indian troops – all to no avail. A full frontal attack launched on 20 January was unsuccessful. By mid-February the difficult and heartbreaking decision was reached that the only way to take the monastery would be to destroy it. It was a controversial decision then, and remains so even today. On 15 February the bombs began to fall on the buildings – from American planes. The ancient buildings and their priceless treasures were reduced to rubble – surely one of the tragedies of the war, even though after the war the monastery was rebuilt to its former glory. However, despite even this action, the Germans were still firmly entrenched in the caves on the hillside. It was then that the Allies decided to use Polish troops for an all-out attempt to take the monastery and the small town of Piedemonte on the all-important Highway No. 6 to Rome.

Preparations were set in motion for this enterprise. The 5th KDP were at Acquafondata by 14 April and immediately began battle preparations. The movements of the Poles had to be concealed from the Germans as surprise was a very strong weapon in the attack. Supplies had to be transported over two mountain tracks as there were no usable roads; as they were under enemy observation and potentially enemy fire, all movement of equipment had to take place at night. The Rapido Valley, just below Monte Cassino, was filled with smoke screens to cover the activity. The plan of attack was to break though the Monastery Hill defences from the north, and to capture two nearby hills, Hill 593 and Colle Sant'Angelo, thus isolating the Monastery. Witold and his colleagues would capture the ring of hills around the monastery and thereby give cover for the 3rd Division to advance on the monastery itself.

Plans were all set to commence battle after dark on 11 May 1944. With a volley of gunfire the battle began and continued without let up until daylight. Losses were great, but fresh troops came to take the place of the fallen. It was becoming clear that some places were easier to capture than to hold. The Germans fought back fiercely, without pause, but the Polish troops did succeed in distracting German troops from other defences, thus enabling the XIII British Army Corps to advance across the Liri Valley. The second phase of the battle began on 16 May; by the following day the fighting had become fierce hand to hand combat. At last the Germans showed signs of weariness after a week of heavy fighting and on the morning of 18 May the 3rd Carpathian Division renewed their attacks. They climbed Monastery Hill and with undisguised joy hoisted the Polish flag over the ruins at 10.25am. What a moment of triumph! Witold, however, was still occupied nearby where the stubborn fighting continued for another day, the Germans only withdrawing on 19 May. The British and Canadians engaged with the Germans on the Gustav Line, at the town of Piedemonte, as Highway 6, the main road to Rome , had to be captured to ensure a free passage to the capital. The exhausted Polish troops also helped with the capture of Piedemonte and after five days' fighting, that town, too, was taken on 25 May 1944.

The road to Rome was now truly free, but at a terrible cost in lives among Witold's colleagues – in total the casualties amounted to 281 officers and 3503 other ranks. The Polish soldiers were rightly praised by all the Allied leaders and the extreme bravery of the troops acknowledged. Proud days indeed for the II Polish Corps. Eventually there was even a message of congratulation from the beleaguered AK (Home Army) surviving in appalling conditions under German rule in Warsaw. This message meant more to the Poles in Italy than any other accolade. On 4 June 1944 Allied troops entered Rome and liberated it.

Witold and his friends, Francis, Jurek Gradosielski and the others could now take some well-earned leave. They naturally climbed up the hill of Monte Cassino, gazed at the pile of rubble and marvelled at the destruction, remembering also their comrades who had fallen in the struggle. Wandering around the ruins, Witold noticed a small statue of St. Benedict, of the kind sold as a souvenir to pilgrims, among the dust and stones. Even this had a piece of the figure's side blasted out by the force of the explosions. He kept the statue and it later had a place of honour on the bookcase in his study – a salutary reminder if any were needed – of the indiscriminate destructiveness and the Poles' moment of glory at Monte Cassino.

There now followed a relatively happy and carefree time. ("Those were the glory days", Witold used to say). They had been through the living hell of the Russian Camps, the horror of life in so-called freedom in the Soviet Union, the period of training in the Iraqi desert and the fierce fighting at Monte Cassino. Of course they were still part of the Allied forces chasing the retreating Germans northwards, but life was easier. They had money in their pockets, they could explore the countryside in their free time, the villas they requisitioned provided an illusion of luxury. Witold could occasionally indulge his passion for good food, good wine and good books. There are stories of how well the Poles got on with the local Italian girls; in fact many Poles eventually married Italians.

However, the Good Life could not continue for ever; the battle may have won but not, as yet, the war. By mid-June the 5th KDP was on the move again, this time to the opposite coast of Italy and the shores of the Adriatic. The supply roads from the major ports of Taranto, Naples, Bari and Ancona had to be improved and upgraded; in fact Ancona itself was still in German hands. It was back to the old task of clearing minefields, repairing broken bridges, fording or swimming across cold, fast-flowing mountain streams: Vomano, Tonto, Tenna, Chati, Portenza, Minesone... Ancona was captured in mid-July 1944. Again the sappers played a key role in the engagement, and the town fell to the Poles on 18 July. With the capture of Ancona the greater part of the task of the II Polish Corps in Italy had been achieved. Back at home the final planning of the Warsaw Uprising was under way. The Uprising began on 1 August 1944, and is described in Chapter 8.

It was at about this time that Witold received what was probably for him the most precious piece of mail during the whole war. The Poles who were abroad were of course very worried about what was happening at home to their families in Poland, and many enlisted the help of the tracing service of the International Red Cross to try and trace their families. As will be seen later, the Red Cross were faced with an almost impossible task but sometimes miracles happened. Probably at the end of June Witold received a telegram via the Red Cross in London, which said in English,

"Parcel no 597 from Ankara[?] already got. Mother died May 1941. The rest of the family well. Wandysia recently died, Marian abroad [he was working as a war artist in the Low Countries], Lunio Oflag, Danek home, Kostek."

These 27 words must have been infinitely precious yet painful to him. It meant that Kostek was alive (although ironically he would be dead within two months), and his father and sister were alive, although his mother, to whom he had always been very close, had died. All through his time in the GULAG Witold had managed to keep the last item of clothing his mother had made him – a crocheted waistcoat. He kept it until the day he died, an infinitely precious momento. We can only imagine his feelings as he read the message. It was tantalisingly short – only such few words were permitted – and printed very small to save space and weight. Witold was normally a quiet man, but these few words must have made him even quieter than usual. So many unanswered questions. What, and who, would be left when this tragic war eventually came to an end? We do not have a reply, although we know that he wrote to Danek (his daughter has the telegram in her possession). It must have been a scene repeated many times over among the Poles abroad.

The next action Witold saw was to provide part of the rearguard for the British Eighth Army between 5 September and 9 October. The Polish troops continued to advance up the Adriatic coast. They reached the River Rubicon by the end of September and were then ordered to turn inland and concentrate their efforts on the Northern Apennines, securing the road between Forli and Faenza and moving towards Bologna. On 17 November Witold passed through or near the village of Predappio Nuovo, the birthplace of Mussolini. A few days later he was transferred to 4 Workshop Company. Faenza was reached by the end of the month, and by the beginning of 1945 they had reached the River Senio. The weather was again very wet so the swollen rivers impeded the progress of the troops. The rain continued throughout January and February. This was another busy time for the Poles; although Witold and Francis had recently been billeted in Ravenna, they had had no chance to visit the famous mosaics there.

At the end of January Witold's name came up for promotion and Francis relates an astonishing incident. The normal practice in Witold's section was that the Commanding Officer of the new enlarged Workshop Company was a professional Lt.-Colonel. The Second-in-Command was the person who actually ran the Company, and Witold was offered this job. The unthinkable happened and Witold refused to take this job! More than this, he said that he was fed up with working with stupid people! This was, technically, a Court Martial offence – but for some reason Witold got away with it, and the incident was not even recorded in his service record. He took instead a job as Planning and Supply Officer, a job much more suited to his temperament, as this involved logistics and brainwork rather than shouting at officers. Francis was offered, and accepted, the Second-in Command post, after consultation with Witold.

The two became very firm friends and used to go to Mantua to see the opera – once it was "Rigoletto" – and later on to the opera in Bologna or Milan. This is another example of Witold's unusual character. He disliked being in charge of people, or having anything to do with hierarchies, and was much happier doing a desk job. He was held in the greatest respect – how did he not get court-martialled? – but had the greatest respect for any-one in a less fortunate position than he was.

The following story is an example of this. One day, as they were passing through a ruined Italian village they saw the remains of a peasant's house. The man and his family had absolutely nothing left but the steaming heap of manure on which they were sitting to keep warm. Some of the Polish soldiers started laughing at the peasant and his family. Witold stopped the convoy and shouted to his men, "You stupid idiots! You laugh at him, and who are you? This peasant sits on his own heap of manure, on his own land, and his own bits of house. You idiots, you have nothing! Even the bloody dirty trousers you are wearing do not belong to you!" At this all the men fell silent. *Pan Inzynier* had spoken. He never suffered fools gladly whether they were his superiors or subordi-nates, but commanded enormous respect from his colleagues. Everyone who knew him would say of him, "*On jest dobry do bitwy i do wypitki*," ie, that he was as reliable in battle as at a drinking party. His toleration of alcohol was legendary; after a night out with his friends, no matter how much he had had to drink, he always seemed to negotiate the way home safely in the jeep!

On 12 February General Anders and the Poles received yet another cruel blow from fate. Roosevelt, Stalin and Churchill met at Yalta on the Black Sea to make decisions concerning the shape of Europe after the war. Once again Britain and America felt that they had to appease Stalin; the Polish Question remained a thorn in the side of the Allies. However, Anders and the Poles were stunned by the decisions of Yalta, whereby the proposals of Teheran were given definite shape, and in some respects, extended. The Eastern part of Poland, including Wilno and Lwow, which had been associated with Poland for six centuries and which had almost no ethnic Russians living there was to be ceded to the Soviet Union. The granting of some of the German Eastern Provinces was no compensation. In addition, the Polish Government in London, which had supported the Allies throughout the war and was recognised by them was to be sidelined, and the Provisional Lublin Government, whose members were all appointees of Moscow, was to be the recognised Polish Government. So all the sacrifice, all the heroism – had it been in vain? The soldiers were numb at first and then as the implications dawned on the men there was a real danger of discontent, or worse, in the ranks. Anders himself felt that under such circumstances he had no justification in asking the soldiers to continue fighting on for a doomed cause. He asked that the II Polish Corps be withdrawn from the fighting, but was told that there was no one to relieve them and they had to fight on. Anders then flew to London and spoke to Churchill. Churchill's comments show that he was still uncomfortable with the Polish Question. He said that the decisions at Yalta were the Poles' fault for not settling the Eastern Question. He tetchily said also that Britain had never undertaken to guarantee these frontiers. Anyway, Britain no longer needed Polish troops as she had enough of her own! What had happened to the Atlantic Charter stating the return of all conquered territories to their pre-war status? Anders could scarcely believe his ears, but despite putting the Polish point of view, he failed to alter Churchill's thinking. This was definite – that the Poles who had kept themselves fighting on with the goal of settling back in a free Poland after the war were now condemned either to living as aliens in a foreign land or in a homeland under foreign rule. There was no victory for the Poles now whatever the outcome of the war; the Allies had consciously or unconsciously decided otherwise.

The final offensive in Italy began on 9 April. Their goal was the assault and capture of Bologna. American bombers flew overhead to start the attack, but some planes dropped their bombs too early by mistake and they fell among the Polish troops, causing several casualties. Despite this, the rivers Senio and Santerno were reached and on 21 April Bologna was taken. Witold was there, but we know that he was in Milan only a week later as he was witness a gruesome piece of history.

By April 1945 Mussolini had been cornered to the northern part of Italy and the village of Dongo on the NW shore of Lake Como. On 27 April he was finally captured by some partisans, together with his mistress, Clara Petacci, and taken to the house of a partisan overnight. The next afternoon they were taken back through Dongo (where that same day 15 of Mussolini's close associates were lined up and shot in the main square facing Lake Como), and at the nearby hamlet of Mezzegra they were ordered out of the truck. Mussolini and Clara were put against the gateway of the Villa Belmonte and shot at point-blank range. Their bodies, together with those of the 15 shot at Dongo, were taken overnight to Milan, where all 17 were dumped on a garage forecourt on the Piazza Loreto at 4am. By 8am crowds had gathered to see for themselves the body of the hated dictator. One woman fired five shots into Mussolini's body, "One for each of my sons he shot," she said, while others performed various obscenities on the body. Mussolini's and Clara's bodies were hanged upside down from the roof of the garage. Someone (Deakin says it was a woman in the crowd, Witold said it was a British soldier) tied a string round Clara's ankles and pushed her skirt between her legs to preserve her modesty. Witold must have been passing nearby and wondering why the crowd had gathered – the sight of those two bodies, hated though they were, disfigured and abused, disgusted him. The memory of that scene always stayed with him. By late afternoon even the partisans had had enough and the bodies were taken down and moved to the local mortuary. (Eventually, after being buried in several different places, Mussolini's body was laid to rest with the rest of his family at Predappio, the village where he had been born.)

By chance the Germans in Italy signed their surrender at Caserta on the same day that Mussolini was shot. Hitler committed suicide in his bunker on 30 April. On 4 May the German forces in NW Germany surrendered and on 7 May a general surrender was signed at Reims.

After the war

The war was over at last, after more than five years of fighting. What did it mean for the Poles? Where could they go, and what could they do? All without exception had lost some family during the war and some came from the Eastern borderlands of Poland which were no longer Polish. Poland had been handed over to the control of Stalin. The Polish Government in London had, in the last few months of the war, been ignored and sidelined; a new Provisional Government formed in Lublin and was considered to be the true government by the Allies. The Government in London became the Government in Exile; as all its power had been removed it was hoped that it would quietly go away and be forgotten about. It bided its time, until Poland should be free again and remained in existence until 1990 when Lech Walensa was elected the first President of a free Poland. The representatives of the Government in Exile travelled to Warsaw and solemnly handed over the insignia of State which they had kept safe for 51 years. Then, and only then, was their job done.

Of more immediate concern was what to do with all the Poles who at the end of the war found themselves dispersed throughout Europe. This not only included those serving in the Armed Forces, many of whom were in Britain and France, but the Poles, over one million in number, who had been deported for forced labour, or put into concentration or forced labour camps. There were 12 000 Poles in France alone, for example. There were approximately one million Poles in Germany, and the numbers were growing as Poles fled from Poland. They were deprived of legal protection because the London Polish Government was no longer recognised and the Warsaw Government was unsympathetic. The 12 000 Poles in France had been forcibly conscripted into the German Army and were held in several camps. In addition, scattered throughout the world there were other Poles, in Africa, Persia, India and the Middle East and they also were helpless. The British Government were faced with a huge logistical problem. General Anders was also faced with a grave problem as to what to do with the 112 000 men in the II Polish Corps. They were, of course, offered the choice of returning to Poland. It is not insignificant that of these 112 000, only 7 officers and 14 200 men applied for repatriation, 8 700 of these being soldiers who had joined after hostilities had ended. Of those who had come out of Russia, only 310 applied.

There was a certain amount of anti-Polish propaganda from Moscow – basically because the belief of 100 000 Poles in a free Poland created a certain threat to the Soviet system.

Further setbacks to a speedy resolution to the situation occurred. The Warsaw Government issued a statement on 20 March 1946 that the units of the Polish Armed Forces under British command could not be regarded as units of the Armed Forces of Poland. Then, curiously, they cited the 1921 Constitution of Poland to say that as members of a foreign Power's Armed Forces they were no longer regarded as Polish citizens.

Deliberations to solve the problem ground on slowly, the Polish troops, whose future, whose citizenship even, was unknown, trying to occupy their time usefully. Sports competitions were organised among the men, but Witold preferred to sightsee. For some time he was billetted in a splendid Abbey in Milan. (He was delighted when, thirty years later, he was in Milan on business and was able to call in at the Abbey. He explained his story, was very warmly welcomed and invited to stay for a meal. This was a happy reunion.) Life went on among the troops, for example his great friend, Jurek Gradosielski, married Danuta on 19 August 1945.

In May 1946 General Anders received intimations from London that the II Polish Corps was to be quickly transferred to Britain for demobilisation. This action would remove all hope of return to a free Poland. Was all the blood, all the suffering in vain? The British Government planned to re-form the Polish troops into a Polish Resettlement Corps (PRC) which would be a first step to demobilisation and a preparation of its members for civilian life.

In June 1946 there was a Victory Parade in London; for some reason the Poles were not invited to participate (although other nationals who had fought with the British, eg., Indian and New Zealand troops were), an action which was considered even by some British politicians as a slight.

The future of Witold and his comrades in arms was still unclear. There was still little news from home, although Witold did receive another telegram from Warsaw, this time from his father. This one said words to the effect, "Mother dead, brother dead, sister dead, I'm still here, Father." That was how he learned of the remaining deaths in the family. The details would have to wait for some years; this message was stark comfort for someone who had effectively lost almost everything.

Eventually the long wait while the Poles' fate was decided was over. In the end 160 000 Poles joined the Polish Resettlement Corps. They were taken by ship to Britain, Witold's and Francis' ship docking in Glasgow on 13th September 1946. From there they were put on a train to Wiltshire, where they were taken to one of the camps for Polish troops. Witold was officially registered there on 9 November 1946.

CHAPTER 8

Poland in the War

Witold's experience of the war was shared by thousands of his fellow countrymen and women, but what happened to those left behind in Poland? The rest of his family had their own share of hardship and tragedy although the details of the story are not as well known as Witold's story.

The pincer-like movement of the two invading armies in September 1939 – the Germans from the west and the Soviets from the east – ensured that Poland as an independent nation had no chance of survival. Both armies crossed the frontiers without a formal declaration of war, and such was the speed and ferocity of Hitler's invasion that the Allies did not realise the full impact of what was happening. Great Britain and France declared war on Hitler on 3 September; by 8 September Warsaw was already under fire. The Polish President, Government, Commander-in-Chief of the Armed Forces and the Diplomatic Corps had left Warsaw on the previous day. They fled south, crossing the border on 17 September, just before it was closed, hoping to find sanctuary in Romania. However, once in Romania, they were interned so the President, Moscicki, appointed Wladyslaw Raczkiewicz as his successor. He escaped to Paris and a new Polish government was formed on 30 September under Wladyslaw Sikorski. This was the Polish Government in Exile recognised by the Allies and when Hitler invaded France in June 1940 the government fled to London.

On 17 September the Russians crossed the eastern border; the battle for Warsaw had been raging since 8 September, by 14 she was encircled and on 28 she fell to the Germans. The fortress at Modlin, where Kostek was stationed, fell next day, but the last Polish units did not surrender until 5 October. On 28 September a Russian-German Pact was signed, dividing Poland between them. The country was divided into three parts, the western part being incorporated into the German Reich, the eastern part into the Soviet Union and the Central part, including Warsaw, Lublin and Krakow, becoming the Nazi-run Central Gouvernment under the command of General Hans Frank, a particularly ruthless and unpleasant man.

Over the next few months approximately 1 700 000 Poles (including 9 500 officers) from the Soviet-run sector were transported to labour camps in the Siberia or the Far North; 1 300 000 Poles were moved from the Central Gouvernment to the Reich as slave labour. If the military are included, the figure deported is nearer 2 million. In addition 2 700 000 Polish Jews were taken in due course from the ghettos of Polish towns, most famously Warsaw and Lodz, and murdered. There was a systematic attempt to eliminate Poland and the Polish nation from the map.

On 5 October Hitler himself took the salute at the Victory Parade in Warsaw, but the beginnings of the Resistance Movement had already come into being the previous week. At first known as the Polish Victory Service (SZP), by 3 November it had become the Union of Armed Struggle (ZWB). In February 1942 it became known as the Armia Krajowa (AK). It took its orders directly from the Polish Commander-in-Chief in London and membership spread rapidly as a means of sabotaging some of the worst excesses of the occupying powers. As a Resistance Movement it was highly successful in the early years. It is noteworthy that although at its height in 1944 it numbered 400 000 men and women in its ranks, making it by far the largest and most successful movement of its kind, there was not a single traitor or Quisling among them. People were fighting for their very existence and the passion, daring and bravery of those of all sections became legendary.

Life took on a nightmarish quality from the very beginning of the German Occupation for both Jew and non-Jew alike. Individual accounts of the sufferings endured by the Poles abound and remain some of the most eloquent reminders of the brutality to which human beings can sink, and also of the indomitable courage and resilience of the human spirit in the face of apparently overwhelming odds. Sadly it appears that we do not learn from history as the same errors and massacres have been repeated in each generation since under different guises.

Hans Frank officially became the Commander in charge of the Central Gouvernment on 26 October; by 6 November the first systematic German attempt at destroying the Polish intellect began with the rounding up of all the Professors of the Jagiellian

University in Krakow, and their subsequent arrest and shooting. The first of the arbitrary street round-ups, which would become so common over the next few years, was on 9 November in Lublin. The Terror began in Warsaw on 27 December with the shooting of 106 hostages in Wawer. No one ever knew when or where the next round-up and shooting would be. Perhaps a tram would be stopped and the passengers lined up and shot, or it could happen to passers by in the street; nobody could be sure that when he or she left home they would return. The systematic rounding up and transporting to mass extermination was still in the future; the concentration camps at Auschwitz (Oswiecim) and Maidaneck (Majdanek) were still being built and would not be functional until 1941. Martial law was maintained with excessive ferocity. Another weapon was to keep the population half-starved. A Reichsdeutscher in Poland at first received food coupons for 4 000 calories a day, a Polish worker, 900, and a "non-productive Jew", nothing.

Harrowing accounts exist of the everyday conditions under which the ordinary citizens of Warsaw were forced to live. Hanson graphically sums them up in her book, "The Civilian Population and the Warsaw Uprising", where on p.14, para 1.5 she describes the methods of Nazi terror thus:-

"Anyone who has not lived through a reign of terror can have no real idea of its implications. They can have no conception of what it means to live in constant fear of arrest, torture, death, transportation or extermination. During World War II every nation under Nazi occupation underwent a reign of terror in accordance with Nazi racial policies. It is probably true to say, however, that no other nation suffered more than Poland.

In other European countries such as Holland, Belgium, France, Denmark and Czechoslovakia thousands were arrested and killed for their anti-Nazi and Resistance activities, for fighting and defying the occupier. But in Poland people were arrested and killed for being out after curfew hours, or for selling black market goods, such as white bread, meat and vegetables in order to eke out a living and keep alive. In the capital cities of Paris, Brussels, Prague and others there was not the fear of being caught in a street round up, lined up against a wall and shot, just because you were there, just because you were Polish. In Warsaw no one was sure when they went to bed that they were going to be allowed to sleep the night out... This was the kind of unimaginable fear that the inhabitants of Warsaw lived under for five long years of the occupation."

The Polish intelligentsia were particular targets for reprisals and shootings. Anyone with a university education, doctors, lawyers, landowners, dentists, executives, writers, etc, were especially at risk. An idea of the scale of the killings and transportations can be gained from considering the statistics. The population of Warsaw in September 1939 was estimated at 1 407 000; German figures in June 1940 estimated 1 306 950. By the end of 1943 it was 954 360 and by the end of the war – nothing, as the city was razed to the ground. Until the Warsaw Uprising of August 1944 it is estimated that 35-40 000 Varsovians were killed, 5 500 in street round ups between January and July 1944 alone. The streets of Warsaw are even today dotted with memorials set into the walls commemorating the site of each execution and after more than half a century fresh flowers are still placed there regularly.

Daily life was a daily nightmare. Employment was very hard to obtain as all normal life had been disrupted. Much of Warsaw had been destroyed when the Nazis besieged it in September 1939, so housing was a constant problem. There was little or no fuel available for heating during the harsh winter of 1939-40. In January 1940 the temperatures in Warsaw plunged to between -20 and -40C. Gas and electricity supplies were very patchy. Clothing was virtually unobtainable, as were shoes; as mentioned above, food rations were set at approximately 20-25% of daily calorific requirements. By September 1942 the monthly ration per person was 4.8kg black bread, 400g meat and 100g ersatz marmalade, averaging 417 cals/day. Somehow people struggled on. Health proved to be a problem but by 1941 there were more deaths due to hunger and emaciation than disease. There was a chronic shortage of medicines and vaccines. By September 1941 there were 3 400 known cases of typhus (the numbers were relatively low because of a huge vaccination programme the previous year). However, dysentery and TB were on the increase and rickets was present in up to 90% of children. Groups of people joined together to form mutual self-help groups and to maintain an extensive system of underground culture, schooling and even universities – activities forbidden by the authorities. Pope John Paul II, as the student Karol Wotyla, was a graduate of such an institution.

182

What happened to the family during this time? Details are few
and sketchy. Kostek seems to have vanished between September
1939 and March 1940. His birth certificate was not stamped by the
Germans until 4 March 1940 and again on 6 March 1942. His registered address was 7 Sierakowski St, Warsaw. What happened to
him during those missing six months? It is most likely that he simply went into hiding in the countryside as he obviously was not
captured nor did he escape abroad. His vocation as a surgeon,
especially in the dark situation of German-occupied Warsaw, must
have driven him back to the capital. He resumed work at the
Transfiguration Hospital where he had been before the war,
although we do not know if he went straight there or was somewhere else at first. He was certainly working there by 1942 as
there are photos showing him at work in the hospital. During this
time Kostek grew very close to a certain Dr. Barr, whose husband
had been deported to the Soviet Union. They obviously fell deeply
in love, two lonely people in a situation of uncertainty. Kostek was
almost certainly a member of the AK right from the beginning of
his time in Warsaw; his hospital was one of several designated as
"safe" by the AK for taking their wounded members.

The rest of the family, Joachim, Anna and Zosia, appear to have
fled from their Warsaw flat in the Zoliborz area of Warsaw and
took up residence in their flat in Radom. Anna and Zosia were
both ill by this time, Anna with heart trouble and possibly stom-
ach cancer and Zosia with deteriorating mental health. By
November 1940 they are registered as living in Radom, confirmed
in February 1942, their address being 68 Zbromskiego St (not the
flat they had lived in before the war). Although they were marginally safer in the country they were not totally immune from the
privations of the war. The provincial partisan sector of the AK had
one of its strongest cells in Radom; was Joachim part of it? The
area was subjected to frequent searches and round ups by the
Germans. In addition, Joachim had to witness the transformation
of the munitions factory which he had built in Skarzysko into one
of the most brutal of all Jewish slave labour camps in Poland. It
was run by a German company based in Leipzig, Hugo Schneider
Aktiengesellschaft, and it is estimated that in total 25-30 000 Jews
were sent there, of whom only 7 000 survived. (see Gilbert,M. *The
Boys*, p.137). Although there were other camps at Radom and
nearby Ilza, this one at Skarzysko must have affected him deeply.

Photographs from the family albums salvaged after the war provide the most clues about this period of family life, although in some cases the pictures are puzzling. In 1940 Joachim is shown in a village garden in the village of Wielge, SE of Radom; in 1941 there is a picture of him labelled as taken in Radom. They may well have had to keep moving in order to stay one step ahead of the authorities. Sadly on 17 May 1941 Anna died (at 13.00h according to the identity card) in the house at 68 Zeromskiego St. She was buried in the cemetery at Radom. Joachim was devastated; he took off his wedding ring, never to wear it again. These were truly dark days as his life seemed to be falling apart around him. His beloved wife was no more, his daughter severely ill, his elder son living in conditions of extreme danger and uncertainty in a city occupied by an invading force, and his younger son a prisoner goodness knows where, maybe not even alive. Perhaps it was at this point that he sought the advice of his clairvoyant friend Ossowiecki to find out whether his son, Witold, was still alive; perhaps he had sought his advice as Anna lay dying in order to comfort her last days. (Ossowiecki correctly said that Witold was at that time alive, but behind barbed wire, near a big river, all of which was in fact true). In the next few weeks after his wife's death Joachim aged visibly; in addition to the constant strain of having to keep one's wits about one in order to survive daily life under a cruel occupying power there was the added anxiety about his family. His was not an isolated case; it is reasonable to assume that every single family in Poland had similar worries. The daily struggle for survival had to continue, some semblance of normality maintained. We do not know how much Joachim and Zosia were "molested" by the Germans but they were raided at intervals. Torn out pages in the photo albums testify to what the Gestapo decided were subversive pictures although looking at the albums today with hindsight it is hard to see why they selected what they did. There are sad pictures of Joachim holding a chicken (where did he find it?), or standing with Zosia, or taking her on visits to old haunts such as Rejow and Ilza, places they had last seen in happier times. He was supported by their faithful housekeeper who performed miracles at finding food and making life bearable. She stayed with Joachim until she died in 1956. Witold was full of gratitude for all she had done in her devoted service in caring for the family in those dark times; he used to send her presents of grey woollen stockings from England when he could.

Meanwhile Kostek was working in the Przemieniena Panskiego (Transfiguration) Hospital in the Praga suburb of Warsaw where conditions were, if anything, slightly easier than in the centre of the city, although by 1943 the hospital was sandbagged against bomb damage.

The single most important factor which kept ordinary people alive and sane was their common support and membership of the Resistance movement. By providing a cohesive focus for resistance by outwitting and sabotaging the hated Nazi conquerors, the AK ensured that the Poles maintained a psychological advantage over their oppressors. Of course they mostly worked under cover while doing other jobs – Kostek was almost certainly a member and his cousin Danek (code name Walek) was an officer in the AK, playing active role in the Uprising of 1944.

The Resistance movement came directly under the command of the Polish Government in Exile and thereby formed a unit which could co-ordinate sabotage and subversive action to maximum effect. Other resistance groups existed such as the Armia Ludowa (AL) of Polish communists but their numbers were much smaller. The ZWZ began to form local units throughout Poland, the earliest being formed in SW Poland in December 1939. Most soldiers of the AK were untrained as nearly all the trained soldiers had been taken prisoner either by the Germans or the Soviets. The principle functions of the resistance movement were to provide intelligence information to the Government in Exile and to sabotage and provide diversionary tactics against the Germans. The penalties for being caught were severe so for safety's sake members were known only by code names. By 1941 there were approximately 100 000 members in the Resistance Movement and, incredibly, they provided amongst other services, a fortnightly courier service to London with the latest intelligence. In a situation where for a Polish household to own such a seemingly innocuous item as an egg was an offence punishable by death, this was bravery indeed. Some of the acts of sabotage were in fact very entertaining, and illustrate the importance of keeping a good sense of humour in the interests of sanity. Bor-Komorowski, in his account of the AK in *The Secret Army* mentions several comical ways in which the Poles outwitted the Germans. False directives sent on Nazi party notepaper were sent out to all German residents – orders to register, invitations to attend non-existent meetings, etc. The effect was to produce chaos among the authorities; eventually the Governor of Warsaw, Fischer, issued a confidential circular warning his subordinates against orders forged by Poles. When a German received an inconvenient order he would consider it forged and the ensuing confusion hampered considerably the work of the authorities. False propaganda, leaflets and magazines were produced on the underground press.

On p.83 of his book, Bor-Komorowaski describes a particularly amusing incident. During the winter of 1942 the Germans removed the plaque from the statue of the astronomer Copernicus [who was Polish] which said "To Copernicus from his countrymen" and replaced it with one which said "To the Great German Astronomer". A few days later a gang of workmen (in reality AK members) casually approached the statue and removed the new inscription. On discovering this theft the Germans issued a proclamation that, as a reprisal, the statue of Kilinski [a bootmaker who led the people during the siege of 1794 by the Russians] would be removed and that any further similar acts be rewarded by suspension of food rations for a week. A few days later Kilinski's statue was removed to the vaults of a museum and next morning an inscription appeared on the museum wall "People of Warsaw – I am here (signed) Jan Kilinski." A week later a new poster appeared, similar in form to Fischer's proclamation -

"Recently criminal elements removed the Kilinski monument for political reasons. As a reprisal I order the prolongation of winter on the Eastern Front for the term of two months. Signed, Copernicus."

Or there was the method used to silence the German farmer from Radomsk who helped the Gestapo by betraying Poles. Two AK men called on the man saying that they had important details to give him about the underground but from fear of their fellow countrymen could only visit after dark. Delighted, the farmer told them to return the next evening, whereupon he welcomed them. Once inside the office he was threatened with revolvers and told that the underground was now taking their revenge. He was made to undress from the waist downwards, to kneel down and to put his head into the oven. They put a board across his backside and told him they were laying a live grenade on it, so if he moved it would fall down and explode. Then they left. After two hours the man's mistress reported to the authorities that he had not returned home. His secretary went to the office and found the man still kneeling, half-naked, with his head in the oven, and on the board on his back – an egg. This ridiculous incident resulted in the man's removal – exactly what the AK had wanted.

The AK was organised very carefully and divided into many different departments. Secrecy was vital for the success of operations and the survival of the members, hence the use of an intricate system of code names. There were three types of soldiers in the AK – people who led a double life ostensibly doing their everyday jobs while also being active members of the resistance. Then there were professional conspirators who had no time for other occupations. These people concentrated on the Intelligence and Liaison aspects of the job. Lastly there were those who had completely broken with their former existence and lived as partisans, hiding in the forests and the countryside. Kostek was a member of the first group and Danek a member of the second.

In April 1943 the Germans announced the discovery of mass graves of five thousand Polish officers at Katyn, near Smolensk in the Soviet Union. The West were horrified as the details emerged. The Germans and the Russians each blamed the other although the Poles suspected right from the start that it was the Soviets who were the guilty party. In fact they did not admit responsibility until 1990. However, international investigations were set up; when the Poles asked the International Red Cross to conduct their own investigation, Moscow broke off diplomatic relations with the Polish Government. Evidence pointed overwhelmingly to the Soviets being responsible, but at last was the answer to the mystery of where the Polish officers had vanished. The full story can be found in books such as the ones by Anders, Fitzgibbon or Zawodny (see bibliography) At the postwar Nuremberg Trials, set up to try and to punish those convicted of war crimes, the Katyn issue was very delicate as the Soviets were allocated to prosecute for these crimes. The Poles were not even called as witnesses and the murderers were never revealed or punished – without protest from the either the Soviet Government or the Communist Government in Poland. Winston Churchill commented in his memoirs, "It was decided by the victorious governments concerned that the issue should be avoided and the crime of Katyn was never probed in detail" (Churchill, W.S. *The Hinge of Fate* p.761, quoted in Zawody *Death in the Forest* p.74). We can only imagine how the beleaguered Poles in Poland (and abroad) must have felt as the news became known and people wondered if their loved ones were among the 5 000. This was aside from the humanitarian consideration as how anyone could shoot so many defenceless men in cold blood. Morale became very low at this point.

As time went by the number and frequency of public executions perpetrated by the Nazis increased and spread throughout Poland, partly because of the success of the AK in sabotaging the German administration. On December 9 1943 the German Governor-General blamed Warsaw for the problems of his government:

"Warsaw," he said, "is the source of all our misfortunes – the focus of all disturbances, the place from which discontent is spread through the whole country." (quoted in Davies Vol. II p.441) Surely a testament to the effectiveness of the AK.

In Warsaw the arrival of a particularly brutal SS man, Kutschera, signalled an increase in the number of vicious killings. Within a very short time of his arrival he had been responsible for the deaths of 2 000 people in street round-ups, not to mention the public execution of a large number of prisoners from the notorious Pawiak Prison in Warsaw. The AK decided that this man had to be assassinated in order to save the lives of thousands of Poles, despite the fact that perhaps 200 hostages may have to pay the price for his death. Plans were laid and very careful research conducted as to his daily routine, etc, in order to ascertain the best time and place for the deed. There were two unsuccessful attempts; the third and successful one was made on 1 February 1944. The AK officer in charge of the attack was codenamed Lot with Cichy as his deputy. Two other men, Sokol and Juno, covered the street with gunfire while the German car carrying the hated Kutschera was stopped. Lot fired at Kutschera's head and while searching for his identity papers was himself shot. The four AK men, Sokol, Lot, Cichy and Juno climbed back into their car with Sokol driving and they sped as fast as they could to the Transfiguration Hospital in Praga – which of course was where Kostek worked as a surgeon. The hospital was one of the Red Cross Headquarters of the AK; many of the doctors were AK members, and wounded AK soldiers were regularly sent there for treatment. So Kostek undoubtedly played an important role in this incident. The two wounded men, Lot and Cichy, were safely deposited in the hospital but the other two were killed as they attempted to escape. Meanwhile the two wounded men were being searched out by the Gestapo, so a cunning plan was executed. At 6pm a police car drew up to the hospital, the "Gestapo" rushed into the ward, doctors and nurses looking on in horror as the "Germans" took them away. Twenty minutes later another group of Germans turned up to collect the Polish "Bandits" but failed to find them despite a thorough search of the hospital. By now, of course, Lot and Cichy were in a safe place, but sadly died of their wounds shortly afterwards. All four men were posthumously awarded the Virtuti Militari Cross, Poland's highest award for bravery.

By 1944 Zosia's state of health was deteriorating and giving the family grave cause for concern. With great reluctance she was admitted to a mental hospital in Warsaw, thus leaving Joachim alone in Radom. As the situation in the capital became more and more dangerous – plans for the Warsaw Uprising had begun in November 1943 – Kostek decided that the hospital was too dangerous so Zosia was transferred to the State Mental Hospital in Tworki, just outside the city, where sadly she died of pneumonia on 20 November 1945, ironically surviving the war itself. Her last months were heartbreaking for Joachim to endure, but she was buried in the hospital cemetery, a calm peaceful place full of trees overlooked by the now very dilapidated hospital buildings, still used as a hospital.

As plans advanced concerning the Uprising – code named Burza or Tempest – news reached the AK from London that Stalin and Molotov were asserting that the Home Army were doing nothing against the Germans and that their sole activities were aimed at the liquidation of Soviet partisans. On 3 January 1944 the Russians crossed the Polish frontiers and German lines; the Poles hoped once again that if only they held out fighting alone the Soviets would come to the aid of the AK and unite with them in overthrowing the common enemy, Germany.

Planning for the Uprising continued throughout the spring and early summer of 1944. In the event it proved doomed to failure as the timing was premature. The officers in command reckoned on seven to ten days of fighting; in fact the Uprising lasted 63 days. Stalin, instead of coming to the aid of the Poles, stood by and watched the Poles destroy themselves in an operation which he knew could not succeed. This was despite a series of urgent telegrams Churchill sent to Stalin begging him at least to send some supplies into Poland.

The Uprising was planned with three main aims. Firstly was the liberation of as much territory as possible from the Germans to create the basis for a free Polish state, secondly to deal another blow to the Germans when the war was going badly for them on all other fronts, and thirdly, the protection of Poland from final destruction. Germans were fleeing from Warsaw throughout July 1944 and the AK were hoping to capitalise on this before the Red Army arrived. The Germans had concentrated all their artillery on the left bank of the Vistula leaving only infantry at Praga itself. On 27 July the Red Army began to advance towards Praga, breaking through towards the suburb next day. On 29 July the Red Army joined battle with the Germans and fought one of the fiercest tank battles fought on Polish soil. Despite being opposed by 5 German Armoured Divisions, the 2nd Soviet Armoured Division continued to advance towards Praga. The control of Praga passed back into German hands on 31 July.

It must have been at this point that Kostek made the supremely brave decision that would ultimately cost him his life. It was decided to evacuate the Transfiguration Hospital, leaving only those patients too ill to risk moving and one doctor. Kostek volunteered to be that doctor and so remained at the hospital in the midst of fierce fighting.

The date for the beginning of the Uprising was set for 1 August. The fighting was terrible right from the start. On the first day alone an estimated 2 000 Poles were killed – by the end a total of 200 000 were killed or died. The German response was to raze Warsaw to the ground. The AK plan was to operate in several distinct areas – Wola, Stare Miasto (Old Town), Powisle, Srodmiescie, Mokotow and Zoliborz. The stories which have come to us from these area are horrifying and the full terror is difficult to grasp for those who have not lived through such times.

The Wola suburb was the first area to fall – where 8 000 citizens were killed. 40 000 were killed when Ochota fell to the Germans on 11 August. Desperate messages were sent from the AK via the

Polish Government in Exile requesting more weapons and equipment. Because of the distance Warsaw was from the Allied bases attempts to supply the besieged city from the West were largely unsuccessful. The only practical way of supplying help was from the Soviet Union, and this Stalin refused to do. As mentioned earlier, correspondence between Churchill and Stalin during August 1944 shows that he begged Stalin for help in this matter but that his pleas fell on deaf ears. Stalin revealed his true feelings in this matter when he replied to Churchill (communication no. 313, 5.8.44 in *Correspondence Between Churchill and Stalin*)

"I think the information given to you by the Poles is greatly exaggerated and unreliable ... The AK consists of a few Detachments misnamed Divisions. They have neither guns, aircraft or tanks. I cannot imagine Detachments like these taking Warsaw which the Germans are defending with four Armoured Divisions including the Herman Goering Division."

Despite further pleas from Churchill on 12 August, Stalin stood by and refused to allow any help for the beleaguered Poles. He knew that he only had to do nothing to let the Poles be totally destroyed. In due course he could pose as its "liberator" and Warsaw would be his; this is in fact what happened.

The Germans began to bomb Stare Miasto on 9 August. By mid-August the food situation was dire, but still the Poles held out. Food and ammunition drops were attempted by some Allied troops but these were sporadic, unpredictable, and into the Kaminos Woods, an area outside Warsaw, so they often fell into German hands. Even those which did get through were hopelessly inadequate. Fighting became fierce, for each building, each square metre of ground. Danek, as a Liaison Officer, had been living in the sewers of Warsaw for some time; this was considered the only safe place to be by the AK (until the Germans tried to gas them out). The sewers were used as a means of communication and occasionally escape. The conditions underground were as unpleasant as may be imagined – slippery, dark, filthy, rat-infested and were such that people were sometimes driven insane by them. In the pitch black it was easy to lose one's way, so people used to travel in groups led by a guide with a torch. Sounds were distorted and as the Germans realised what was happening they sometimes threw hand grenades down manholes. A graphic account of this way of travel in given in Bor-Komorowski's account of the

Uprising. Danek lived underground at great danger to himself. Once he entered the system via a manhole in the Mokotow district (strangely only yards from where his daughter would live decades later), to emerge the other side of the river, in Praga, opposite the Transfiguration Hospital. He found Kostek in the hospital, and he immediately gave Danek an anti-malarial quinine injection. Unfortunately Danek experienced a severe reaction to the injection and nearly died!

As the Stare Miasto was fighting for its life, Kostek was a virtual prisoner in the hospital so on 24 August he started to write his memoirs. He comments on the scene from his window:-

"... I see smoke and explosions in Warsaw and I can hear the sounds of the battle. The dominating noise is from a terrible mine-thrower, called a "Marrillo" by those in the hospital. Instead of an explosion there is a sound like someone dragging a heavy wardrobe across a floor. Two days ago a bomb exploded and 32 people were injured. The building where I am sitting on the fourth floor is shaking. From time to time German planes fly overhead to bomb the Stare Miasto. There are not as many fires now, everything has already been burned down. The fifth anniversary of my call-up papers makes me feel even more melancholy, if that is possible... I think that on the whole the idea is to be busy, to do something to forget the hard times of the present and the depressing future. The past has also been bad – we have not been lucky in this war. But up to now we had always been a subject [ie felt some control over events] and not as now, an object, a rat in a hole waiting to be hit by a blow from an outsider."

Meanwhile the awful battle continued in Stare Miasto. When the sound of firing from the bank of the Vistula could be clearly heard by the people on 25 August, it was decided to evacuate the Stare Miasto via the sewers. The order for the evacuation was given on 31 August and the whole population of the Stare Miasto disappeared in a carefully organised operation down a single manhole, to emerge in a safer area of the city. During the night of 1 September 1 500 people used this escape route.

The Germans were still attempting to hold Praga against the advancing Russians, whose troops included captured Poles conscripted into the Red Army. One of the officers was General Berling, who had been with General Anders in the USSR but who decided to remain in the Soviet Union and join the Red Army. The

Red Army finally entered Praga on 15 September although fighting continued well after that. Nine days later Kostek was in the middle of operating on a patient when the hospital suffered a direct hit – killing the patient and most of the others in the theatre instantly. Kostek himself was very badly wounded. His arm was almost blown off, but due to the fact that he was the only doctor in the hospital no one was able to save him, and he died a few hours later on 24 September 1944. His courage, and unstinting work for the freedom of Poland, was still remembered over half a century later among Varsovians. Although not apparently mentioned by name in official accounts of the Uprising he was awarded the honorary title "Bohater" [hero] for his part in the war. He is buried in the military cemetery of Powazki in Warsaw.

There is a postscript to this sad ending. Each year, on 1 November, All Saints Day, it is the custom in Poland for families to visit the graves of their loved ones and to place candles and flowers on the tomb. It is an extraordinary sight to see every cemetery crowded with people on that day and the dull November day brightened with thousands of bouquets and burning candles. During the few days beforehand the family visits the grave to tidy it up. Danek and his family undertook to perform this annual task for Kostek's grave, but every year when they came to do this, they found that someone had already been there before them and the grave was neat and tidy. Who could be doing this? One year Danek decided to find out, so for several days he hid behind a nearby tree and kept watch. In due course, someone did appear and set to work on tidying the grave – it was none other than Dr Barr, the doctor with whom Kostek had become very close during the war. Each year, for at least 45 years and possibly longer, this woman has been faithfully performing this act of devotion for the man she loved – her own husband had never returned from the Soviet Union. She did once visit us in London. I can just remember an elegant woman with very white hair, but I was far too small to know the real story behind the phrase "friend of the family".

The Uprising continued in the face of overwhelming odds as district after district fell to the Germans – Srodmiescie on 1 September, Powisle on 6, Mokotow on 26 and Zoliborz on 30 September. The Poles finally capitulated to the Germans on 2 October. The terms of the capitulation stipulated that all AK

193

members and other resistance units would be treated as POWs according to the Geneva Convention of 1929. By the surrender some 20 000 AK members had been killed and 225 000 civilians and the entire population was to be evacuated. 550 000 were taken to a concentration camp at Pruszkow (ironically very near to the hospital where Zosia was a patient) and 150 000 were deported to Germany. The pre-war population of Warsaw had been 1 407 000, so this evacuation left Warsaw empty. The retreating Germans set about systematically razing Warsaw to the ground. They dynamited almost all the remaining buildings but had not quite completed the task when the Red Army finally entered Warsaw on 17 January 1945. What the Russians found was a scale of destruction hard to take in. It was a ghost capital; there was not a single inhabitant left. 93% of all dwellings were destroyed or damaged beyond repair, in the Stare Miasto 94% of all the buildings were destroyed. Overall, 90% of hospitals, 90% of the city and state buildings, all railway stations, telephone exchanges, road and railway bridges were blown up or otherwise demolished. The exact figures vary according to the source.

However, once the war was over, reconstruction began almost immediately. The Soviets claimed to be the liberators of Warsaw and they did indeed help to reconstruct the city, but at a terrible price. For the Poles realised that the Soviets were intending to turn Poland into a satellite state of the Soviet Union and that she would effectively be run from Moscow. The AK had lost its influence after the Uprising and officially disbanded in January 1945, the same month as Moscow officially recognised the pro-communist Lublin Provisional Government of the Polish Republic as the official government, henceforth ignoring the Polish Government in Exile in London. Soon other Allies followed suit.

Joachim remained in Radom after the war, moving back to the flat they had occupied before 1939. Soon after that he returned to the flat in Zoliborz, miraculously still standing. The destruction was terrible. Joachim, now in his 70th year, had lost his wife and his elder son. His daughter was in hospital and his younger son abroad. He was effectively left alone. Joachim went through all their remaining possessions to see what was left. The family fortune had long gone we do not know how. Most of the family documents were safe and there were some photograph albums – with some pictures ripped out by the Gestapo during their

rigorous searches. However, that which he had held most dear –
his family – were all but destroyed, and what would the future
hold under the Soviets? Gone was the old, comfortable way of
life, surrounded by family and friends. Gone was the prospect of a
gentle old age to look forward to – the house in southern Poland
would never now need to be built. He would not now be eagerly
following the career of his surgeon son or have his wife to comfort
him in his advancing years. And what had happened to his
younger son? It was truly a sad time of grieving for him. Indeed,
such situations were being repeated all over Poland at this time.

A fitting epitaph for this chapter of the family – and Polish –
history is an extract from one of the last broadcasts from Warsaw
to London, quoted in Davies *God's Playground* Vol II p. 479.:-

"This is the stark truth. We were treated worse than Hitler's
satellites, worse than Italy, Romania, Finland. May God, who is
just, pass judgement on the terrible injustices suffered by the
Polish nation, and may He punish accordingly all who are guilty.

Your heroes are the soldiers whose only weapons against tanks,
planes and guns were their revolvers and bottles filled with petrol.
Your heroes are the women who tended the wounded and carried
messages under fire, who cooked in bombed and ruined cellars to
feed children and adults, and who soothed and comforted the
dying. Your heroes are the children who went on quietly playing
among the smouldering ruins. These are the people of Warsaw.

Immortal is the nation that can muster such universal heroism.
For those who have died have conquered, and those who live on
will fight on, and again bear witness that Poland lives when the
Poles live."

CHAPTER 9

Afterwards

At the end of the War the future for many thousands of Poles was extremely uncertain. British attitudes towards the Poles had been ambivalent throughout the War, especially after the high point reached in 1941. When the USSR joined the Allies in 1941 Soviet attitudes helped to reduce sympathy for the Polish cause. Ignorance of Polish history led the British to consider Poles to be intransigent and unrealistic in her dealings with the Soviets. Confusion and ambivalence was particularly marked with respect to the Eastern Border Question. Churchill felt obliged to help the Poles only out of a sense of duty. The Press reinforced these attitudes in 1944 when much was made of the desertions from the Polish Armed Forces in the Middle East, especially of the Jews who deserted in Palestine. The British public were led to believe that all was well in post-war socialist Poland and that the vast majority of Poles would freely return to their homeland. It was thought that to date 30 000 Poles had opted to return to Poland, leaving approximately 160 000 who were stateless and homeless. The Polish Government in Exile, the legitimate and internationally recognised representative of the Polish people since the start of the War, had been passed over in favour of the pro-Communist Provisional Polish Government of National Unity by the Soviets in January 1945 and by the Allies on 6 July 1945. Of the 112 000 men in the Second Polish Corps at the end of 1945 only 7 officers and 14 200 men applied for repatriation, 8 700 being men who joined after hostilities had ended. Only 310 of those who had come out of the Soviet Union chose to return.

The Poles were still in a state of considerable shock in 1945. Contrary to British belief, they had not voluntarily abandoned their homeland; in fact it had been snatched from them and occupied by a foreign power. The political situation was such that many, especially those from Eastern Poland whose home no longer lay in Poland but in the Soviet Union, were simply unable to return home. The Poles felt betrayed by the Teheran, Yalta and Potsdam Conferences which allocated Poland to Stalin's sphere of influence without consulting any Poles for their opinions. On 20 March 1946 the British Government announced their earnest hope that most Poles abroad would return to Poland. There was widespread disapproval of any plans for large numbers of Poles to settle in Britain; indeed plans, later abandoned, were outlined to deploy the Polish troops in post-war Germany. Both the Polish Government in Exile and the Polish Armed Forces were an embarrassment to the British Government and the issue of what to do with them was the subject of much debate. From the British point of view the formation of a Polish Resettlement Corps followed by demobilisation was a generous one as much help would be given to help Poles settle down in their new country.

If this happened there would no longer be a distinct, identifiable force capable of continuing the fight for free Poland, and Poles would therefore have to abandon all hopes of a free Poland in the foreseeable future. In May 1946 General Anders heard rumours about the transfer of the Second Polish Corps to Britain. On 21 May he was summoned to London to be told of the plans to form a Polish Resettlement Corps. His opinion was not sought and he felt he had no choice but to agree. This decision was announced in the House of Commons next day. How were the Poles expected to respond to behaviour which amounted to a betrayal on all fronts? How could General Anders keep up the morale and a spark of hope alive among the Polish troops when he heard of the British intentions?

The Polish Resettlement Corps (PRC) officially came into being on 13 September 1946, by chance the same day that Witold and Francis arrived in Britain, landing in Glasgow before being transferred to camps elsewhere, and by the end of October all the Second Polish Corps had been transferred from Italy to Britain. On 27 September 1946 Warsaw publicly withdrew General Anders' Polish citizenship (and by implication every other member of the Polish Armed Forces and PRC), citing the 1921 Constitution of Poland – which had in fact been superceded by the 1935 Constitution. This put Poles into even more of a dilemma – *wracac czy nie wracac* – to return or not to return: on the one hand they lost their Polish citizenship by joining the PRC and on the other they were disowned by the Polish Government in Exile if they returned. Even among those who chose to remain abroad there was the hope that one day they would return especially if they had loved ones in Poland. Was all the suffering, the fighting, the hoping against all odds worthwhile if in the end they had lost everything? Europe was carrying out a policy of appeasement to Stalin and apparently ignoring the wishes of Poles regarding their future. Poland's borders had moved 150 miles to the West and her total land area decreased by a sixth. More than one in five of the entire population of pre-war Poland had been killed, a higher proportion than in any other country. According to figures cited by Rozenbaum in Wiles, T., for every 1000 Polish citizens, 220 were killed in the war, compared with 108 in every 1000 in Yugoslavia, 40 in the USSR, 15 in France and Czechoslovakia, 8 in the UK and 1.4 in the USA. In the end a mere 25% of all Poles abroad at the end of the War opted for repatriation. There was the question of what to do with the rest. Polish civilians were already scattered throughout the world and many decided to emigrate further. Some 20 000 decided to settle down in India, mostly in Chela, Balachedi and Kolhapaur, where the refugee camps had been. Others went to Persia, Uganda, Tanganyka, Kenya and New Zealand. Some were granted visas to USA and Canada where there were already well-established Polish communities. Others set their sights on Mexico or South America.

Approximately 160 000 Poles enlisted in the PRC when it came into being. They were housed in military-style camps (265 of them) spread throughout Britain. The Second Polish Corps were allocated to 160 camps. They were given two-year commissions unless they found suitable civilian employment before that time. Meanwhile they were enlisted as part of the British Armed Forces and were under British Army Regulations. The aim of the PRC was to help members of the Polish Armed Forces settle down into civilian life either in Britain or elsewhere if they wished to emigrate further. Pending civil employment members of the PRC were usefully employed in military tasks or reconstruction work. They received British Army rates of pay. They were given opportunities for learning a trade, the English language and the British way of life. Some universities gave special consideration to Polish students in particular faculties, for example, the Faculty of Medicine and Veterinary Science at Edinburgh, Law at Oxford or Architecture at Liverpool in order to help make up for lost opportunities in education. Employment was allocated either by "loaning" Poles to carry out work of national importance –

198

clearing bomb sites, harvesting, etc, or by individual release to a job considered suitable by the Ministry of Labour. As a group the Poles soon made a good impression on the local population by their willingness to work hard and to support themselves and their families, who were allowed to join them until Poland's borders were effectively closed in 1947.

When Witold and Francis arrived in Britain in the autumn of 1946 they were initially allocated to a camp in Codford, near Warminster, Wiltshire, but were soon moved to the nearby Longbridge Deverill camp after a few months. Witold's Identity Card showing him to be a member of the Polish Armed Forces is dated 9 November 1946. Other documents show that he had been awarded, though not necessarily received, his service medals by this time. The Monte Cassino Cross was awarded on 22 November 1945 and the three British medals (1939-45 Star, the Italy Star and the War Medal 1939-45) on 27 December 1945. He also received the Polish War Service Medal at this time. By a strange twist of fate Witold was awarded the prestigious Silver Cross of Merit with Swords on 31 August 1945 for his work in training the Polish Army in the Middle East.Thirteen years before Joachim had received the Gold Cross of Merit in such different circumstances; the irony would not have been lost on Witold. It was rare to award the Silver Cross to one of such lowly rank as Witold (he was a 2nd Lieutenant at the time) and it is a tribute to his exceptional qualities. He was also an extremely modest man who never wore his medals and never talked about them; in fact he had been sent the wrong version of the Silver Cross (the civilian version) and never corrected it. For him his medals were no compensation for all that he had lost through the War.

Witold and Francis began to adjust to life in the PRC Camp. Together they struggled to make sense of their shattered world and to plan for the future. Witold thought that he would emigrate to South America but in the meantime time hung heavy on their hands. The tasks they were allocated were very tedious so to while away the time they decided to have some English lessons. Witold had learned English at school and was a gifted linguist (he listed English, French and Russian as his languages) as Joachim was. A local clergyman, Canon Meyrick, gave them English lessons. When Witold and Francis were told that they were moving Camp to Longbridge Deverill, they wanted to continue with their

English lessons, so Canon Meyrick wrote to the Rector, a Mr Lance, asking if he would be able to give the lessons.

Mr Lance himself was heavily committed but a young teacher, Rosemary Edwards, was moving into digs in the Rectory with him and his wife. He asked her if she would be prepared to take on these two pupils, and despite the misgivings of her colleagues, she agreed to meet them. Francis, Witold and Rosemary met for the first time on 12 March 1947 and seemed to get on well from the outset. Two weeks later, on 26 March, Witold received his Discharge Certificate from the Polish Armed Forces and was officially commissioned in the PRC. He still gave his place of birth as Radom, as on previous documents. He wanted to look for work, but in common with many professional Poles he knew it would be hard to find a job which used his vocational training. He was luckier than some as his Diploma was relatively recent (1936). For those Poles over the age of forty life was much harder as their qualifications were a mixture of Russian, German or Austrian documents. Also in many cases the relevant pieces of paper had not survived the chaos of the war so there was no written proof of their qualification. This group proved the hardest to place in work and many were forced to take unskilled jobs to earn a living. By June 1947 20 000 Poles had been found jobs. By the end of the year only 38 000 remained unemployed out of a total of 108 000 registrations.

Witold and Francis found their English lessons and growing friendship with Rosemary a welcome diversion from the tedium of Camp life. As well as the serious business of adjusting to the British way of life – the order and "neatness" of Britain and the British Sunday were often cited as examples of novelties to adjust to – Francis and Witold participated in local village life. Francis, the more extrovert, met Marjorie his future wife at a village dance so the friends became a foursome. By November 1947 Witold and Rosemary were becoming close, but Witold was suddenly transferred to Reading. He also had a spell at Bruntingthorpe, near Lutterworth, Leicestershire, which he hated. Just after Christmas Witold spent a few days with Rosemary and her parents in Shaftesbury, Dorset, the first of many weekends they would spend together. There was also an old family friend from pre-war days, a Mrs Zaleska, living in Westward Ho! with whom Witold also stayed sometimes. She used to think of him as her grandson so she used to make a fuss of him and spoil him. He wrote to his father about Rosemary; Joachim responded by writing to her in March 1948. In May 1948 Rosemary and Witold were invited to Clovelly to stay with her aunt for a few days.

At the camp in Reading Witold was supervising the demobilisation of the Polish troops – an exceptionally tedious task. He was by now beginning to adjust more easily to British life. Rosemary and he spent as many weekends as possible together, Rosemary staying in a nearby hotel in Reading. Witold was having problems finding work – it seems that ideas of emigration to S. America had been abandoned by now – he sent off approximately fifty job application forms and letters but nothing seemed to materialise and he was now into the second year of his commission. On New Year's Day 1949 Francis and Marjorie were married in the tiny village church in Longbridge Deverill, Wiltshire, and soon moved to West London where Francis had found a job and Marjorie continued her career marking exam papers.

Witold was on the move as well – firstly to Lutterworth briefly and by February 1949 he was staying with friends in Challoner Mansions, Kensington. On March 10 he went for another interview, this time with Balfour Beatty, the electrical construction company. Those who interviewed him were undecided as to whether he would make a suitable employee, but he had a strong advocate in a member of the interviewing panel, a Mr Marr, who saw his potential and was in favour of taking him on. One week later Witold was formally offered the job at Balfour Beatty, to start immediately. He was to remain with the firm until he retired 27 years later, moving with them from offices in the City to Croydon following the merger with BICC. Witold's relief at getting a job must have been enormous and he thankfully resigned his commission with the PRC, with effect from 25 March 1949.

Settling down to a "normal" job for the first time for ten years was difficult. The harsh world of work made few concessions to the foreigner with the unpronounceable name and the pay was poor. Witold moved out of Zygmunt and Rosemary Nowakowski's flat in Challoner Mansions and rented a tiny flat in Courtfield Gardens, Kensington. The new job was tedious but Witold soon acquired a reputation as a steady and reliable worker, a reputation which enabled him to escape redundancy some years later. Life was beginning to look a little more hopeful. He had a job, his own flat, a girlfriend. He would often spend his evenings walking round West London, exploring the area. Several friends from pre-war days had also found their way to London so he was beginning to renew acquaintances and to discover other people's experiences of the war. Irenka, for example, arrived from North Africa with her new husband. She was the daughter of an old family friend. Before the war her father had been a judge, the Vice President of the Law Court in Lwow. He perished in Katyn. Her first husband shot himself and her son, aged 12 (born only two years before Rosemary) was murdered by the Gestapo. When Witold and Irenka met there was much weeping for the life that was lost and much catching up to do. Witold would sometimes visit the Polish Hearth, a club in Kensington, but he disliked evenings spent in morbid reminiscing enhanced by large quantities of vodka.

Witold and Rosemary became engaged at Easter 1952. In order to save some money to get married, a friend recommended that Witold took on extra work preparing charts and drawings for lecturers at the Royal Marsden Hospital. Once he came home from his day job in the City he would set to work on this work, often continuing until well into the night. The work continued until 1960, when the demand ceased. To avoid the complications of the time in a Roman Catholic marrying a Church of England person, they were married on 7 February 1953 in a very quiet ceremony at Kensington Register Office. Witold was almost 42 and his bride fourteen years younger. Like many couples at that time they could not afford to spend much money on the occasion, so Rosemary wore a black suit (the subject of many family jokes in later years). The honeymoon was short – five days in Seaton, Devon – then Rosemary moved in to the minute flat in Courtfield Gardens.

In due course their first child was expected so Witold and Rosemary moved on 6 March 1954 to a small house with a garden suitable for growing vegetables in Greenford, Middlesex, and their daughter was born in July. Her arrival delighted not only the proud parents but was especially precious for Joachim, who had long given up hope of grandchildren. In fact, Witold had been concerned about his father for some time, as he was by now almost eighty years old and becoming much more frail. The situation in Poland was not easy; the borders had been effectively closed since

1947. The crisis came when Joachim's faithful maid, who had looked after the family for so many years, died and there was no one who could look after him. Fortunately this also coincided with the general political thaw in Eastern Europe in 1956 so travel became possible in a very limited way.

For some time Witold had benn making enquiries about the formalities he had to undergo enable Joachim to emigrate to Britain and to spend his last years with Witold and his family. Finally, on 2 October 1956 Witold and Francis went to Heathrow Airport to meet the flight arriving from Warsaw. They found an elderly gentleman with a long white beard who seemed lost. In his hand he was clutching a pile of cards written in English on one side and Polish in the other, in Witold's writing. One said "My name is JOACHIM CHRZCZONOWICZ. Please help me find my son." Recognising his father, Witold fell into his arms and they wept together. They had last met seventeen years before in the summer of 1939 – and such a lot of water had passed under the bridge since then. Their world, their family, had literally fallen apart, the rest of the family dead or killed, their country once more occupied. Joachim knew that he had now left his native land for ever, that at the age of eighty this was the last exile of his life. After a lifetime of exile and travel – to Russia, to Siberia and back to Poland – this was to be the final chapter. There was so much to catch up on, so much to talk about. Joachim brought over as many of the family treasures as he could – a porcelain dinner service, the wall tapestries which had hung on the walls of their flats, books, the family silver monogrammed AK (for Anna Kokoulina), monogrammed linen sheets, what could be salvaged of the photograph albums and family documents, the precious seal of the Pilawa *herb*. There were his and Anna's wedding rings, a ruby and diamond pendant which had belonged to Anna and a pair of diamond earrings which had belonged to Zosia (These were later made into finger rings and one became my engagement ring in due course).

More importantly there were the stories – the accounts of life during the war, the story of Anna's last years, of Zosia's illness and death, a subject which Joachim found so upsetting that he was not able to tell the story for some years. Joachim needed to tell his son about Kostek's part in the terrible events in Warsaw in 1944 and of how life had been in Warsaw under the Communists. They needed to keep alive the memories they had of the family in happier times, recognising, too, that some memories were too painful to dwell on.

When Joachim first came to London he was able to get out of the house and visit old friends who had settled in London. There was a distant cousin who had settled in South London whom he visited sometimes. He also read a great deal, keeping in touch with events in Poland by reading papers and journals sent by friends in Warsaw. There were also various papers published in Britain or France which gave a different perspective, unfettered by censorship. The leading literary newspaper published in London was *Wiadamosci*. Joachim's eye was caught by an article published on 13 January 1957. This vividly described the countryside and lifestyle of Polish *szlachta* in Lithuania and Byelorussia at the turn of the century and it instantly took Joachim back to his very early childhood. He wrote to the editor in response giving his personal recollections and this reply was duly published. Taken together the two articles are the best, indeed the only, source material for Joachim's early years and have been extensively drawn upon for information.

By the end of the year there was another baby on the way so as the house was getting crowded Witold and Rosemary went house-hunting again. In February 1958 the family moved again, this time to Eastcote, a Middlesex suburb between Harrow and Uxbridge. Their second child, a boy, was born in July 1958.

Witold continued working for Balfour Beatty but he was concerned that he was still technically a Stateless Person without citizenship. All he possessed was his Alien's Registration Certificate. So he decided to apply for naturalisation, which was granted on 7 April 1960. His place of birth is given as Radom, Poland, as had appeared on all official documents since September 1939. However, there was in existence an English translation of his Birth Certificate dated 1 September 1956 clearly giving his place of birth as Usole, Irkutsk. Presumably other documents were sufficient for obtaining the Certificate of Nationality

Money was still scarce for the family so when the income from the chart designs for the Royal Marsden Hospital dried up, Witold was fortunate to find an alternative. He decided to take up translating work, translating Russian technical journals and books into English. The work started in 1960, but it was extremely difficult and tedious to do. The text was peppered with socialist propaganda and the technical standards were on average 10-15 years behind those of the West. Understandably, there was not a huge market for this kind of work, nor was it particularly well paid. However, the work continued until 1984. Witold and Rosemary worked as a team, Witold translating and Rosemary editing and typing up the manuscript. The earnings from their second book translation paid for the first holiday together for the family. As relaxation Witold cultivated his beloved garden, growing most of the family's vegetables and some of the fruit as well. The early 1960s was a period when large numbers of books about the Second World War were published and these he read with keen interest. He was eager to have a more complete picture of the events of the war than his own experience had given him.

Joachim's health was declining steadily by this time. By 1963 he needed extensive care which Witold and Rosemary struggled to provide, not an easy task with two small children and Rosemary's own mother to look after as well. In October 1965 Joachim was admitted to hospital where he died of pneumonia a week after his 90th birthday, on 30 October. So ended an extraordinary life, which began as a child of Polish gentry in rural Lithuania, then study in St Petersburg, exile in Siberia, return to Poland. He saw his family grow up, then came the tragedy of the Second World War with its losses and uncertainties, and finally peace in his declining years with his remaining son – at the cost of a final exile. He was cremated in Middlesex. A memorial service was held on 17 November 1965 at the Carmelite church on Krakowskie Przedmiescie in Warsaw.

Witold and Rosemary calculated that they could afford a holiday abroad on the strength of their earnings from the Russian translating. In 1966 Witold, Rosemary and the two children, by now twelve and eight, set off for the Adriatic coast of Italy. The children and Rosemary had a marvellous adventure; Witold was revisiting his wartime haunts from over twenty years before when he was taking part in the Italian Campaign. They saw Ravenna, where Witold and Francis had been billeted for a time, Urbino, the Rubicon, and the wonderful Italian countryside which Witold loved so much. For Witold the area was full of memories of comrades in the 5 KDP, some of whom perished at Monte Cassino, and of his experiences of the mid 1940s.

The question of Witold's incorrectly listed place of birth as stated in official documents had always made him feel uneasy and he felt he now wanted to put the record straight. The original reasons for giving in 1939 at the time of his arrest by the Soviets his place of birth as Radom, Poland, were twofold: to save his own life by clarifying that he was Polish (as the Soviets would have considered him Russian) and to protect his family. Now, almost 30 years later he did not need to be so cautious, but the myth had been carried forward on each official document. In 1967 he sought the advice of the family solicitor, who after careful enquiries gave the following advice: as he had given false information on his passport application form he was thereby technically liable for a term of imprisonment; as he had no evil intent this could be ignored if he never revealed his Siberian birthplace. Thus the fiction of the Radom birthplace was perpetuated until his death; not even his children knew the real story. This explanation solved some mysteries: why Witold was so reticent about his Siberian childhood (he never even admitted that his mother was Russian; I was told this by my Polish cousins in 1990), and the improbable explanation that the family returned to Poland for the birth of each child. He would never show his children his Birth Certificate, using a variety of excuses not to do so. Some inconsistencies remain however, for example, how the existence of the 1956 translation of the Birth Certificate fits into the picture.

With the death of Joachim Witold became the legal owner of the plot of land which his father had bought over thirty years previously for his retirement. After the War Witold had resolved never to return to Poland as he would have found the memories and the changes too difficult to cope with. So he realised that he would never be able to use this piece of land and as there was an interested buyer he decided to sell it. The son of Joachim's great friend from student days, Klukowski, was an artist and his wife was very interested in the land. Witold decided to make the land over legally as a gift to his cousin Zosia in Gdansk, so that she could sell the land and have the money from it as she was struggling to live on a tiny pension. This arrangement suited everyone and so the deal went ahead and the Deed of Gift was completed in February 1968 (and interestingly gave Witold's place of birth as Usole, Irkutsk).

By the late 1960s life had settled into a peaceful routine for

Witold. He had his day job and was now an Associate Member of the Institute of Electrical Engineers (and would eventually become a full Member). He had his job as a Russian technical translator. There was a good sized garden to cultivate and a well-stocked local library for reading on a variety of topics. There were his Polish friends from before and during the War, although he did not enjoy Old Boy Reunions. His children were growing up, one destined for university and the other for a career in the Civil Service. His experiences and wounds of the war he kept mostly to himself, locked deep within. The impression he gave to others was of an extremely shy man who expertly hid his feelings. Even his closest friends, such as Stan Harknett, who knew him for forty years, would say that he hardly knew him. He had nightmares about the war and he suffered flashbacks for the rest of his life. Apparently innocent events could trigger these – for example the Russian folk song *Kalinka* took him straight back to the Camps and a prisoner who played the tune constantly all day. Once when the children put up a tent in the garden and wanted him to crawl inside it he panicked and became both tearful and vehement in his refusal. The sight of hair clippings at the barbers brought back scenes of compulsory shaving in the Camps. He wrestled with the issue of how much Polish culture to teach his children. There was no nearby Polish Church or Social Club so the children did not attend the Saturday School which was the experience of so many first generation Poles. Both were taught Polish at home and certain Polish words and phrases slipped into the family vocabulary. He could sometimes be persuaded to show the family albums, but few photos of his Russian childhood survived. Questions about his past were usually met with a philosophical "Well, you know ... " thus indicating that further enquiry would be fruitless. Rosemary tried hard to persuade him to write his memoirs, but to no avail. The family knew that his past was horrifying and unimaginably painful.

Current thinking encourages victims to talk about their suffering and to express their feelings. Witold was of the generation of Poles (and other groups of victims) whose experiences were so unspeakable that they felt that only those who had undergone similar suffering could understand what they had been through. The rest of the world often regarded such accounts with disbelief or hostility so it was felt better to contain the experiences within.

The first accounts of the Holocaust to reach the West were greeted with disbelief on the grounds that no human being could behave in such a way towards their fellows; it was only after the war when the Allies liberated the Camps that the full extent of the horror became apparent. It is the cruellest irony of all to have lived through such experiences and survived and then to be told that the whole experience was exaggerated or invented. More than one survivor committed suicide as a result of other people's disbelief. To talk about the terrible events and to relive the horror was a course few felt able to contemplate, so it is understandable that the vast majority of people kept silent.

It was a great joy to Witold when the political situation eased enough in Poland for some of his friends and relatives still in Poland to come to Britain on visits. Stefcia, and much later her daughter and son in law Anna and Wieslaw paid visits as did Dr Barr, Kostek's faithful admirer. Emil Skulski, Witold's companion of the Camps, had emigrated to the USA in the 1950s, but they still kept in touch by letter, as did Zygmunt and Rosemary Nowakowski, by now in Canada. But Witold was probably most pleased to see Danek when he came over on business trips, and in due course his children Wojtek and Joasia.

In 1973 and 1975, not long before his retirement in 1976, Witold was asked by Balfour Beatty to oversee a project of theirs near Basra, in Iraq. So in another twist of fate Witold was again revisiting the scenes of his 5 KDP Army life in Iraq; it must have been a strange experience for him to go back to Iraq for that three month spell. After retirement Witold continued with the translating until 1980. He spent much time gardening, reading and visiting London. He took on one or two private pupils for Russian or Polish lessons and kept in touch with his old friends. He remained physically fit, although by the late 1980s was beginning to show signs of Altzheimer's Disease. Together with most Poles he was hugely relieved when on 26 March 1990 the Soviets finally admitted responsibility for the Katyn massacre in an article published in *Moscow News* (Gilbert, *Atlas of Russian History* p.159) – almost fifty years after it had happened. However, when communism toppled in the Soviet Union in August 1991 his delight knew no bounds. It was as if a dreadful chapter in his life had closed, that he could now die at peace having witnessed the end of a system which had destroyed everything he loved and held dear. His last few years were ones of gentle decline and he died peacefully in hospital on 23 July 1993 at the age of 82, the only one of Joachim's three children to live to old age. He was cremated locally, expressing no wish even for his ashes to be returned to Poland.

His story was unique, as all our stories are, and yet thousands of Poles and indeed other exiles will find resonances in this story. This was an ordinary family involuntarily caught up in the seismic changes of history which have affected the world, both over the centuries and more especially during the last hundred years. It is a story of how politics and history shape each other and what this means in affecting the lives of ordinary men and women. It also poses the question – by understanding the mistakes of the past, can we avoid repeating them in the future? Sadly, it would appear not as we can look around the world stage and see the same tragedies played out today. It is as if people's cruelty to each other is part of the human condition – and maybe this potential is present in all of us. It is also a story celebrating the triumph of the human spirit over apparently impossible odds, of people who refused to give up hoping and proof that not even the most oppressive regime can destroy the human soul.

BIBLIOGRAPHY

Anders, W. *An Army in Exile,* reprinted Nashville, Tenn, 1981

Anon., *Okupacja i medycyna* publ. Ksiazka i Wiedza, Warsaw 1977

Anon., *The Dark Side of the Moon,* preface by T. S. Eliot, London 1946

Armstrong, T. *Russian Settlement in the North* Cambridge University Press 1965

Ascherson, N. *The Struggles for Poland* Michael Joseph 1987

Beable, W.H. *Commercial Russia* Constable, London 1918

Begin, M. *White Nights,* transl. K. Kaplan, Steimatzky's Agency, Jerusalem, 1957

Bialoszewski, M. *A Memoir of the Warsaw Uprising* NW University Press 1977

Bor-Komorowski, T. *The Secret Army* London 1950

Broido, S. *Gorod na Vitime* Irkutskoe Kruzhnoe Izdatelstvo,1959.

Bruce, G. *The Warsaw Uprising of 1944* Rupert Hart-Davies 1972

Brus, A.(et al) *Zeslanie i katorga na Syberii* PWN, Warsaw 1992

Children's Friend Annual 1897

Ciechanowski, J. *The Warsaw Uprising of 1944,* London, Cambridge 1974

Clarke, W. *The Lost Fortune of the Tsars* Weidenfield & Nichilson London 1994

Correspondence between Churchill & Stalin vol. I 1941-5 Moscow 1957

Conquest, R. *The Great Terror* MacMillan, 1973

Council for the Preservation of Monuments to the Resistance & Martyrdom *Scenes of Fighting & Martyrdom Guide to the War Years in Poland 1939-45,*Warsaw 1966

The Crime of Katyn, preface by W. Anders, Polish Cultural Foundation, London 1965

Crowley, D. *National Style and the Nation-State* Manchester University Press 1992

Dallin, D.J. & Nicholaevsky, B. I. *Forced Labour in the Soviet Union* London 1948

Davies, N. *God's Playground* (2 Vols.) OUP 1981

Davies, N. *Heart of Europe* OUP 1984

Deakin, F. *Brutal Friendship* Weidenfield & Nicholson 1962

Devlin, J. *Shostakovich* Short Biographies, Novello 1983

de Windt, H. *The New Siberia* London 1896

Dobson, C. & Miller, J. *The Day We Almost Bombed Moscow - The Allied War in Russia 1918-20* Hodder & Stoughton 1986

Edelman, N. *Lunin, adiutant* PIW, Warsaw 1976

Edwards, S. *The Polish Captivity* 1863

Evans, G. *Tannenburg 1410 / 1914* Hamish Hamilton 1970

Fic, V. The *Bolsheviks & the Czech Legions* New Delhi Abirov 1978

Fitzlyon, K.& Browning, T. *Before the Revolution* Penguin 1977

Footman, D. *The Civil War in Russia* Faber & Faber 1961

Fitzgibbon, L. *The Katyn Massacre* Corgi Books 1977

Forsyth, J. *A History of the Peoples of Siberia* CUP 1992

Foster-Fraser, J. *The Real Siberia* Cassell & Co 1912

Garlinski, J. *Poland in the Second World War* 1985

Gilbert, M. *An Atlas of Russian History* J. M. Dent 1972

Gilbert, M. *The Boys* Phoenix, 1996

Gradosielski, J. *5 KDP Saperz w walce 1941-5* London 1985

Great Soviet Encyclopaedia 3rd Edn, transl. MacMillan, NY 1973

Halecki, O. *History of Poland* Routledge & Keegan Paul 1978

Hanson, J. *The Civilian Population and the Warsaw Uprising of 1944* Cambridge 1984

Hapgood, D. & Richardson, D. *Monte Cassino* Congdon & Weed NY 1984

Herbasz Armorials:-

Boniecki, A. *Herbarz polski* Vol III 1900

Herbarz polski Vol I Lwow 1855

Niesiecki i Bobrowicz *Herbarz polski* Lipsk 1841

Paprocki, B. *Herby rycerstwa polskiego* Krakow 1858

Pilawa Herb author & date unknown

Uruski, Kosinski, Wloderski Vol II Warsaw 1902

Herling, G. *A World Apart* New York 1951

Jackman, A. *Russian Mines* 1916

Jefferson, R. L. *Roughing it in Siberia* 1897

Johnson, A. *Consolidated Goldfields – a Centenary Portrait* Wiedenfield & Nicholson 1978

Kapuscinski, R. *Imperium* transl. K. Glowczewska Granta Books London 1994

Karski, J. *Story of a Secret State* Hodder & Stoughton 1945

Kennan, G. *Siberia & the Exile System* University of Chicago 1964

Kochan, L. & Abraham, R. *The Making of Modern Russia* Penguin 1983

Komarnicki, T. *The Rebirth of the Polish Republic* London 1957

Ksiega Pamiatkowa inzynierow technologow Polakow w Petersburgu Warsaw 1933

Kudryatsev, V.N. *Historia Irkutska* publ Irkutsk 1971 edn.

Leslie, R.F. *The History of Poland Since 1863* CUP 1980

Lincoln, W.B. *Conquest of a Continent* Jonathon Cape 1994

Lincoln, W.B. *Red Victory* Jonathon Cape 1989

Linklater, E. *The Campaign in Italy* HMSO reprinted 1977

Litewski Metryka [National Archives of Grand Duchy of Lithuania] Vols 6,8,etc, 1993-,   Vilnius

Maclean, F. *Portrait of the Soviet Union* Weidenfield & Nicholson London 1988

Majdalany, F. *Cassino, Portrait of a Battle* Longmans 1957
Massie, R. K. *The Romanovs – The Final Chapter* Jonathon Cape 1995
Mawdsley, I. *The Russian Civil War* Boston 1987
Medvedev, S. *Irkutsk na Pochtovikh Otkritkakh* Moscow Galart
    Publishers 1996
Mining Manual, years 1909-38 Entry: *The Lena Goldfields Ltd*
Mowat, F. *The Siberians* Readers Union 1973
Moynahan, B. *The Russian Century* Chatto & Windus 1994
Nansen, F. *Through Siberia – a Land in the Making* 1914
Norem O. *Timeless Lithuania* Chicago1943
Perira, N.G. O. *White Siberia – the Politics of Civil War* McGill-Queens
    UP 1996
Pipes, R. *The Russian Revolution* Fontana Press 1990
Pipes, R. *Russia Under the Bolshevik Regime 1919-24* Harvill 1994
Pogonowski, I. *Poland – a Historical Atlas* Hippocrene Books NY 1987
Polak. W. *Christian Poland's Millenary* Hosianum, Rome 1966
Polonsky, A. *The Politics of Independant Poland 1921-39* Oxford 1972
Polski Slownik Biograficzny Vol III Krakow 1933
Portisch, H. *I Saw Siberia* London Harrap 1972
Read, C. *From Tsar to Soviets 1917-21* UCL Press 1996
Richards, D. *Modern Europe 1779-1945* Longmans 1957
Roos, H. *A History of Modern Poland* transl Foster, J.R., Eyre &
    Spottiswode 1966
Roseberry, E. *Shostakovich* Midas Books 1981
Salisbury, H. *Black Night, White Snow* Da Capo 1977
Schmitt, et al, *Poland* Univ. California 1947
Semyonov. Y. *The Conquest of Siberia* Routledge 1944
Senn. A. E. *The Emergence of Modern Lithuania* London 1959
Seroff, V.I. *Dmitri Shostakovich* Alfred Knopf NY 1947
Shamanskii, V.I.. *Usole Sibirskoe* publ. Irkutskoe Vostochno Sibirskoe
    1994
Smele, J.D. *The Civil War in Siberia* CUP 1997
Sollertinsky, D.& M. *Pages from the life of Dmitri Shostakovich* transl. G.
    Hobbs & C. Midgely Robert Hale England 1988
Solzhenitsyn, A. *Gulag Archipelago* Collins & Harvill Press 1974-7
Stephan, J.J. *The Russian Far East* Stanford 1994
St. George. G. *Siberia, the New Frontier* Hodder & Stoughton 1970
Strzembosz, T. *Oddzialy szturmow Konspiracynej Warszawej 1939-44*
    PWN, Warsaw 1983
Suchitz, A. *Poland's Contribution th the Allied Victory in World War II*
    Polish Ex-Combatants Association in GB 1995
Swain, G. *The Origins of the Russian Civil War* Longman 1996
Swianiewicz, S. *Forced Labour & Economic Development* Royal
    Institute of   International Affairs London 1965
Sword, K. *Deportation and Exile to the Soviet Union* Macmillan 1994

Sword, K. *The Formation of the Polish Community in Britain* 1939-50

Treadgold, D. *The Great Siberian Migration* Princetown, NJ 1957

Tupper, H. *To the Great Ocean* Secker & Warburg 1965

Wandycz, P. *The Lands of Partitioned Poland 1795 - 1918* Seattle 1975

Whittle, P. *One Afternoon at Mezzegra* W H Allen 1969

Wiles, T.(ed) *Poland Between the Wars:1918-1939* Indiana Univ. Polish Studies Center, Bloomington, Indiana 1989

Wright, R. & Digby, D. *Through Siberia* Hurst & Blackett London 1913

Zamoyski, A. *The Polish Way* Hippocrene Books, 1990

Zaprudnik, J. *Belarus at a Crossroads in History* Boulder, San Francisco 1993

Zawodny, J.K. *Death in the Forest* Hippocrene Books 1962

Zawodny, J.K. *Nothing but Honour – The Story of the Warsaw Uprising 1944* London 1978

Zubrzycki, J. *Soldiers and Peasants* Orbis Books, London 1988

ARTICLES

Bukchin. S. *The Singer of Lithuania at a Crossing of Nation & Tradition* 1997

Chrzczonowicz, J. *Letter to the Editor* "Wiadomosci" January 1957

Collins, D. *British Interests & Interests in Siberia 1900-22* "Revolutionary Russia" Vol.9 no2 Dec.1996 pp. 206-33

Kokoulin, V. article in "Gold & Platinum" January 15 1909

Koltz, A. "Journal of Modern History" Vol 48 no3 Sept 1976 pp. 483-91

Marshall, A.G. in "Russian Review 1913"

Melancon, M. *The Ninth Circle: The Lena Goldfield Workers & the Massacre of 4 April 1912* "American Quarterly Review of Russian & Eurasian Studies" Vol 53 no 3 Fall 1994

Pawlikowaski, M. *Borsukowa grzeda* in "Wiadomosci" 2 / 563 13 January 1957

Shostakovich article sent by M. Shostakovich, source unknown

OTHER SOURCES

Personal papers of the Chrzczonowicz family

Personal memoirs of E. Skulski & F. Marten

Stock Exchange

Newmont Mining Corporation, USA

Leeds Russian Archive

Alexander Bely, Minsk

MOD, British Army Records, Hayes, Middx

Polish Institute and Sikorski Museum, London

GEOGRAPHICAL INDEX

218

219